WRESTLING IN HONEY

Martin Kelner

Scratching Shed Publishing Ltd

First published by Scratching Shed Publishing Ltd in 2023
Registered in England & Wales No. 6588772.
Registered office:
47 Street Lane, Leeds, West Yorkshire. LS8 1AP
www.scratchingshedpublishing.co.uk
ISBN 978-1739247638

A catalogue record for this book is available from the British Library.

Typeset in Cheltenham Bold and Palatino
Printed and bound in the United Kingdom by
Ashford Colour Press
Unit 220, Fareham Reach
Fareham Road, Gosport, Hampshire, PO13 0FW

WRESTLING IN HONEY

To John Motson, Dickie Davies, Jimmy Hill,
Sid Waddell, George Carlin, Diego Maradona
and others who died before this anthology could appear;
and especially Steve Callaghan, kind sponsor
and titan of the UK concrete industry.

Contents

Foreword

Gary Lineker

It would be wrong to say I was honoured to be asked to contribute a foreword to this collection of Martin Kelner's work. Surprised would be more accurate, because many of the pieces come from his Screen Break column in *The Guardian* about broadcast sport, which wasn't always entirely appreciative of my efforts.

Some weeks Martin took delight in rubbishing my pun-heavy sign-offs from *Match Of The Day*, even suggesting at one stage that I had a team of scriptwriters working on them. I am therefore grateful for this opportunity to put on record that the very worst of them were all my own work.

Mind you, even though there was every chance of being skewered in the *Guardian* sports section on a Monday morning, I still looked forward to reading it. After all, there was also the possibility the flak might be directed elsewhere, at one's loved and respected colleagues, very much enlivening the morning tea break. Schadenfreude, I think the expression is, unless that's a German midfielder I'm confusing it with.

But all is forgiven now, and would have been forgotten had Martin not chosen to anthologise these pieces from *The Guardian* and other places. They're mostly from the early 2000s, which makes them particularly worth revisiting – quite apart from the quality or otherwise of the writing – as a reminder of a sports broadcasting landscape radically different from the one we inhabit now.

It was a time before streaming services, VAR, social networks, a time when it was possible to think of a joke and publish it in a newspaper the next day without it already having been thought of by 200 other people and turned into a full-scale YouTube production.

But what Martin has that is absent from today's Twitter hubbub is a certain elegance of expression, displayed to its best advantage in these pieces.

That, together with – and I write as something of an expert – some half-decent jokes.

Gary Lineker, February 2023

Introduction

Wrestling In Honey, Maradona's Backside, and other wonders from the World of Sport and beyond...

This collection of pieces stems from a conversation I overheard in a publisher's office. An autobiography of an entertainer not quite celebrated enough to be considered in the pantheon of showbiz, nor obscure enough to be a cult figure, was being discussed.

'Look, I'll be honest,' said the publisher, words that very rarely precede 'That's a million dollar idea you've got right there. I see it as a book, a Netflix series, a Hollywood movie, a radio show, a podcast, a Sunday newspaper serialisation, a takeaway Chinese meal.'

No, what followed was more like, 'There'll be a specialist audience, nobody's going to make any money out of it, but if you're just looking for some kind of legacy project, I'd be happy to have a look at it.'

Hmmm, a legacy project. The problem with legacy, I have always thought, is one is often too dead to enjoy it. Then again, the concept of nobody making much money out of it seemed to fit in quite neatly with what I laughingly call my career trajectory, so I gave the idea some thought and decided, yes, a legacy project, put me down for one of those too.

In fact, my sudden enthusiasm for legacy was such that I suggested we gazump any Z-list entertainers looking in that direction and call this compendium *The Legacy Project*, maybe filching a few sales from the airport novel market, from weary travellers seduced by the title into expecting something Dan Brown-ish or Forsyth-esque (that's Frederick, not Bruce), eagerly pulling this volume from the shelf thinking, 'What is this mysterious 'Legacy Project'? Is it maybe a shadowy underground movement of holocaust denying fanatics with a mission to restore the reputation of the Third Reich?'

I was quite happy to foster that kind of misunderstanding for barefaced commercial reasons. Indeed, I was a little miffed when my suggestion of a big red swastika in relief on the front cover, dripping blood, was rejected on grounds of taste.

That, by the way, may be the last encounter with good taste you enjoy in this collection of pieces, many of which were written for *The Guardian* in the 2000s, shortly before Culture Wars were declared, or at least before everybody started lobbing poison gas canisters into each other's trenches.

Frankly, as I undertook the selection process, I was shocked how many off-colour jokes and questionable asides about Clare Balding's hairstyle were permitted – in *The Guardian*, for goodness sake – back then.

Alongside the *Guardian* Screen Break columns there are also pieces from the *Independent*, the *Racing Post*, rugby league magazine *Forty20*, online articles and unpublished stuff. A lot of it is about sport on TV, which has accidentally become my specialist subject over the past quarter century, but I cover other important topics too, including chicken and Bristol.

Introduction

I have hundreds of thousands of words on my laptop, many of them still perfectly serviceable, and ordered in such a way to evince a smile even now, and when I die – I've just passed the three-score-years-and-ten, which, in the famous gag from Leviticus should just about see me into the terminus – what will happen to them?

Nobody's going to read through, looking for the good stuff. Oh yes, my jackets and shirts, carelessly chosen from town centre stores in a matter of moments just so I could get out of the damned shop and go for a coffee or a beer, they'll be carefully sorted into piles destined either for charity shop donation or recycling, yet my words, agonised over on many a Sunday afternoon, deadline clawing at my shins ('what sounds funnier, chicken or turkey?') will disappear unloved, unremembered. There's irony for you right there.

In fact, what does happen to the old man's laptop when he's gone? We boomers are the first generation to face that dilemma. I assume it gets wiped clean and bequeathed to a young person to write their history project, and watch TikTok, on.

So this legacy project is, if nothing else, a means of recycling some of the more viable words, giving them a second life. It's not about ego (yeah, right). On my desk I have a plastic bottle of water carrying the slogan, 'bottle made out of other bottles.' I'm doing the same thing only with words.

I mean, there is a point of view that eschews the idea of legacy, and it's one we've established I have sympathy with. When I see a footballer pointing to the heavens after knocking in a last-minute equaliser at the Bridge, dedicating it to his recently deceased granddad, I'm inclined to respond with, 'Your grandpappy doesn't care, you doughnut, he's dead. He's not filling in his coupon.'

That certainly summed up my view before the summer

of 2013 when I almost died. I had what we doctors call a big fuck-off abdominal tumour, about which you may read more presently. Suffice to say, it burst and I was immediately admitted to the life and death ward at St James's Hospital, Leeds.

Managing my legacy was the last thing on my mind, at least until I came off life support a week later, and found others doing it for me.

At the time, alongside a weekly column about sport on TV for the *Racing Post*, I was presenting the lunchtime show on BBC Radio Leeds, whose management, bless them, were very concerned about me and, knowing I had a bit of a hospital stay ahead of me, arranged for my stand-in to present 'A Show to Cheer Martin Up.'

It was a kind gesture, and well meant, but the thought did occur that they were broadcasting my obituary without bothering to wait till I was dead. And of course they got it all wrong. I know it's curmudgeonly to complain, but they played my 'favourite' tunes which weren't really my favourites, and clips of me interviewing various local worthies rather than the stuff I was really proud of, which was basically me fooling around to no particular effect, and certainly not in any way fulfilling the terms of the BBC Charter.

Incidentally, on the subject of local worthies, I can only thank my obituarists that they didn't include the programme I presented at Christmas 2011, paying tribute to much loved family entertainer, philanthropist, friend of Prime Ministers and the Royal Family, and celebrated son of Leeds, Jimmy Savile. It was a hagiography, nothing less, and it was not a commission I sought, not because I had any idea of the horrors that were about to be revealed but simply because I thought he was a bit shit.

He never made me laugh, and on his disc jockey shows he gave no indication he had any interest in or knowledge of popular music. I couldn't see the point of him, apart from the fact he was a safe pair of hands, a family friendly, non-threatening entertainer (that's the kind of spot-on, incisive media analysis you will become used to in this collection), perfect for Saturday evenings when I was out, a safe distance from the TV.

In my defence, though, because I was a Radio 4 listener and occasional contributor I was aware of a programme Savile had done in 1991 called *In The Psychiatrist's Chair*, a kind of inquisition by therapist Dr Anthony Clare, which hinted at a darker side to Savile.

I got hold of a CD of the programme and included a clip in my tribute. Clips from the programme are everywhere now – YouTube and so on – but I believe I was the first to dig it out. (What's the point of a legacy project if you can't correct the balance sheet a little?)

Mind you, at Christmas 2011, amid the welter of praise the BBC was showering on the beloved entertainer, there wasn't really any appetite for balance. In Leeds, of course, he was one of our own, as away fans at Elland Road never tire of reminding the locals, but that hadn't caught on yet.

On the day of Savile's funeral, conducted by the Bishop of Leeds, all normal programming was halted on Radio Leeds. The funeral service was broadcast live, commentated upon with due solemnity by *Guardian* writer Martin Wainwright. It truly was a 24-hour grovel-fest, which I'm guessing doesn't figure too prominently in Martin's *cv*.

As we now know, Savile's legacy turned out not to be hospital wings and *Jim'll Fix It* badges, but a change in the culture of the BBC, which may incidentally and ironically have led to my departure from the Corporation.

Two incidents come to mind. I was interviewing Robin Colvill, a member of the comedy troupe The Grumbleweeds, the main part of whose act was a wickedly accurate impersonation of the formerly much-loved etc. etc, but now discredited family entertainer – look it up on YouTube, it's hilarious – a bit of business he could no longer do for reasons of taste, leaving him with a much reduced repertoire.

'So in many ways you're the final victim,' I said, which was not the sort of attitude the BBC was looking for to make up for all the years they ignored the bastard's appalling behaviour (that's Savile, not lovely Robin Colvill).

At dead of night you could find executives striding round the ramparts of Broadcasting House in the style of Lady Macbeth, endlessly, pointlessly, and tragically washing their hands to get rid of the stain of Savile.

The main strategy seemed to be to pretend Savile had never existed, which helped no-one, especially not the poor blighter who had to edit the vintage editions of *Top Of The Pops*.

But that clearly wasn't all that was going on. In 2016, I paid tribute to the recently departed Beatles record producer George Martin, referencing his earlier work with Bernard Cribbins, Peter Sellers, and other old school comics. I played, 'Goodness Gracious Me', a hit single for Sellers and Sophia Loren on Martin's Parlophone label.

Despite my protestations that this was illustrative material, the station manager accused me of playing a racist song (Sellers's Indian accent), and shortly afterwards my contract was not renewed, just like the old bugger down at Radio Devon who got the push for playing a 1930s version of 'The Sun Has Got Its Hat On', which includes a racial epithet. I bet he got the same number of listeners' complaints as I did, which if you take an average of the two of us would work out at precisely nought.

But I shall not be railing against the BBC in this book – there are two TV stations and several newspapers that will do that for you all day long – there is no agenda to these extracts of mine. If I have any political attitude at all, it's kind of like my football, hanging around on the left wing, not achieving very much.

Mostly, though, this collection takes as its overarching philosophy advice given to me by my smarter brother when he was at *The Independent* and I wrote some pieces for him. 'Get a joke in the intro, and then run like fuck for the end' were his wise words.

I can't deny you will find the odd piece that is slightly unkind to one or two television personalities, but as I always say, in the context of a weekly semi-humorous sport-on-TV column there will be casualties.

I write about programmes on BBC, ITV, Channel 4, Channel Five, and occasionally explore the outer reaches of the Sky remote, looking for a joke. I'll put them into context where I can, but mostly this book is a response to what politicians hardly ever call 'The Lack of Humour crisis.' I'm fulfilling a need, it's not about ego (enough already).

Don't worry about me, by the way. When the BBC decided there was no place any more for slightly irreverent middle aged white males, I got a job with Ken Bates's Leeds-based radio station – keen billionaire-watchers will hardly be startled to learn that political correctness was not one of his absolute priorities – and was later picked up by talkSPORT, not for their highest profile gig it's true, but if you happen to be awake at three o'clock in the morning on a Friday or Saturday night, or are in Ho Chi Minh City (a couple of our listeners are), you may have heard me being irreverent. And old and male and white.

I also carried on reviewing sport on TV on the Hawksbee

and Jacobs show on talkSPORT on a Friday afternoon. As I suggested earlier, writing about this stuff was never a plan. I was doing capsule reviews of film and TV for a different newspaper, and my editor got a job as number three on the *Guardian* sports desk. He took me with him despite my professed ignorance of sport. If I'd known how funny sports broadcasters could be, I'd have started watching it sooner.

Some of the jokes may seem cruel, and occasionally to broadcasters you hold in high regard. But in amongst the cruel humour there is celebration too.

Is there any point to it all? Absolutely not. Articles about TV broadcasts from ten or 15 years ago? They're about as relevant as the old newspapers you find lining that chest of drawers you're painting. But you'll read them too, of course you will. And in this collection, there will be the odd piece that could easily pass as humour, promise...

There are some blog pieces as well, and unpublished stuff which could be loosely categorised as 'memoir'.

Feel free to skip over those bits as they're about my life, and therefore not that funny.

1. Wizards of The Green Baize

'When that final black ball rolls smoothly and sweetly into its pocket, it is a moment of closure unrivalled in sport...'

Semi-finals day of the Snooker World Championship, The Crucible, Sheffield, Saturday 5 May, 2007. Memoir, previously unpublished.

A full-size snooker table in prime condition is a thing of beauty, its playing surface so smooth and deep green, its sturdy yet shapely mahogany legs so prettily fluted, its coloured balls so shiny and perfectly spherical.

At the 2007 World Championships I find myself sitting just a few feet away from a particularly fetching example. It is, I believe, the Riley Aristocrat tournament champion snooker table, and during the interval, when the Crucible Theatre is drained of fans and players, I am left alone with it.

I could wander over and touch it, stroke its wood, maybe lay my cheek against its green baize, but I daren't. Instead, I get my friend George Riley (a journalist, not a manufacturer of top-end snooker tables) to take a picture of me standing by the Aristocrat, like a tourist in the Sistine Chapel, or a kid at Disneyland wanting to prove he met Mickey Mouse.

It is a thrill for me simply to be in the presence of such a table. During my own playing career I never got the chance to perform on a surface like this. In fact, I rarely encountered a table on which the wooden surround was not decorated with cigarette burns.

My heyday, if you can call it that, was round about 1973, when I made my record break of 14, comprising two reds, a black, and a blue, on the balding, slightly sloping, baize at the now defunct Bristol United Press social club.

It was a doubles match; myself and another junior reporter, Jim Townsend, a gangly, fresh-faced lad from Dursley, against a couple of grizzled veterans, Leo Clancy and Rob Gibson (at least, they seemed like GVs to us, they were probably about 25). The contest took place at the height of the snooker craze that briefly gripped myself and fellow journalists on the *Western Daily Press*.

We worked shifts; 2.00pm–10.00pm, 3.00pm–11.00pm, or 5.30pm–1.30am. Somewhere around the middle of the shift was a strict one-hour break – the unions, who held sway in the newspaper industry in those days, insisted on it – during which those of us who liked to think of ourselves as proper cynical hard-boiled hacks (in Bristol, for goodness sake) went over the road to the club, where we smoked, told filthy jokes, and played snooker.

I never recall seeing a woman in there. Why would they want to be? The newspaper had a perfectly serviceable canteen in the building, catering for women and married sub-editors, where you could get a plate salad, a freshly made sandwich on Mother's Pride bread, or a hot meal, like shepherd's pie with chips and peas. You know, the stuff that passed for food in 1973.

The club, frankly, was a dump – everything else being in much the same state of repair as the snooker table – and the only sustenance available was something called cobs; sandwiches made from small, round, very crusty, bread rolls, which needed to be at maximum freshness to avoid having the consistency of Dunlopillo, and in the club rarely were. Two fillings were available; a very mature Cheddar cheese served with a thick, uncompromising slice of raw onion, or ham.

I have Proustian memories of biting into a cheese cob – the onion was never given a name check in those days in the West Country, it was just taken as read – and encountering the onion, to which I had a strong aversion. Even two pints of subsidised cider did little to alleviate a feeling of revulsion. I shudder even now.

No wonder we were all leaner in those days. If you wanted something to eat outside of strictly proscribed meal times, you had to work at it.

A sandwich was cheese or cold meat, end of story. The BLT was a distant dream, and while there may have been an avocado pear somewhere in Britain, it had yet to make its way to our end of the M4. There were no takeaway pizza shops that I can remember, no McDonald's or KFC, and fish and chip shops routinely closed on Mondays. There were Chinese restaurants, but not many, and none in Bristol that I can recall serving anything edible. Such supermarkets as there were lowered their shutters at six o'clock prompt.

If you were a married chap, the little lady might have something hot waiting for you at home – *autres temps, autres mœurs* – but I honestly cannot remember what we single guys and girls subsisted on, beyond some vague memories of steak and kidney pies, which I ate cold, and milk drunk straight from the bottle.

There was one place you could eat after a late shift, a Greek(ish) restaurant called The Famagusta, rammed in amongst the second-hand furniture shops at the bottom end of Gloucester Road. It was primarily a drinking joint, but they would serve you omelette and chips at two in the morning.

That was more or less all anyone ate in there – I am not even sure there was anything Greek on the menu at all – until the famously thirsty Rob Gibson, who introduced us to the place and was a regular *habitué* himself, decided one night to vary his evening meal to include some food, and struck out with something none of us had ever ordered before called a 'Vienna steak'.

This turned out not to be a steak at all but a hamburger, and its connections with the Austrian capital were tenuous at best, but as the item came in at under two pounds when Berni Inn steak houses were charging a fiver for the genuine article, it seemed churlish to cavil.

Not to Rob, though, who may have reached that point in his food-to-drink cycle when truculence became a first resort. He railed against the failure of the faux Viennese dish on his plate to be a proper steak, and accused the gentle proprietor in none too complimentary terms of false advertising.

Violence may have been offered, if not accepted. In any case, newspaper reporters were barred from the Famagusta from then on, and it was back to the steak and kidney pies.

If LP Hartley's famous gag about the past being a

foreign country where they do things differently springs most readily to mind when thinking of food, the sporting landscape back in the early 'Seventies was pretty alien too.

There was sport on television, but, like dinner, you had it when you were told you could. Snooker was restricted to a strange little programme called *Pot Black*, which ran from 1969 on the newly-launched BBC Two, a channel chiefly associated with arts programming, and unavailable in some parts of the country.

Bizarrely, such passing customers as the programme picked up, on their way to a season of continental cinema or a Pinter play, were often viewing in black and white, hence the famous and probably apocryphal quote, 'For those of you watching in black and white, the blue is behind the yellow,' said to have been uttered by *Pot Black*'s commentator, a chap known as 'Whispering' Ted Lowe.

(There was an awful lot of whispering going on in the early days of BBC Two. 'Whispering' Bob Harris presented another of the fledgling channel's shows, *The Old Grey Whistle Test*. Maybe it was part of the BBC's plan; to launch the station not with a bang, but a whisper.)

Pot Black, which was comprised of one frame, once a week, recorded in a BBC studio in Birmingham, became surprisingly popular. It was notably short on showbiz razzmatazz. Its theme tune, a plinky plonky piano piece, *Black and White Rag*, played by Winifred Atwell, was deliberately retro, and most of the players, with the exception of Alex 'Hurricane' Higgins, looked like junior clerks in a particularly dull insurance office. It did serve, however, to remind some of us what an intensely satisfying game snooker is.

The joy of snooker, I think, derives from a deep-seated human desire for things to be neat and tidy. That, essentially, is what snooker is; a tidying-up game. Someone breaks up the triangle of red balls, they bang into the other balls, leaving a mess all over the nice clean table, and the rest of the game is more or less about clearing up the mess.

It is something we find difficult to do in real life. There is always a ball or two left over – a tax bill, an unresolved relationship – but on the snooker table they can all be cleared away, which is why when that final black ball rolls smoothly and sweetly into its pocket, it is a moment of closure unrivalled in sport.

I am not altogether sure these considerations played much of a part in the frenzy for snooker at the *Western Daily Press*. We were undoubtedly, though, for a short while, snooker loopy, despite pre-dating the expression, and indeed the careers of Chas and Dave, who coined it, by at least half a decade.

We probably played simply because there was a full-size snooker table there, something often provided in pubs and clubs in those days. These days the space might be filled more profitably with three pool tables and a raft of games machines, or used as a dining area, but how many pubs needed dining tables back then, when the most ambitious item coming out of the kitchen was a scotch egg?

I was a very keen competitor, despite having a game that was more Maureen than Ronnie O'Sullivan (one for the teenagers there). I even used to go in on my day off sometimes to see if any of my mates was around for a game. If not, you could usually find a printer or two ready to take on and probably humiliate a journo, especially if their opponent could be persuaded to risk hard cash on the outcome.

None of us journos was frankly much of a match for the inky-fingered artisans of our trade, who could do things like read type back to front and inside out, bang phalanxes of metal firmly into a galley with a little hammer, and carry on a conversation over the mighty roar of huge rotary presses, and so had little difficulty in lining up a green for the top left hand corner, and what is more doing it without ever removing the cigarette between their lips.

It is a lost skill, in these smoke-free days, not unlike the hot metal malarkey the boys performed to get the paper on the street. The best of those guys could crouch over the table, fag in mouth with about one and a half inches of ash teetering off the end of it, complete the shot, and execute a half-turn so the ash fell on the lino rather than the baize.

Someone set up a league table, with my name more or less inked in at the foot of it, but I did make a break of 14, which no one can take away from me.

Unfortunately, I was deprived of the chance to build on that, as the *Western Daily Press* sent me to work in district offices in Chepstow, Taunton, and Weymouth, effectively putting my snooker career on the back burner, and giving me the opportunity to spend the next twenty years or so going out with girls, not going out with girls, falling in and out of love, changing jobs, moving to entirely different areas of the country, and eventually getting married and having children.

During this fallow period, I played the occasional game in The Kersal Hotel, a cavernous, careworn, pub on the edge of Kersal Moor in Salford, with loads of space never likely to be pressed into service as a gastropub. The table was not dissimilar to the Bristol United Press one, thinning and pocked with cigarette burns. My brother and I sometimes used to meet up there for a game or two with my late dad prior to going to a rugby match together, when we were both home for the weekend.

Apologies, by the way, to the Kersal if it has undergone a refit – become a gastropub maybe – because I am finding it increasingly difficult to keep pace with developments in provincial towns and cities. It is not just the old hardware shops that have turned into Costa Coffees or the banks that have been J D Wetherspoon-ed, but whole areas that have been transformed.

Sheffield, for instance, where I travel to on a warm and sunny Saturday 5 May for semi-finals day in the 2007 World Snooker Championships, does not remotely resemble the city I arrived in some twenty-nine years earlier to take up a job as a radio newsman.

Then, Sheffield was recognisably an industrial – about to become post-industrial – town, full of rough and ready pubs, with fine old Victorian buildings like the Town Hall, blackened by decades of soot, sitting rather uncomfortably among new ones, like the market, or the tower blocks built on the hills above the city centre, slabs of brutal 'Sixties concrete, which seemed to look down and say, 'Come and have a go if you think you're hard enough.'

In some comically misguided rush to modernity in the 1970s, they even extended Sheffield's classic late Victorian Town Hall by building a hideous concrete office block next to it, dubbed the 'egg box' by locals. One year, my radio station broadcast an April Fools' Day hoax in which we reported that prominent civic figures, stung by the widely expressed criticism that the Town Hall extension did not blend in with the original, had decided to knock down the original Victorian building and rebuild it in the style of the egg box. The fact that half the city was taken in by the stunt owed less to the brilliance of its execution than the fact it was the kind of daft thing the city fathers were capable of doing in those days.

The egg box was demolished in 1999. Today Sheffield gleams. In the late morning sunshine, it could be Barcelona or Brussels. Sheffield Midland Station, for instance, which used to be one of the most dismal entry points of any city in Britain, stuck at the bottom end of town among a ramshackle collection of mini-cab offices and dubious greasy spoon cafes, has been tarted up beyond belief. The station is now glass fronted with automatic doors, and is full of those franchises selling posh coffee and fancy-schmancy baguettes, which might not seem much, but this is Sheffield.

Sheffield, where, when I was working at the radio station in the late 'Seventies, a reporter newly arrived from London complained: 'If you ask for a cocktail in Sheffield, they give you a pint of lager with a piece of coal in it.' Sheffield, where, ten years after female emancipation hit the rest of the country, they would still ask if your girlfriend wanted her lager 'in a lady's glass.'

In the old days, you stepped out of the bleakness of Midland Station, took your chances crossing the Chesterfield Road, and then had to climb a hill past a couple of dangerous looking pubs before you encountered anything resembling a town centre. Now the council has created a sweeping approach to the station – they would probably call it a piazza – bordered by a kind of sloping stainless steel wall, off which the sun glints. There are water features, of course, and it is very impressive. You still have to walk up the hill to the Crucible Theatre, but it is up a proper tree-lined walkway now, hung with banners proclaiming, 'Sheffield Snooker City.'

The city has hosted the World Championship since 1977, so it must have been going on when I was living there, but I was only dimly aware of it, and certainly never went to the Crucible to watch.

Today it is inescapable. The city is running something called the *Sheffield On Cue* festival alongside the snooker, with the games being shown on a giant screen adjacent to the theatre, and street entertainers and market stalls in Fargate,

Sheffield's main shopping street. I do not think it is overstating the case to say Sheffield is *en fête*.

The walk from the station up to the Crucible takes me past what used to be the Polytechnic, where I did a weekly disco when I was a local radio 'personality' around 1979 and 1980. It was a typically soulless concrete aircraft hanger of a student union, smelling of roadies, rancid chip fat, and plastic glasses. My clientele seemed to be predominantly male, studying metallurgy or civil engineering, subjects deemed appropriate, I suppose, to the Sheffield of the time. Denim jackets and acne were what the young men were wearing then, as they shook their heads rhythmically to the music of Rainbow and Status Quo. Occasionally we brought on to the stage competent, enjoyable, but undemanding rock 'n' roll acts like Dr Feelgood.

The Poly is called Sheffield Hallam University now, and I suspect there is still the odd metallurgist clinging on, but this is a thoroughly modern seat of learning, offering customers in this new bracing commercially minded education environment the products they want; courses in media, cultural studies, community needlework, that kind of thing. Its bright airy new student union does a rather impressive imitation of a shopping mall. It has cash dispensers in it, high street shops, and ciabattas (in the new Sheffield you are never more than a minute away from a fancy sandwich).

I meet a couple of its students outside the Crucible. They are waiting to collect autographs and maybe exchange a word or two with the players, who remain far more approachable than most participants in professional sport. James King and Mark Sultara, both about 20, are equipped with the panoply of enthusiasts; plastic carrier bags, souvenir programmes, albums of photos and cuttings.

James, who comes from Hull, tells me he is studying

human geography (I nod sagely, although I have little idea how that might differ from the geography Mr Esplin taught us at Stand Grammar School, except that I suspect ox-bow lakes are not involved), and that he has followed on the TV every World Championship since 1990. This is not the entire reason he has chosen Sheffield for his studies, but it certainly played a part.

His favourite player, he says, is Stephen Hendry, which figures, as Hendry won seven out of ten championships in the 1990s, and I suppose you might latch onto a successful snooker player in your formative years in the same way kids in Bournemouth become Manchester United or Chelsea supporters.

'He was my childhood hero,' says James, 'I just loved his style of play,' which is an interesting comment, because Hendry was never much of a crowd pleaser, and in fact came over as a little sulky at times.

But commentators who know more about the game than I do say he remains the best snooker player ever to draw breath. It all goes to show that kids love a winner. My son was the same, conceiving at ten years old a passion for Tiger Woods that has never died. The vulnerability or flakiness of a Ronnie O'Sullivan or Hurricane Higgins does nothing for children. It speaks more directly to adult males who can identify and empathise with the flaws, and to women who want to mother these child-men, or, I suppose, sleep with them.

James and his friend Mark, a business and financial services student and an equally keen Hendry supporter, paid the £20 to watch their hero's second round defeat, but will not be joining me in the theatre for the semi-final, there being only so many £20 sessions of snooker the student loan will stretch to. Instead they will follow it on TV, and attempt later to emulate their heroes on the snooker tables in the University Union. TV has truly pitchforked the sport out of smoky back rooms of pubs and clubs and into the modern age, and I doubt anyone these days would suggest dexterity on the green baize as the sign of a misspent youth.

Hendry's defeat was at the hands of Ali Carter, a 27-year-old who has only recently broken into the world rankings after a setback in 2003 when he was diagnosed with Crohn's disease, a debilitating gastro-intestinal condition.

This seems like a shock result to me, but my friend George Riley, who is chairman of the Snooker Writers' Association, tells me Carter, or the Tiptree Cueman as he is known, is an up and coming star with a good record against Hendry. (You should know, by the way, that they cannot do nicknames in snooker, and frankly I do not know why they bother. Where other sports have Hunters and Destroyers, snooker has the Leicester Cueman and the Sheriff of Pottingham. Maybe it is a reflection of snooker's genteel beginnings in the Officers' mess in the days of the Raj.)

Hendry is still, at 38, a great player, says George, but has lost his focus a little, and no longer seems to have quite the same appetite for the game. The late Canadian writer Mordecai Richler, who was a huge fan of snooker, and particularly Hendry, reckoned it was family life – Hendry is married to Mandy, his childhood sweetheart, and the couple have two sons – that had dulled Hendry's edge.

Snooker is a game played so much in the head that amateur psychoanalysis becomes the lot of the snooker writer, several of whom I meet when George takes me into the press room at the Crucible.

The last time I was in this room, some 26 years previously, it was to interview Ken Dodd before his *Laughter Show*, a staple of the Crucible's programme in those days, cleverly slotted in alongside the Strindberg. I had my girlfriend, a teacher, with me, and Doddy commented: 'By Jove, if I'd had teachers like you when I was at school, I'd be ten years older now.' He has, as comedy folk sometimes say, got a million of 'em; and likes to work his way through an unwieldy number in his *Laughter Show*, which is why it went on, if memory serves, till well after midnight.

The Crucible's most famous marathon, though, was in 1985, when the affable Irishman – that may even have been his nickname – Dennis Taylor, wearing his newly adopted upside down glasses which helped him to see down the length of his cue, pulled off an unlikely victory in the final ball of the final frame against the reigning champion, the seemingly invincible Steve Davis. At 12.23am on BBC Two, there were 18.5 million people watching, the highest figure for any televised sport bar football, and the largest British television audience after midnight.

Both the participants in that final now work on the BBC's commentary team, and Davis wanders into the press room while I am there, as does Stephen Maguire (the Merlin of Milton; see, I told you), one of this year's semi-finalists.

The ease with which players and writers mix in this room is rare in sport these days. In football the atmosphere between the two camps falls somewhere between mutual suspicion and open hostility. After a European championship qualifying match in 2007 between England and Andorra, the Sky TV and *Daily Star* football specialist Brian Woolnough was crossing the road in front of the England team bus, when coach Steve McLaren playfully instructed the driver to run him down. There remains doubt within the press corps about exactly how playful McLaren's suggestion was.

Here, though, the members of the fourth estate can walk the streets of Sheffield with impunity. It helps, I suppose, that some of the snooker writers have been around since the days when the sport was little more than a pub game, and have actively helped it develop into the lucrative entertainment it is today; but probably more important is the fact that this leisurely-paced game fosters a certain courtliness in its participants. Snooker breeds young gentlemen. With a few notable exceptions, of course – and thank goodness for them.

My colleagues in the press room, I find, follow the action mostly on the TV screens, which seems odd to one condemned to experience almost all his sport this way. Do these chaps – and two women – not realise how privileged they are actually to be at a tournament like this? Sometimes I watch an event on the TV and only realise later I have missed most of it, by fast forwarding to a panel discussion or a feature of some sort I can lampoon in the newspaper. So this Saturday morning I am determined not to miss the opportunity to be in the theatre alongside the players, sampling the atmosphere, and maybe getting a deeper understanding of what is going on.

A common complaint about snooker is that there are no characters in the game nowadays, which I think may be one of those often expressed laments for a bygone golden age which do not bear too close an examination; like *Viz* is not as funny as it used to be, or window cleaners don't whistle any more.

Shaun Murphy and Mark Selby, whose semi-final I pick up with Selby leading 11-9 in a 33-frame match, are probably the kind of characters people are thinking of when they voice this opinion, but I think they may be more interesting than their nicknames.

Murphy, billed in the programme as the Rotherham Cueman, won the title in 2005 when he was number 48 in the world rankings, the lowest ranked player ever to win the championship. He is 24 years old, but looks younger, maybe because of his round, fleshy, face.

The youth of the players is the first thing that strikes you when you see them at close quarters. They somehow seem more adult on TV. Television is said to add ten pounds. I wonder if it adds ten years as well. Without wishing to be unkind, Murphy, despite a recent impressive weight loss, still looks like the kid in class the others might have called Podge; and indeed, checking up on Murphy's history, I read that he was bullied at school.

Not just bullied, but bullied to the extent that he was taken out of school and taught at home by his father Tony; so it is fair to assume that part of the sub-text behind Murphy's rise to the top in his chosen sport might read: 'Where are you now, those of you who called me Podge and Porky, now I'm a 24-year-old millionaire?'

Tony was the archetypal pushy dad, not just schooling Shaun, but driving him on in the sport the father loved. We have all done it with our sons to some extent. I have lost count of the Sunday mornings I have spent on windswept playing fields urging my boy on from the sidelines in junior football matches. I was happy if he showed just a little more fight than I used to, but some dads were brutal with their kids, to a level that you do not have to be a strict Freudian to suspect might be unhealthy.

Still, however wrapped up we become in our sons, I doubt many have been as intensively reared as Shaun.

Tony, for whom snooker was not only a passion but also a living – he was an executive of World Snooker Ltd., the company that arranges tournaments, and a director of the World Professional Billiards and Snooker Association – bought eight-year-old Shaun his own snooker cue and miniature table, and spent most of his spare time driving his boy round to junior tournaments. By the time Shaun was 10 he had chalked up his first century break. Recognised as a prodigious talent from his early teens, Murphy became one of World Snooker's first Young Players of Distinction.

He tells a touching story about that first snooker table: 'I found out that Father Christmas didn't exist because I came downstairs to find my dad asleep on the couch having put the snooker table together. Before I was 9, I had joined a club and I was down there every night with my dad, and at weekends. I loved every minute of it.'

This childhood idyll was shattered when Shaun was 14, though, when his mother walked out. 'I came home from a cycle ride one morning to find she had gone,' says Shaun. 'I felt my world had turned upside down. I would never have imagined her walking away from us.' He was so hurt he never spoke to his mother for six years.

His religion helped him eventually to forgive her, but now, remarkably, he is not talking to his father. For 18 months the two have not exchanged a word. The story of the bitter row is in several newspapers. Before Shaun will speak to his father again, he tells the *Sheffield Star*, Tony must apologise for some of the 'horrible' things he said.

Since Shaun's championship triumph at the Crucible in 2005, it transpires, his father has attended not one of the tournaments in which his son has competed. Tony suffered a heart attack a few months after Shaun's championship win, and Shaun believes 'things came to a head' after that.

What things? Clearly Shaun's evangelical born-again Christianity, about which he has been very forthcoming, has something to do with it, because he is quoted as follows in Scotland's *Daily Record*: 'My dad's not a Christian but I am, and nowhere in the Bible does it say I have to accept blasphemy. I wasn't going to roll over when we had the row.

I thought "enough is enough".' It probably would not be an amateur psychoanalytical step too far to say there might be some unresolved issues around Murphy's mum.

Maybe Shaun's wife Clare, whom he met in an Internet Christian chatroom, was the subject of the disagreement, because another quote reads: 'I just had to stand up for myself because what he said to me was wrong. As a husband, as a person, I just wasn't going to take it.'

The story of the rift between father and son appears in the papers on the morning of Shaun's quarter-final against Matthew Stevens, which you might think would seriously affect Murphy's play.

Well, up to a point. He falls behind 11 frames to 5, leaving Stevens just two frames from victory, but then stages a remarkable fightback to win the match, 13-12. See, that was my problem at the Bristol United Press social club. If there was anything on my mind – and there usually was, even if it was only whether Liz Davies was ever going to sleep with me – my game was shot.

These snooker players are obviously special characters. The bullying, the absent mum, the rift with the beloved dad, the unsought publicity; Murphy puts them all to one side to pull off one of The Crucible's great comebacks. Some would say it is a good advertisement for having Jesus Christ in your corner, although Murphy gives some of the credit to Ray Reardon, one of the pioneers of the modern game having won BBC Two's *Pot Black* tournament, and the 1978 World Championship at the Crucible.

Reardon, now 75, bridges snooker's smoky back room years and the glamorous television era, and so has become a kind of snooker guru, whom the eternally troubled Ronnie O'Sullivan, for instance, acknowledges helped him win two Crucible titles. Murphy says it is one of Reardon's tenets that has helped him develop the defensive side of his game. 'Ray said to me, "If they can't see it, they can't pot it,"' says Murphy, explaining how he prevented Stevens from shutting out the match.

At 12-8, says Murphy, he sensed a shadow of doubt fall over Stevens. 'His leg started to wobble a little, and he was doing strange things with his feet.'

Steve Davis says you can pick up this kind of 'vibe' off your opponent in the Crucible because you are sitting much closer together than at other tournaments, and also the theatrical atmosphere serves to intensify that kind of thing. 'It is literally a crucible,' adds Davis's BBC colleague Hazel Irvine.

In the Crucible/crucible for Murphy's semi-final against Selby I notice, to my surprise, that the crowd is favouring Selby. Murphy is the local boy, so I should have thought he would garner most support; but though the audience is not exactly against him, Murphy seems to command respect rather than affection.

Some people, I expect, find the Christian thing a little off-putting. Such public piety tends not to be the way we do things in Britain, where the Church is expected to be more about organising fêtes and sending unwanted woollies to earthquake zones. Murphy has said in interviews that he believes his steadfast Christianity – he was 'born again' at the age of 16 – gives him an edge in his sport, which is the kind of statement that does not play well with a British audience.

Anything that gives a player an artificial leg-up, in sport or in life – religion, freemasonry, American-style self-improvement techniques, plastic surgery – tends to be viewed here with far more suspicion than elsewhere. We revere the gifted amateur who muddles through, armed with nothing more than a smile. That may be why our footballers don't practice penalties.

Mark Selby definitely has the smile. I am sure he is as dedicated and single-minded as any player who has ever reached a Crucible semi-final, but he enters the arena in the style of one breezing past the doormen into a nightclub.

He is wearing all black, whereas Murphy has a white shirt on, which sort of adds to the impression that he is the young racy gunfighter riding into town to take on the sheriff.

In fact, Selby is 23, just one year younger than Murphy, and the two are good friends who often practise together. Selby wears his hair short and neat at the back, but longer on top, carefully arranged in spikes, with the help of what we used to call Brylcreem or hair oil, but is now referred to as 'product'. This is the default look for young snooker players, something that passed me by watching on TV but strikes me quite forcibly in the theatre. The precision needed to maintain this hairstyle, it occurs to me, is not a million miles from the skill you might call upon to extricate yourself from a tricky snooker.

It is a fantastically exciting match, although had I been watching at home I suspect I might have formed a different view, especially when it was poised at 11-11, with the players swapping safety shots. In normal circumstances that would have been the trigger for an extended bout of tea making, biscuit selecting, email checking and other favoured displacement activities.

There is an awful lot of walking round the table, sucking in of teeth, and unnecessary cue chalking, which is boring on the TV – I am sure I have said as much in one of my columns – but in the theatre it serves to build the tension as you wait for a player to make the mistake that will afford his opponent an opportunity. It is like waiting for the moment in a Hitchcock movie you know is going to arrive, when the decent normal hero is plunged into danger and darkness.

At one point, Selby wanders over towards the press bench while contemplating a shot, and I catch a whiff of a bracing male fragrance, a clue maybe to the undoubted sex appeal of these players. Male grooming is something they take seriously, so you can see why women who complain it is impossible to find a well-dressed, well-mannered, neat, good-looking man who is not gay, like these young sportsmen so much.

Given the tension – tied 12-all, then 14-all, then Murphy ahead 16-14, before Selby wins three straight frames to take the match 17-16 – Selby not only maintains the sangfroid we have come to expect from snooker players, but seems to approach it with a light heart, clowning around a little; throwing up the chalk and catching it, smoothing the baize as though his ball has hit a divot, and at one point trying to drop balls into the pocket by jumping. All of this, I should say, was for the benefit of the crowd – and much appreciated it was, too – and did not take place when it might undermine his opponent.

When you think of the tense, grim faces of Premiership footballers at work, it was all rather refreshing. On TV after the match, Dennis Taylor congratulates Selby on remaining calm in the heat of battle. 'I wasn't,' says Selby. 'I felt like I had Parkinson's disease.'

The fact there is no spin doctor warning Selby off light-hearted references to serious and debilitating conditions is one more reason to love snooker and the people who play it. Despite the huge amounts of money in the game, and the focus needed to perform at the highest level, the players still come across like amateurs.

It is ten years or so since I last hit a snooker ball myself. One Christmas we bought a junior table for my son, who is now 22, and he and I used to play fairly regularly. By the time he reached the age of about 12, though, he could beat me too easily, and he found himself more credible opponents. That break of 14 on the Bristol United Press social club's scabby table is looking increasingly like being the pinnacle for me.

The point is, snooker is a very difficult game, and it is only when you spend some time in the crucible feeling the tension that you realise just how difficult. Getting the cue ball to nestle against the cushion so that the next play is awkward for your opponent is boring when you see it on TV, a hiatus before some exciting potting action, but when you witness it close-up you appreciate the skill that goes into that kind of shot.

I could never do it. It may be that I am racially unsuited to the sport. I hesitate to end my visit on a controversial note – I know all the fuss that was made over theories that the East Africans' success in distance running was a racial thing – but one of the joys of getting off the sofa and onto a train is that I can read a book on the journey, and on the way home I read Mordecai Richler's brilliant monogram *On Snooker*, in which he tells how he scoured his *Encyclopaedia of Jews in Sport* (I did not know there was such a book) for snooker players of our religion, without success. There are boxers, footballers, even ice hockey players, but among all the sons and daughters of Moses, not a single wizard of the green baize.

It does not surprise me. Though it is clearly wrong to ascribe to an entire race my own character traits, I am sure I am not alone in the Hebrew corner as an emotional, impatient man, who would no more have the patience and cool-headedness to effect an escape from a particularly recondite snooker, than he would to change the cylinder head gasket on a 1975 Skoda Octavia.

But my admiration for the modern snooker player is not merely because he is different from me. My feelings were summed up in a leader in *The Guardian* published the day after John Higgins had won the world championship.

'In great matches players must show startling wizardry with the cue,' it read, 'but also endurance in a gruelling mind game. The hush – broken only by the hypnotic clinking of the balls – only adds to the intensity. When so much entertainment panders to short attention spans with noise and movement alone, snooker's slow-burning tension deserves to be cherished as never before.'

I would only add that on a shimmeringly beautiful Saturday in one of Britain's most attractive cities, it is a damned good day out.

2. Valedictions

'Jimmy Hill's passing was kind of a result for me...'

Obituaries of famous people, as I'm sure most of you realise, are prepared in advance, while the people concerned are still very much alive. Thus it was, in the late 1980s or early 'Nineties when I was working at BBC Radio 2, I got a call asking me to write an obituary of fellow broadcaster David Jacobs.

I was happy to do so, as an admirer of Jacobs, having grown up with his TV show Juke Box Jury, *one of the few shows to feature pop music on the TV in the early 'Sixties, and knowing a little bit about the broadcasting business.*

What complicated the matter a little was the fact that the great man was sitting in the next studio at the time, presenting the show that followed my 6.00am slot.

That's how obits work anyway, leading to the definitely apocryphal story of the late night editor who, when faced with the sudden death of war hero Robert Chester-Smythe, pulls from the shelf in haste the obit of an entirely different Robert Chester-Smythe, a distinguished veteran of the diplomatic corps, who, as luck would have it, was at home reading the paper the very next morning, while eating a soft boiled egg, and doing all sorts of things that live people do.

He telephoned the newspaper to share the happy news of his continued existence, whereupon the late editor was admonished: 'You've printed the obit of the civil servant Robert Chester-Smythe and he's still alive.'

'Well, you got yourself a bit of a scoop there then,' was the reply.

And that partly explains how I got into a celebrity death match with Jimmy Hill. I posted this on my website a few days after my tribute appeared in The Observer.

My Celebrity Death Match

Blog post, 21 December 2015

Clearly one mourns the passing of not just an innovator in the world of football, but a major figure in broadcasting, but still I felt Jimmy Hill's passing was kind of a result for me.

Let me explain.

A few years ago I got a call from *The Guardian*'s sports desk telling me Jimmy Hill wasn't too well, asking me to write a piece about him. I was pleased to get the call, because I'd grown up with Jimmy on the TV, had written about him in my book about sport on TV, and felt he was an even more significant figure in broadcasting than he is given credit for.

I was doubly pleased because at the time I was not too well myself. I had recently returned home from the life-and-death ward at Leeds's St James Hospital, after surgery to remove what we doctors call a big fuck-off abdominal tumour. I was lying on my day bed, anxious to do some work to convince myself there was a way back, and to keep me away from daytime TV.

So I wrote the piece, only to be told, in an, er, uncharacteristic case of *The Guardian*'s right hand not being entirely conversant with what the left one was doing, that the fine staff writer Barney Ronay had written a similar piece which had appeared in the paper two days earlier. But mine, they said, would be saved for when Jimmy carked it – these sort of conversations go on all the time among the heartless bastards who put your newspapers / websites together – so would I rewrite it as a sort of sidebar for the obit.

This I did, not being over-busy at the time, and the paper paid me. But still, you like your stuff actually to see the light of day, so about six months later, when Jimmy appeared to be stubbornly refusing to check out – I told you we were heartless – and I was still convalescing, I spoke to the sports desk, and asked if I might use the piece on my website. They demurred, feeling Jimmy was very much in the pending tray, and my piece might be called upon to enliven *The Guardian* any day now.

I told them about my tumour, and some later complications, and offered the opinion that the way things were going there was every chance I might cross over before him. 'Tell you what, if I go first, get him to do mine,' I said.

As Jimmy, bless him, remained a going concern for two more years, I began to tell those few people who were interested in what I was doing, that I was involved in a Celebrity Death Match with Jimmy Hill.

And now, fully recovered for the time being, I appear to have won.

Of course, our thoughts are with his family and all that, but we all have to go some time, and if we assume this life is the only one we have, Jimmy made the most of it. A life well lived, certainly.

Anyway, yesterday I'm eating lunch with my family in a pub in the beautiful garden city of Leeds, when Matthew Hancock, one of the *Guardian*'s top sports guys, calls to tell me Jimmy has finally succumbed and my two-and-a-half year old piece is to appear on the website and in *The Observer*.

This was followed by several texts from friends giving me the news, including this one:

> **Friend:** 'Jimmy Hill's died – does that mean your obit goes in?'
> **Me:** 'Yes. Online this PM. In Obs tomorrow. He died before me. Result!'

Heartless, moi?

Appreciation of Jimmy Hill

Obituary of the broadcasting and football legend,
The Guardian, *19 December 2015*

While Jimmy Hill's football career recedes into a monochrome era of Woodbines and reinforced toecaps – he was a wing half, which tells you everything you need to know – his later role as a TV football pundit will be more readily recalled.

Hill was the first former professional to do the job, a

trailblazer as he was in so many areas of the national game, and more forthright in his views than many of those who followed.

Not that this made him a national treasure. Jimmy wore hostility like a badge of honour. The current presenter of *Match of the Day*, Gary Lineker, told me about a match at Goodison, where Des Lynam and Alan Hansen were gently barracked, as is traditional, on their way to the TV gantry, but when Jimmy appeared the good-natured banter turned venomous. 'Jimmy Hill, you're a wanker, you're a wanker' was the refrain. Jimmy turned to his colleagues, beaming. 'There you are, that's fame for you,' he said.

'To Jimmy, it was justification for what he did on TV,' Lineker told me. 'He knew football, having had experience of every role in the game; fan, player, coach, chairman, director – he was a qualified referee for goodness sake – but he also knew television, and his view was there was no point in being mealy-mouthed. It wasn't an act. He was passionate about the game and had strong opinions he believed in expressing. Sometimes, of course, they came from left of field.'

But not from the political left. If your experience of Jimmy on TV dates no further back than his latter days at the BBC – who terminated his contract amid some acrimony at the end of the 1990s – and his *Sunday Supplement* on Sky from 1999 to 2007, you may view him as a grumpy old man with values distilled in the 19th hole at a suburban golf club, a kind of Peter Alliss-lite.

That is not to say the *Supplement* was not enjoyable, like pretty well every project of Hill's in 40 years of television. Admittedly, some of the fun came from Jimmy's pretence that the Sunday morning paper review was broadcast from his lovely rural home. To foster this illusion, he used to introduce the commercial breaks saying he had to attend to some domestic duty, many of which seemed straight from a *Carry On* script. 'Well, I'm off to peel the turnips now,' he would announce, or: 'It's high time I went and basted my meat.'

But late-period Hill misrepresents the man grievously. From a pretty decent footballing career with Brentford and Fulham, aided by a speed of thought not always present in his team-mates, through his successful campaign, as chairman of the PFA, to topple the feudal regime under which footballers were kept, his innovative management at Coventry City, and his time as head of sport at London Weekend Television from 1968 to 1972, Hill was nothing less than a revolutionary.

The effects of Jimmy's revolutions in football and broadcasting are still being felt today. Take the panel of four outspoken pundits he introduced to ITV for the World Cup in 1970. Quite apart from its effect on football punditry, it's a format that thrives more than 40 years later on programmes such as *Strictly Come Dancing* and *X Factor*.

Also at ITV he brought the much-loved Brian Moore, authoritative without being strident, to London Weekend, to commentate and to host *On The Ball*, a Saturday lunchtime football magazine show way ahead of anything the BBC was doing at the time. 'We devised as many innovative ideas as possible to attract a young audience,' Jimmy wrote in his autobiography. 'One idea was a penalty competition where kids took spot-kicks against professional goalkeepers,' a tradition that lives on in programmes such as Sky's *Soccer AM*.

Under Hill's stewardship *World Of Sport*, of blessed memory, was spruced up, too, with the introduction of the ITV Seven, combining the races covered into a handy betting format.

Away from TV, Hill's innovations as manager of Coventry City in the 1960s – his espousal of all-seat stadiums and proper readable match programmes, and his rewriting of the 'Eton Boating Song' as the 'Sky Blue Song' – have passed into legend in that part of the Midlands (A statue of Hill at the Ricoh Arena was unveiled by the man himself in 2011).

What is less well advertised are Jimmy's 'pop and crisps' nights at Highfield Road, when he got his players to stay behind and sign autographs and hand out free snacks to hundreds of young fans – not a million miles away from the 'community work' football makes such a fuss of these days.

Decades before fans' forums, footballers' Twitter feeds, and radio 'phone-ins, Jimmy was an advocate of interaction with fans, which did not always go as smoothly as Jimmy wished. In his early days on *Match of the Day*, he introduced a feature in which a supporter got to interview the manager of his club, but was requested not to ask anything too personal or controversial, a plan that was scuppered by the Spurs fan who kicked off his chat with then manager Keith Burkinshaw by asking: 'Why, did you sell Pat Jennings to Arsenal? Why?'

Jimmy was what is sometimes described as 'a real football man,' but he was a real TV man as well. He is undoubtedly godfather to Gary Neville, until this month making waves as a Sky analyst, as well as Lineker at the BBC.

'My first presenting job was the Euro 96 highlights,' said Gary. 'Jimmy was my pundit and he was hugely helpful to me. I was shaking like a leaf, of course, but he was very encouraging. He was totally involved in all aspects of the programme, and gave me lots of advice, some of which was obvious, some not, telling me to slow down, when to listen more, that kind of thing.'

The former Arsenal goalkeeper Bob Wilson is among many broadcasters who pay tribute to Hill in their autobiographies. Wilson praises Hill's versatility, recalling that when the 1971 Arsenal Double team needed a Cup final song – all teams had one back then – Jimmy altered the lyrics of Rule Britannia to 'Good old Arsenal, we're proud to say that name, While we sing this song, we'll win the game,' for which, given his massive contribution to football and broadcasting, he should be forgiven.

This is from the monthly rugby league magazine, Forty20, *lamenting that these days there's 'nothing to laugh at at all,' to borrow words from the great monologuist Stanley Holloway.*

Holloway wrote of Blackpool in The Lion and Albert*: 'They didn't think much to the ocean; The waves they were piddlin' and small; There were no wrecks and nobody drownded; 'Fact, nothin' to laugh at at all!'*

The Death of Comedy

Any Other Business, Forty20, *August 2022*

The problem with writing for a magazine, especially one as lovingly put together as this one, is that there can be a fairly long 'lead time', the time between writing something and it actually appearing in print.

Try anything too topical and there's a good chance that by the time the customers are enjoying your words they will be hopelessly out of date – which is why I rejected my latest piece about the folly of women playing association football, and why no good will ever come of it.

However, lead time or no lead time, I think I am fairly safe in assuming that we will still be more or less going to hell in a hand basket as you pick up the current *Forty20;* with inflation roaring away, a tank full of petrol costing about the same amount as I paid for my first car (true), and a nervous nation waiting to see if it's wild fires or pandemics that are going to be the death of us.

What we all need in these desperate circumstances is a good laugh, so it's especially galling that comedy seems to have disappeared. Let me explain.

I have been reading Mel Brooks's autobiography, *All About Me!*, which is mostly just Mel writing about the people he's met, how wonderful they all were, and how much they all laughed at Mel's wacky japes. But in amongst this rather tiresome self-congratulation – and give the guy a break, he's 95 – what strikes you most is how remarkable Mel's body of work is; from *The Producers* in the 1960s, via *Blazing Saddles, Young Frankenstein, High Anxiety* and others, to the stage musical of *The Producers*, for which Brooks also wrote the songs for goodness sake.

I remember seeing these movies when they were first released, as well as his hilarious TV spy spoof *Get Smart*; and at the same time as Mel was tickling our funny bones, Woody Allen was producing a comedy a year, the *Monty Python* team gave us *Life Of Brian* and the *Holy Grail* (*Holy Grail*, by the way, is the better of the two movies, don't let anyone tell you different), Zucker and Abrahams were turning out the *Airplane* and *Police Squad* movies, and there were one-offs like *Planes, Trains and Automobiles, Dirty Rotten Scoundrels*, and *What's Up Doc?*

But when was the last time you went to the cinema with no other motive than to have a bloody good cleansing laugh? No, I can't remember either.

Why, I asked a screenwriter friend of mine, is no one making comedy films any more, films that have no other intention than to tickle ribs? Because they don't sell in Russia, he said, or China. It's as simple as that.

Wrestling in Honey

An endless supply of Marvel Comic movies and superhero actioners is what translates into international sales. Comedy as a genre is dead. Rowan Atkinson realised this years ago and *Mr Bean* was the consequence. It's why Atkinson's *Man Versus Bee,* a sort of grown-up *Bean* best categorised as sporadically mildly amusing, is a worldwide hit on Netflix, and why Atkinson has a selection of racing cars and half a dozen Baby Bentleys in his garage.

Of course we have stand-up, arguably too much of it. The late Canadian comedian Norm Macdonald once said, 'When I started doing comedy in Los Angeles there were about 500 comedians, of whom about 50 were funny, then there were 5,000 comedians, of whom about 50 were funny, now we have more than 50,000. Of whom about 50 are funny.'

So good luck finding something to lighten the gloom in that department.

All I can do for you as we await the coronation of Liz Truss as Prime Minister is quote my favourite joke from the Mel Brooks autobiography. He's writing about his time in the so-called Borscht Belt, the resorts in the mountains north of New York, where Jewish New Yorkers liked to spend holidays in the 1950s and 1960s. You'll be familiar with the milieu from the film *Dirty Dancing.*

An old-time comic, Myron Cohen, is describing a scene in a deli. (You may have to indulge in a little cultural appropriation and adopt a Brooklyn Jewish immigrant accent to enjoy it fully). A chap goes into the store and finds the shelves crammed with tins of salt: 'Boy, you must sell a lot of salt,' says the customer. 'Not really,' the shopkeeper replies, 'Hardly any really, I can't sell it. But the guy who sells salt to me, boy can he sell salt.'

Work a little harder on the accent and I'm sure you'll appreciate it.

As a postscript to the previous piece, we have a game we play at home where we name celebrities we have worked with, or know in some way, who have the reputation of being generally a good thing, occasionally even national treasures, but in fact, in some people's experience, are absolute nightmares.

In Bristol, I worked briefly with the son of a famous actor who passed on his dad's opinion of Stanley Holloway, who he'd worked with on My Fair Lady.

At one point in the film, Stanley did a dance with some youngsters. Apparently, he'd give them a right mouthful if they were less than perfect, and wasn't above giving one of the stage school darlings a clip round the ear if they caused a re-take. We've shared similar stories about personalities who are alive and enjoying successful careers, who I shall not name as they are still alive, and I suspect the publishers have more rewarding things to do than answer lawyers' letters.

Obituary of David Coleman

The Independent, *21 December 2013*

It takes a kind of genius to turn the phrase 'one-nil' into a catchphrase. David Coleman did, because of the tone in which he delivered it in football commentaries, momentously, as if he knew it was coming all along. And we believed him. That is the kind of authority Coleman wielded for most of his four decades with BBC Sport.

Coleman changed the game for the BBC in any number of ways. Before 1958, when he was plucked from local news in Birmingham to present the new Saturday afternoon show *Grandstand*, announcing on the BBC – and it *was* announcing in every sense of the word – had been a stuffed-shirt, plummy-voiced affair. Coleman, with his no-nonsense, virtually classless vowel sounds forged in his native Stockport, was something different – at last a BBC figure who spoke like your geography teacher, rather than Lady Isobel Barnet (kids, ask your dad).

He was a journalist too, editor of the *Cheshire County Press* at the age of just 22, and those journalistic instincts never left him. If you want to see Coleman at his editorialising best, there's a clip of him on YouTube introducing highlights of Chile v Italy in the 1962 World Cup. 'The game you are about to see,' he says, staring straight down the barrel of the camera, 'is the most stupid, appalling, disgusting and disgraceful exhibition, possibly in the history of the game. The national motto of Chile reads "By reason or force". Today, the Chileans were prepared to be reasonable, the Italians only used force, and the result was a disaster for the World Cup.'

Manifestly, he cared about sport. He had played football, for Stockport County reserves, and before injury blighted his athletics career, had been a promising middle-distance runner. In 1949, at the age of 23, he became the first non-international to win the Manchester Mile, and were it not for a persistent hamstring injury forcing him to hang up his spikes, he may have fulfilled his ambition to compete at the Olympics. Instead, he covered 11 Olympic Games, from Rome in 1960 to Sydney 2000, and six football World Cups, arguably making a greater contribution to sport than he would have as a mere competitor.

Maybe it was Coleman's empathy with his fellow athletes that prompted what *Private Eye* christened 'Colemanballs', the unintentionally comic one-liners he spouted in the heat and passion of battle. They have been flying round the social networks – 'Juantorena opened his legs and showed his class' – but it should be noted some of them are not strictly as spoken. In fact, some of them do not emanate from Coleman at all. They were ascribed to him because he was the dominant voice in sports broadcasting. And if he did say, 'There you can see her parents – her father died some time ago,' it would have been because he was utterly transfixed by the action.

As columnist Harry Pearson noted in *The Guardian*, he was given to saying 'Oh my word... has he gone too early?' as a runner moved into the lead, 'But viewers often feared it was Coleman himself who had gone too early... he reached a pitch of excitement in the final curve that seemed unsustainable without access to helium. But just when you thought he might yodel his lungs out through his nostrils, he found something extra.'

The one thing Coleman cared as much about as sport was broadcasting. He was – and this is sometimes ambivalent praise – a perfectionist. There's a famous clip of Coleman, unaware he was still being taped, berating a producer for a fluffed pre-recorded opening of a *World Cup Grandstand* programme from Mexico in 1970, stinting on neither swear words nor vituperation. But the producer involved, Jonathan Martin, later a head of BBC Sport, told me: 'He was difficult to work with, but that was because he had high standards and he expected the same from everyone else.'

I spoke to a number of BBC executives for a book I wrote about sport on TV, and even the ones with whom he had clashed over the years – he was off-air for a year in 1977 protesting at young upstarts like John Motson and Frank Bough getting gigs he thought he should have had – spoke of him in the most glowing terms.

Some idea of his status at the BBC, and his journalistic credentials, can be gathered from the fact that when the Beatles flew back into Heathrow in February 1964 after their triumphant tour of the United States, it was Coleman who was chosen to meet them. Ever the journalist, he put the difficult question, asking what they might do to reclaim the spot in the top ten they had just lost. John Lennon later said he knew the Beatles had really made it when they saw Coleman waiting for them.

Coleman's journalistic training became even more relevant at the 1972 Munich Olympics when he broadcast live and unscripted for several hours when the Israeli athletes were held hostage in the Olympic village.

When he called it a day after the 2000 Olympics, sports broadcasting was already melding into showbiz, and Coleman, you felt, was never the sort of chap who saw it as a stepping stone to *Strictly Come Dancing* or joshing with Ant and Dec. Indeed, he refused to take part in tribute shows that were planned, wrote no newspaper pieces about how much better it was in the old days, and told the BBC he didn't want anyone to make a fuss about him. Now, I feel, he will have no choice.

Channel Four lost the racing to ITV in 2016. Both the BBC and Clare Balding seem to have got over the loss.

The BBC says farewell to the Grand National

Screen Break, The Guardian, *16 April 2012*

Totemic is not a word I bandy about lightly – nor is bandy come to that – but it sums up the importance of the Grand National to the BBC. It is just one race, but for the Corporation its loss is the broadcasting equivalent of the ravens leaving the Tower. When Clare Balding brought down the curtain on

52 years of BBC coverage at 5.10pm on Saturday, a mighty empire had fallen.

Clare, by the way, did her usual bang-up job and will surely be found a berth at Channel Four, the new custodians of this crown jewel, while BBC Sport, assuming it hasn't spent its last penny covering the Olympics, will oppose the greatest horse race in the world with what? Rowing? Second division darts? Yet more of what former phone-in host David Mellor used to call, with unerring inaccuracy, red-hot soccer chat?

As luck would have it, I can enlighten you on the significance of the National in the story of our great national broadcaster. I recently spent a day with Peter Dimmock, one of the pioneers of BBC outside broadcasts, and he detailed nearly ten years of chivvying and cajoling before the formidable Mirabel Topham, Aintree's owner, agreed to allow the cameras in.

In 1960, the BBC was already showing the FA Cup, Test match cricket, and more or less all the other sport worth watching, but the National reached out far beyond its sports constituency. By the 1970s, it had become one of the great BBC days of the year, a *Radio Times* cover, crumpet-toasting family get-together. And while the race cemented the BBC's reputation as a great sports broadcaster, the television coverage, so staunchly resisted, helped elevate the race and undoubtedly contributed to its survival when its continued existence looked like economic madness. It was a marriage made in heaven.

As Keith Wilson's poem, recited over the montage of great National moments kicking off this year's coverage, pointed out, 'It's in the country's DNA.'

So, if it's in the country's DNA, was it not worth fighting to keep it on our BBC?

I am no expert in sports rights, and I know it is no

longer the 1970s – whatever the evidence inside my wardrobe might suggest – but the 50-year marriage did seem to end with a barely audible whimper. The irony is that while goodness knows how many millions have been spent to ensure Gary Lineker and Alan Shearer sit in Salford to blether about football matches played at Tottenham or West Bromwich, one of the North West's biggest sporting days of the year will be on Channel Four.

There will doubtless be a perfectly logical reason for this, but your man on the sofa is puzzled.

Not that Channel Four will short change racing fans – its Cheltenham coverage was exemplary – but the sense of national occasion will necessarily be lessened. I used to enjoy it when the national treasure comedian or TV personality of the day would anoint the occasion with his presence; Peter Kay bantering with Sue Barker comes to mind. The National was the first place light entertainment met sport. I accepted hospitality on National day one year – normally, like most journalists, I am incorruptible – and not only saw Cliff Richard in a lift, but also stood next to *Coronation Street*'s Ken Barlow in the gents' urinals (this was before his revelations of prodigious feats in the boudoir, or I might have paid closer attention).

The coverage has become less showbizzy in recent years. Clare is all about the horses, and According To Pete was the horse she took a particular shine to this year, visiting him at home in Yorkshire, and cooing over him in the saddling boxes. 'The coolest person in this team is the horse himself,' she said.

As we know, horses aren't people, but the anthropomorphism that underpins racing blurs the distinction, so Clare was naturally visibly affected by the fate of According To Pete, and Synchronized, the Gold Cup winner. It made for one of the most difficult sign-offs in sports broadcasting history.

In the few minutes between the replay of the race, and the closing titles, Clare not only had to lay to rest two much-loved horses, but all those years of Peter Kay and crumpet toasting. Being the pro that she is, she soldiered on, exchanging weasel words with Richard Pitman about how the shooting of the two animals 'was the kindest thing to do,' where really what was needed was a philosophical debate about our relationship with the animal world, taking in the wearing of leather shoes and eating of pork chops.

Two minutes with Balding and Pitman was never going to begin to approach that Beecher's Brook of an issue. Nor probably were they equipped to answer the other big question of the day; if the BBC is not for the Grand National, what *is* it for?

Sid Waddell (10 August 1940 – 11 August 2012) is sadly missed. When I was writing Screen Break in The Guardian, *the only similar column was Giles Smith's for* The Times. *I saw Giles once in the press box at a West Ham v Chelsea match, and remarked that if a bomb were to fall on the stand that night there would be nobody left to make sarcastic remarks about Clive Tyldesley. We agreed that when we were short of funnies for our work, we only needed to follow Sid on the darts and make notes on the commentary.*

The late great Sid Waddell, and the joys of Blackpool

Screen Break, The Guardian, *30 July 2007*

Oh, to be in Blackpool now that wet July is here, as no poet ever wrote; and Dave Lanning and Sid Waddell's commentary from the Stan James World Matchplay darts on Sky Sports last week made it abundantly clear why.

As they described steady drizzle falling onto a grey promenade, and angry, sludgy sea the colour of mushy peas, this viewer got vivid flashbacks of childhood holidays in the resort, hunkered up with the family in Uncle Mac's snack bar, zipped into a garment known as a pac-a-mac, a kind of plastic straitjacket which did not so much shut the rain out as shut the misery in. We would stare glumly at the rivulets of water making their way down the steamy, greasy, windows, and someone would invariably clear a little patch, peer into the gloom, and say: 'It looks like it's brightening up a little.'

Plus ça change apparently. Mind you, those responsible for promoting the jewel of the Fylde Coast would point out with some justification that it is not exactly *la même chose* these days. There are attractions beyond Uncle Mac's chocolate milkshakes. As Sid and Dave pointed out endlessly, it might have been raining outside, but the atmosphere inside the Winter Gardens for the darts was, variously, electric, buzzin', bubblin', hummin'. And yet, said Sid, when a player was going for a difficult winning double, 'you could hear the drop of a fly's dandruff.' The crowd, agreed Dave, was in a good-natured holiday mood.

To emphasise the commentators' manifesto, the camera swooped over the spectators every time the catchy little jiggy jiggy tune signalled a break, and demonstrated that, though the seaside town may have missed out on a super casino, and the party political conferences might opt these days for the relative *gemütlichkeit* of a Manchester or Harrogate, Blackpool is still the world capital for women wearing pink cowboy hats.

Sid loves the crowd shots. When the camera moves in on a table of well-upholstered females taking advantage of the cocktail hour, he comments admiringly: 'Juggin' it and lovin' it – a couple of beers and a bit of tungsten,' his great skill being to champion and celebrate the pleasures of the working classes, while simultaneously ever so slightly sending the whole business up.

Sid would, of course, deny any element of mockery, but consider this exchange between Dave and Sid. We get a shot of Freddie Flintoff in the crowd and Dave comments: 'It's the sport of the people, but it has a magic very much of its own. We've had footballers, cricketers, and people from *Coronation Street* turning up to watch.' 'Yes,' says Sid, 'Joe Longthorne and two of The Grumbleweeds were in earlier this week.'

If that is not post-modern irony – or taking the piss, as it used to be called – then I will take my box set of *Seinfeld* DVDs back to the shop.

Blackpool itself was something of a gift to the commentary box, with references to the resort's most famous fast food crackling over the airwaves like the nylon sheets in a £15-a-night guest house, and as plentiful as used condoms under the North Pier (don't blame me, Sid started it). 'This is a banquet,' said Sid, of the match between Michael van Gerwen and Ronnie Baxter. 'Good old Blackpool fayre. This is fish 'n' chips with saveloys, steaming hot and dribbling with vinegar – tongue-smacking tungsten... You will never see a better match anywhere between here and planet Venus.'

Though I am no expert on interplanetary pub games, it seemed to me he had a point. The match was just one of several that came close to justifying Sid's hyperbole. Another he described as 'like Chelsea v Manchester United, on roller skates, on ice.'

I loved it all. Not just the commentary and crowd shots, but the players' entrances, led into the arena to their chosen music – 'Eye Of The Tiger' or its closest equivalent – by two young women in swimwear, almost certainly still known in

Blackpool as dolly birds. Peter Manley's is my favourite because he does a little half-dance, half-twirl when he gets on stage. It is probably wrong to laugh at a fat man dancing, but sometimes you can't help yourself. The sport was more competitive than expected, too, with at least four players, alongside Barneveld and Taylor, now looking like potential world champions.

All in all, it was a palate-cleansing experience after another dismal Beckham-in-Los-Angeles documentary. Matt Smith and Beckham sat in ridiculous dazzling white armchairs on the terrace of some California wet dream apartment overlooking a deep blue swimming pool. As the opening scene of a porn movie, it would not have been bad, but instead the two talked about Beckham's 'challenge.' It was all 'pretty incredible,' said the sage of the midfield. 'To see people like John Travolta and his wife saying how great we are as people, me and Victoria are saying "Oh my god." It's pretty amazing.'

The more you saw, the more convinced you were that the move was about the three ms; money, money, and money. Not necessarily on Beckham's part, but the quote from LA Galaxy general manager Alexei Lalas was the giveaway: 'Having Beckham is a wonderful thing for any product.'

Beckham told Smith he had no ambition to be in the movies. I have news for you sunshine, you are already in one.

All you need to know re this next piece is that, after one hundred years, Steve Wright in the Afternoon *is no more; not one hundred per cent sure about Tupperware parties, and the reference to Paris Hilton mystifies me. Something topical, I suspect.*

The legend that is Eurosport's David Duffield (1931–2016), Cycling in the afternoon

Screen Break, The Guardian, *18 June 2007*

One does not wish to be unkind, but the thought that crops up when watching cycling on Eurosport – not, I have to admit, a daily occurrence in my case – is: forget the riders, what on earth is David Duffield on?

Duffield, well into his seventies now, is Eurosport's venerable cycling commentator, a former competitor who has been covering bike racing since the birth of the channel, and expects any day now to complete his first sentence.

His problem, quite apparent during last week's *Critérium du Dauphiné Libéré,* the 219 kilometre race from Grenoble to Roanne, is that in his mind he is addressing several different audiences; Brits, foreigners, people watching live, those watching recorded highlights, cycling enthusiasts, casual viewers who like looking at pretty pictures of rural France, and, I suppose, the odd passing pharmacist interested in the latest developments.

Duffield will begin by addressing one of these groups, then interrupt himself with an apology to all the others for whom the information is not strictly relevant, and finally lose the thread of what he was trying to say in the first place. It would not be strictly accurate to describe Duffield as the king of the dangling participles, but there is definitely something dangling there.

On the afternoon I was watching, he started praising Bradley Wiggins, the British rider wearing the Yellow Jersey, before remembering the overseas viewers: 'Do bear with me if I do get carried away, because I know Eurosport coverage goes to 90 million, er, 99 million...' – at this point, I am sure he said 99 million countries which, even with the break-up of the old Soviet Union, and Eurosport's massive penetration, seemed to be overstating the case a little – 'and of course we're interested in what Biggins will do. You can understand the bias, and what a weekend with the result in Formula One.' (Whether this Biggins he speaks of is Christopher, whom I do not like to think of in Lycra, or some other Biggins, he did not specify.)

'Do bear with me' is one of Duffield's catchphrases, and you know that when he craves forbearance in this way he is about to come out with an absolute pip, and it is time to reach for the notepad and pen. Obviously, this applies particularly if you are charged with producing a semi-humorous column about sport on television, but is also worth noting if you are one of those people collecting Duffieldisms for one of the various websites dedicated to them.

'Rough end of a ragman's trumpet' and 'blast on the old banjo' are Duffield favourites apparently, but I never heard them on the afternoon I was watching. Maybe he is saving those for the Tour de France. 'Ooh, steady the bus,' as the riders rounded a bend, is the best I can contribute to this valuable internet resource.

Duffield also has a rather quaint idea of the daytime audience. 'Many people watch us in the afternoon,' he said. 'Women, the kids haven't come home from school yet, and they switch on. Obviously, there are cycling specialists wanting to know about the gears, and what they had for breakfast...'

And so another thought was left just dangling there, but I assume what the Duffster was beginning to articulate was that he felt obliged to go through some of the tedious basics of the sport for the benefit of full-time mothers, who, briefly and temporarily liberated from maternal duties, would eschew such competing attractions as quiz shows, programmes about people doing up property in Spain, repeats of that ancient detective series with Dick Van Dyke in it, re-reading the poetry of Gerard Manley Hopkins, sitting in an easy chair listening to a favourite album, extra-marital affairs, marital affairs, and *Steve Wright in the Afternoon*, in order to whack on the old Eurosport for stage two of the *Critérium du Dauphiné Libéré*.

Yes, they are probably all at it in the suburbs, David. Maybe they combine it with a Tupperware party.

Duffield, as ever, was having a party on his own. When he wasn't going into raptures about the riders – 'Look at the faces, guys at work, puffing and panting...' – he was marvelling at the pictures these modern cameras were bringing us.

'Great photography, isn't it?' he enthused. 'There are cameras in the helicopters sending the pictures back, and those chaps on the motorcycles, and there's a van just by the finish, and the director has one, two, three, four, five pictures to choose from. This costs a lot of money. It is not like covering football or tennis with static cameras, and I know we do tennis wall-to-wall...' where the thought again sort of tailed off, just as the director chose a close-up of a rider's buttocks in full hill-climbing mode – from the arsecam, I expect.

You can sympathise with Duffield. For the general audience there is not a lot going on in the middle period of a cycle race, and the Dufferino comes from a generation that believes in value for money, so he just keeps on commentating regardless, ill-advisedly some would say.

Still, you pick up some stuff. The riders have radios in their crash helmets, you know, so team managers can convey tactics. Get on your bike and pedal like hell, I should have thought would cover it, but apparently not. It is a highly tactical business. The Tour de France is next, and Duffers is the man to interpret it for us – if, like Paris Hilton, he ever manages to complete a sentence.

All Our Yesterdays

No 43: **Take Your Pick** (1955–1968),
The Independent, 1 June 2002

I did 70-odd of these for the Independent in the paper's glory, glory days. I'll slip one in from time to time as a palate cleanser between the meatier stuff.

● *Take Your Pick* must have seemed like the devil's work to a generation reared on the wholesome paternalism of the BBC.
A smarmy host called Michael Miles – a New Zealander no less – waved £5 notes under the nose of some hapless punter trying to tempt him or her to give up the key to a secret box.
How demeaning. How humiliating.

Have you any idea what one single five-pound note could buy you in austere post war Britain? A night out for two at the local palais, half a pound of monkey nuts, and a two bedroomed town house in Islington. And here was some suntanned encyclopaedia salesman from a land of plenty flaunting great fistfuls of them. Of course the poor saps were going to give up their key. Sometimes, though, they would gamble and, urged on by the audience, would spurn Miles's grubby handful of notes in the hope of winning a treasure chest full of money.

When, instead of the money their secret box was found to contain a booby prize of a box of spent matches or an elastic band, Miles said 'Doh!', while the contestants slunk off to drown their sorrows in such harsh home made liquor as was available in those dark days.

3. The Value of Investments

'They gave a chimpanzee a pin and a racing card. I could be that chimpanzee...'

Newly signed up by The Racing Post, *after departing* The Guardian, *I felt obliged to point out that readers might be disappointed if they were hoping to read my column for fun and profit. Fun, maybe.*

What Kind Of Klutz Am I?

Racing Post, *8 January 2014*

I know nothing. You need to know that, as it runs counter to the whole ethos of this journal, which is to provide facts and informed opinion to those seeking guidance on which dumb animals – and obviously I include footballers in that – it might be wise to invest in.

Elsewhere in the paper you will find great phalanxes of figures, which may help with that sort of reckoning, but there is minimal financial advantage to be gained from this column. That's certainly what I've found over the years.

I know you study the statistics, because I sat next to one of you once on the train from Waterloo to Kempton Park, and he guided me through evidence proving beyond reasonable doubt that a particular horse, priced at 7/2, would reverse the form of a previous meeting and beat its more fancied opponent.

'Ah, but has anyone told the horse?' I asked, as he suddenly remembered an urgent appointment in the buffet car. (The only buffet car, incidentally, where you can be pondering which biscuits to buy, and somebody will sidle up, tap the side of his nose knowingly, and say, 'Hobnobs.')

As it turned out, my statistically minded friend was spot on, but I failed to invest. I was enjoying lavish hospitality from the sponsors who had mistaken me for an influential media figure, and was distracted by a rather fine looking herb-crusted rack of lamb just as betting for the race closed. I was actually wiping flecks of gravy from the corner of my mouth as I watched the unbacked (by me, at least) 7/2 chance stride over the line. That's the kind of klutz you're dealing with here.

I have, however, watched a lot of TV in my time, so I fancied I might be able to help a little with *Celebrity Big Brother*, which has just begun on Channel 5. Some hope. I suspect I am not the natural audience for this programme. I could tell they did not want me hanging around with the young folk, when they kept advertising something called 'Old Skool Garage Anthems'.

To me, a garage anthem is 'Little Red Corvette' by Prince, or the Beach Boys singing, 'We'll have fun, fun, fun till her daddy takes her T-bird away,' but judging by the racket coming out of the TV set, they meant something else entirely.

Apart from the very young and heavily medicated, I can never work out who Channel 5 is aimed at. People who have had their brain removed and replaced by a clockwork mouse, possibly. Certainly, *Celebrity Big Brother,* which I wasted two hours of my life on the other evening, might as well have been in Sanskrit for all I could grasp. For a start, they introduced housemate Rylan Clark, currently favourite to win, as '*X Factor* legend.' No, I shouted. A legend is Sir Lancelot Du Lac or Stanley Matthews, not this grinning clothes horse without a significant accomplishment to his name.

The next contestant will be known to you, the currently suspended jockey Frankie Dettori, who is reputedly being paid a sum not unadjacent to 'How much? How much? You're joking,' for his participation.

I assume there is a sliding scale for these fees, under which the glamour models and minor soap stars get ten grand or so, while producers have to go up into six figures to secure people like Frankie, or Gillian Taylforth, veteran of many TV dramas and a brief period of notoriety when she was caught with a gentleman enjoying an impromptu snack in a lay-by just off the A1 (well, anything beats the Little Chef).

Neil 'Razor' Ruddock, whose Wikipedia entry describes him rather optimistically as a 'TV personality,' was the only other housemate known to me. Razor now goes from reality show to reality show picking up the fees, and good luck to him, I say. In his time at my team West Ham, we rose to fifth in the league, our highest position for years.

So much of a fixture is Razor on reality TV, that he was available to be drafted into *CBB* at the last minute to replace Jim Davidson, otherwise engaged helping with inquiries into sexual improprieties back in the dark ages.

Wrestling in Honey

Readers of my blogs will know that I suggested some time ago that rather than turning aside from this regrettable business, *Big Brother* accept it, and help Operation Yewtree expedite the unfortunate process. As the whole thing is being played out in the glare of the media anyway, with much loved entertainment figures – and Jim Davidson – forced to appear on the news to defend themselves, why not allow Plod to place its chosen names in the *BB* House to be questioned there? That way, that ludicrous basement could be turned into a real dungeon.

Needless to say, TV has spurned my idea, so *CBB* will meander on in its monumentally uninteresting way, in which case my tip is former Steps singer Claire Richards, 9/1 at time of writing, as she should get the nostalgia vote. Although, be warned, if I haven't already made it sufficiently clear, that the value of investments can go down as well as up.

Having left The Guardian, *the then-editor of* The Racing Post *Bruce Millington had sent me a sweet email asking if I'd do a weekly column. My lack of expert knowledge of horse racing was one of the more noticeable snags to this brave if slightly baffling appointment, which I'm sure is why, unlike other pundits from the paper, I was never asked to go on preview show,* The Morning Line. *Then I picked a 28/1 winner, and still the invitation never came.*

Mistaken Identity

Racing Post, *9 March 2014*

The more observant among you will have noticed I wasn't on Channel 4's *Morning Line* on Saturday. I waited all week for the call, having advertised via all electronic means currently available my perspicacity in backing Bally Legend, 28/1 winner of the Betbright Handicap at Kempton Park. My lack of any horse racing background, I felt sure, would be merely a minor impediment for a man in such blistering form.

Imagine, then, my disappointment on checking my emails and texts early on Saturday morning – not in any kind of a desperate way, you understand – to find no last-minute booking, this paper being represented instead by Tom Segal, aka Pricewise.

Admittedly, Tom's suggestions were likely to be more helpful than mine – he was said in one show to have 'whipped up a punting storm' with one of his tips, something I could never be accused of – but still, in the same way as Paul the psychic octopus was recruited to predict the scores in the 2010 World Cup, remember, I could have had a bash.

In fact, I am sure in the past I have read a newspaper feature where they gave a chimpanzee a pin and a racing card and tested his picks against those of an expert, finding little difference in profit and loss accounts.

I could be that chimpanzee.

I think they tried it with stock market tips as well, with similar results, proving that deep down none of us knows anything much about anything. I know I don't. Since my recent brush with death, I find myself moving closer to the *Monty Python* view that we are all just 'spiralling coils of self-replicating DNA.'

All right, I'm probably not the perfect fit for *Morning Line*. While Clare Balding was being brought up with horses – possibly even BY horses – I was brought up with a variety of unreliable motor vehicles starting with my dad's second-hand Hillman Husky, which was in the repair shop so often it may have done more miles vertically than horizontally.

In any case, the best I could do last Saturday was a few

bob each way on Renard in the Grimthorpe Chase, which went some way towards financing my other useless picks. In short, I seem in no immediate danger of losing my amateur status, so it's probably just as well the phone never rang.

Actually it did ring. It was a young chap called James, a producer at BBC WM radio in Birmingham, asking for my views on the possibility of a televised debate between deputy PM Nick Clegg and UKIP leader Nigel Farage ahead of the European elections.

I raised an eyebrow at this – inasmuch as it's possible to do that over the phone – but, not wishing to be rude, said I thought Clegg's invitation to Farage to face him on TV was either a high-risk strategy by the Lib Dem leader or a last desperate throw of the dice depending on how you look at it. TV debates can influence elections, though, I added, citing the famous 1960 Kennedy-Nixon meeting which as good as secured the Presidency for the telegenic young Senator.

'Great,' said James. 'Can you come on our breakfast show in the morning to talk about it?'

'Well, OK,' I said, still with eyebrow raised. I knew there was no money in it, what with BBC local stations being strapped for cash, but am always happy to share my views on subjects about which I know nothing, as regular readers of this column will confirm, so agreed.

I assumed I had been chosen to address the heartland of England as a famous watcher of telly rather than for any political expertise.

'How should we describe you?' asked James.

'Journalist, legendary lover, and inventor of Cling Film, will do,' I replied. 'No seriously, just journalist is fine.'

'And of course, you work in political polling,' he said, which was when I twigged that he had confused me with near-namesake Peter Kellner, proper political journalist and president of YouGov. 'You mean you're not him?' was the response, followed by the stunner, 'Well, can you come on anyway?'

So I did, informing the West Midlands that as Clegg's last big triumph was in the TV debate before the last election he was probably trying to recapture past glories, 'rather like Spandau Ballet going back out on tour,' at which point they cut – a little too rapidly, I felt – to the travel news.

This is not the first time this has happened either.

A few years back I took a call from talkSPORT, asking if I could come on and talk about 'the Portsmouth situation.' (It was when Tony Adams was manager) 'Well I can,' I said, 'But I only know what I've read in the newspapers.'

'Well, there's a story in one of the papers that he is going to bring you in as defensive coach,' the young chap replied. I had to tell him that despite some success in junior football and the odd showbiz XI, such a move was unlikely, concluding that his call owed more to my proximity to Martin Keown in the talkSPORT contacts book than my undoubted tactical acumen.

I was that close to going on, though. Meanwhile, I live in hope that *Morning Line* may one day mistake me for someone who knows something about horse racing.

Clare Balding on Channel 4, and a dodgy World Cup tip

Racing Post, *13 July 2014*

There was a sweet moment on *Channel 4 Racing* the other day, when the sainted Clare's welcome to the show, from the pre-parade ring at Newmarket, was interrupted by a loud whinny as one of the horses passed.

'Ooh, steady,' said Clare, but it whinnied again, and though I'm no horse whisperer, I swear I heard the horse say to its mates, 'Blimey fancy that, Clare Balding on Channel 4 on a wet Thursday afternoon.'

Newmarket's July Festival is probably one of the events the Queen of All Media is contracted to present for the channel, but still it was a surprise to me – and maybe to The Great War too, the horse making all the noise – to see Clare out of the context of the big showpiece occasions like the National and Ascot.

Maybe it was because it was raining. Huddling for warmth under an umbrella with Mick Fitzgerald seemed a little incongruous for the celebrated broadcaster and paragon, whom we last encountered anchoring BBC radio's coverage of Wimbledon, and before that in an ambassadorial role for BT Sport.

Increasing numbers of revered figures from the world of sport – and Robbie Savage – are hawking themselves out as ambassadors these days.

An advertisement used to be a simple matter; your agent would ring and tell you you'd got an ad, at which you'd high-five the family, tell them they could have shoes this year, hasten to a studio in Soho, and extol the virtues of Weetabix or Toilet Duck.

But now it's not enough for commerce to own your tonsils. They want you, body and soul, for which I believe they pay a sum of money if not strictly beyond the dreams of avarice very much in that neighbourhood.

José Mourinho has been signed up for that amount plus ten per cent as the latest BT Sport ambassador, and is now in a head-to-head contest with David Beckham, who is Sky Sports' ambassador. The two providers are eyeing each other across no-man's land.

You'll have seen a shiny smiling Becks during the ad-breaks in the World Cup, hawking Sky's new dedicated European football channel, whereas José does not appear to have been launched in earnest yet. Maybe he's doing those other things an ambassador does; handing out Ferrero Rochers, going to the opera.

Behind the smiles, though, it's all about flogging us broadband. I've already had a call from BT warning me that if I want to 'continue enjoying BT Sport for free,' I need to carry on buying my broadband from them.

I told the young lady I wasn't about to switch anyway, being from the generation that got its gas from the gas board, its books from the library, its bins emptied by the Corporation, and free milk in little bottles warming by the radiator. It's amazing how quickly you can get rid of cold callers if you try.

On World Cup Final day tomorrow, our choice is between ITV and BBC, and I expect the audience breakdown to go something like this; BBC – pretty well everyone, ITV – Adrian Chiles's mum.

For what it's worth, I marginally favour the commercial channel's commentary, but not enough to endure the ads and Chiles's still slightly desperate chumminess. (You've got the gig, Adrian, calm down). I could do with Clive Tyldesley not talking quite so much, but he is a hugely experienced commentator and you feel pretty safe in his hands.

His sidekick, Andy Townsend, rarely adds a great deal in the way of penetrating analysis, but at least he doesn't get heavily involved in banter, for which relief much thanks.

The BBC, on the other hand, has gone banter crazy this World Cup. I blame its main commentator, Guy Mowbray, who encourages his second banana in the commentary box to join him in a stream of pointless blether. Danny Murphy is the worst, and whatever your views on how the two of them call the game, the one thing you can say for certain is they are not Morecambe and Wise.

On the pundits' sofas it has been a score draw. The BBC's Rio Ferdinand has been a hit; fluent, personable, occasionally revelatory, and with the kind of relaxed insouciance that is as pleasing on telly as it was heart-stopping sometimes at the centre of the West Ham defence. But Martin O'Neill, playing wide left for ITV, in every sense, remains the undisputed star.

His disputes with Fabio Cannavaro have been endlessly entertaining. I particularly enjoyed the exchange, in the discussion before the semi-final, over Netherlands manager Louis van Gaal's late late substitution of his goalkeeper for the penalty shoot-out against Costa Rica.

Cannavaro made the interesting point that while the move might have brought short-term gain, its effect on team spirit could stifle further progress for the Dutch. Never one to disregard expert advice, I duly made a small profit on Argentina's progress. I may have to tune into ITV's build-up tomorrow to pick up on any re-investment advice Fabio has.

It's predicted the final will be the most wagered upon event in sports betting history, which must exacerbate the hard times horse racing is facing.

One assumes there's a limit to the mug punter pound, which means four legs having to fight ever harder against 22 for a share of it.

What the business probably needs at this stage is a well-known, respected, ambassador, and really there's only one candidate.

Who knew, a few short years later I'd be writing for the Racing Post*?*

The low-cost way to enjoy the Cheltenham Festival

Screen Break, The Guardian, *21 March 2011*

A friend of mine who met his wife on an internet dating site (which was a shock to him, as he thought she was ordering a book on Amazon at the time) tells me he used to eliminate potential partners, however toothsome they might seem in other respects, if they answered the question about religion with the single word 'spiritual.'

That spoke to him of multiple cat ownership, oversized jewellery, inappropriate teddy bears in the bedroom and pointless arguments about the existence of some higher power, because otherwise, like, how did we get here?

That is certainly not a conversation I would feel able to contribute to, at least not until last week when an unseen hand – I hesitate to talk of guardian angels – helped save me from financial embarrassment at Cheltenham.

I rarely bet on horse racing, believing racehorses to be flighty creatures capable of capricious behaviour it is folly to try and predict.

I do not buy the anthropomorphism that marks out certain horses as keen competitors, having never seen any concrete evidence that the animals even know they are in a race.

We only really have Clare Balding's word on that, and as she tweeted last week that James Corden was 'a genius' (No Clare, Einstein and Leonardo da Vinci are geniuses, Paolo Di Canio at a pinch, James Corden is something else), I do not feel comfortable risking the children's university money on her say-so.

I prefer to back my judgement on events like the Eurovision Song Contest, the Booker Prize – I write as someone who lumped on Howard Jacobson, if you will pardon the expression, at 8/1 – and the cricket World Cup, where the non-human element is less crucial.

However, the Cheltenham Festival is such spectacular television it invariably reels me in, and has me signing up for special offers from various betting web sites.

But this year – and here is where the force beyond our ken comes in – on the eve of the Festival, I lost all my bank cards which meant, despite the inducements being offered ad nauseum on TV and radio, I was unable to set up any new online betting accounts, making it my most profitable Cheltenham for years.

I still do not know how the wallet containing the cards disappeared from the inside pocket of my jacket, and reappeared by the pumps at an all-night petrol station in Sheffield, but that is what I found had happened after exhausting every other possible scenario, and some at the very edge of possibility (what combination of circumstances did I imagine might have placed it at the bottom of the fridge in the cheese compartment?)

It meant I was able to enjoy the festival purely as a television event, and once again Channel 4's coverage was terrific. The combination of HD and super slo-mo makes the re-runs of the races something to marvel at. Channel 4's cast of characters is well chosen, too.

The great joy of going racing is that it is one sporting event at which you genuinely meet people from all walks of life, united only in the futile quest to predict which combination of horse flesh and undernourished pilot might be worth investing in, and Channel 4's team reflects this democracy brilliantly.

John McCririck summed it up on the *Morning Line*, dubbing the patrician Nick Luck 'Lord Snooty', and the permanently rumpled and windswept (even in the studio, somehow) Alastair Down 'Fat Al'. Between Lord Snooty and Fat Al, meanwhile, there are a number of amusing and attractive broadcasters, provided you realise that the views they propound are for amusement only, which was not a problem for me this year.

I did, by the way, get my wallet back once the racing was safely over, with my British Library card and all my cash still in it, proving either the existence of an unseen force, or that Sheffield is the most honest city in Britain.

Finally, referees cannot win – it's official.

In the Tottenham v West Ham match on Saturday, Carlton Cole went to ground in the penalty area, after being leant on by Spurs captain Michael Dawson. No penalty was awarded, and pundit Glenn Hoddle duly delivered the line beloved of Sky analysts: 'That happens anywhere outside the penalty area, and it's a foul.'

Fellow expert Robbie Keane (who I hope has invested his money wisely because I do not foresee a glittering media career after he hangs up his boots) agreed.

However, had Mike Dean given the penalty, would he not have been excoriated for awarding 'a soft penalty?' So what is a referee to do? Should he be allowed to exercise a little common sense, or forced to stick to the rules?

Do not ask me, I have my work cut out keeping track of my possessions, but maybe Glenn can find an answer from somewhere, being a little on the 'spiritual' side himself.

I have absolutely no idea what the reference to the Sharm El Sheikh sea bathing club was about, but I'm sure it was funny at the time.

It's all about the in-play. A mug's game.

Screen Break, The Guardian, *13 December 2010*

I wonder if any of the bets Ray Winstone suggests on the Bet 365 advert ever come off.

You will have seen the commercial: 'It's all abaht the in-play,' Winstone snarls, as he saunters around your screen like he owns the place (and having seen him in *Nil By Mouth,* if that is what he wants to do, it is fine by me), 'the total goals, the next scorer, the method of scoring.'

He looks you straight in the face, daring you to go to the kitchen for a cup of tea and a fairy cake, and says: ''ere's the latest odds,' while some vaguely plausible bet on the match in progress appears.

Now, though I cannot claim to watch every football match shown live on TV, I have yet to see a single one of these bets turn out to be anything other than a passport to the poorhouse.

I may be wrong, and the last thing I want to do is upset Ray, because he looks like the sort of chap who has ways of dealing with an uppity smartarse at *The Guardian* traducing his life's work. But as someone who has been known to have a financial interest in a football match, I feel that of all the reasons you might have for risking your money in what we are obliged to call these difficult times, probably the worst is; because Ray Winstone told me to.

Not that I am taking the gambling high ground. Anybody following my tweets knows the overwhelming message that emerges from my investments is that it is extremely difficult to predict the outcome of a football match.

That, and the fact that the value of investments can go down... and, er, that's it. In terms of cash receipts, I am currently running about neck-and-neck with the Sharm El Sheikh sea bathing club.

Saturday was typical.

Having argued with so-called experts that Alan Pardew was nowhere near as bad as advertised, I backed Newcastle to hold mighty Liverpool to a draw. I should have gone the whole hog. Curse my timidity. That is five pounds I shall never see again.

I am beginning to feel about football betting the way the American gag merchant Henny Youngman felt about Las Vegas: 'I'll tell you how to beat the gambling in Las Vegas,' said Henny. 'When you get off the airplane, walk right into the propeller.'

That might be a smidgen extreme, but if you need a cautionary tale about where it can all end, the excellent documentary series *30 for 30*, on ESPN Classic last week, provided one with *The Legend of Jimmy The Greek*.

Jimmy The Greek (real name, Demetrios Georgios Synodinos) was a pundit from 1976 to 1988 on *The NFL Today*, a legendary American show screened by CBS Sports on Sunday lunchtimes, looking ahead to the day's matches. Jimmy managed the difficult task of suggesting betting opportunities without actually mentioning odds, points spreads and so on, in keeping with the puritan nature of the American networks in those days.

He became a huge star, 'getting cards and letters from people he don't even know, and offers coming over the phone,' as Glen Campbell put it in an entirely different context.

'He was born for television,' said Dan Rather, a CBS news anchor from 1981–2005. 'What you look for in television is someone who can get through the glass, and become a real person to people in living rooms and bars, and Jimmy could.'

Trouble was, he was a gambler as well. Like all gamblers he was full of stories of his big wins – Jimmy died in 1996, his words were spoken by a voice-over – but less forthcoming about the ones that went awry. His greatest coup was backing Harry S. Truman at 17/1 to win the 1948 presidential election, when press and pollsters were united in the view that the contest would be a walkover for Thomas E. Dewey. Jimmy's hunch was that women voters would be put off by Dewey's moustache – and having seen it on Google images, I see the point – and he backed it with every penny he had.

What Jimmy did not see coming was his sacking from CBS. Dan Rather, unafflicted by the gambler's romance, had a more clear-eyed view of how television works: 'Jimmy was an American tragedy. To get all the way to the mountain top, and then plummet to the bottom. He came to the end of his 12th year and his contract was up for renewal. He was perhaps an easier victim than he thought, of the dark side of television. Network politics can really stink.'

Jimmy provided the ammunition himself, with a racist comment about black athletes, and never worked in TV, or advertised shaving cream again. In his latter years, a CBS director went to see him and found a shambles. After he bought Jimmy lunch, the former TV star asked him for a few dollars. Jimmy died, penniless, and near friendless. It was a stunning documentary, wise about television, and even wiser about gambling. From now on, I shall be giving Ray Winstone the gimlet eye.

After a disastrous World Cup under Roy Hodgson in 2014, I was looking to Andy Murray to restore national pride, and backing it with hard cash, the very definition of irresponsible gambling. Also, anyone remember White Dee? The wheels of the television mill keep on grinding.

Please Gamble Responsibly.

Racing Post, *23 August 2014*

I'm sure I'm not alone in finding it difficult to adjust after a few weeks away, but in fairness there's a lot to take in when you return to find the former Frank Maloney now a woman, Cliff Richard apparently on Britain's Most Wanted list, and Roy Hodgson still England manager.

It's the Hodgson thing I'm finding most difficult to come to terms with. The sight of the man I'm itching to call the former England manager during Sky's coverage of Liverpool's opening match against Southampton was genuinely disconcerting. Ah, I remember him, I thought. What's he doing there? Blimey, he must be checking out players for the 2016 European Championships. And there I was, thinking the FA was having a laugh saying Roy was sticking around for a couple of years to continue with his plan, whatever that might be.

I think we got just the one shot of Roy and certainly no post-match interview. So Sky clearly sees him as an irrelevance too. Not like those balmy days of a couple of months ago, when the telly couldn't get enough of him. It was all so different then, as the great philosopher Barbra Streisand put it in her song 'The Way We Were', although she was not referring directly to Hodgson.

Anyway, dreamer that I am, as keen readers will remember I put money on England to win the World Cup.

Not to get out of the group, or to progress to the quarter-finals, but to actually win the tournament. That's what we doctors call comedy – but I was wrong to suggest it was your patriotic duty to follow me on this suicide mission.

Few of you did, I suspect, about which I am happy, since the exhortation ran counter to my mantra, shared by the Government, most bookmakers, but not necessarily Cash Converters – Please Gamble Responsibly.

You'll find the slogan on online betting sites, and on the wall of any betting shop, somewhere near the notice telling you how to get access to the disabled toilet. And this paper does what it can in this regard by providing full disclosure on antecedents and historical precedent in discussing the animals and their human helpers contesting the various horse races, ensuring that placing a bet does not become a mere reflex action, like lighting up a cigarette.

In this environment of sound common sense, I like to delude myself into thinking you might have missed, over the past three weeks, my tales of slightly less responsible gambling (self-delusion is one of my hobbies, alongside studying the lives of the Hollywood greats, and sitting on the toilet till my legs go to sleep, two activities I have managed to combine quite successfully). If it is the classically bad bet you want to read about, I have what the Americans would call a doozy for you.

Think back to the early days of summer, when we were cursing the lamentable England football team, holding out little hope for our almost equally inept cricketers, and before our athletes had smashed the likes of Tuvalu and St Kitts in the Commonwealth Games.

This genius looked at the contenders for the *BBC Sports Personality of the Year* award, in which market I have some form, and concluded that the very lukewarm favourite Lewis

Hamilton was worth taking on, given the poor recent record of Formula One contenders.

I mulled over the candidates lower down in the betting and decided the winner might be someone who lifted our spirits in the autumn after what I was sure was going to be a miserable July and August. And that was what led me – or rather my tenner – to Andy Murray at 33/1.

I figured that was tantamount to backing Andy at 33/1 to win the US Open, and he was looking half-decent at that stage. I mean, who else was likely to win anything, I asked, just weeks before Rory McIlroy went and won both the Open and the US Open? He's now 1/6, and you can get Andy Murray at only slightly shorter odds than on Kellie Maloney changing back again.

I've not given up hope, though. If Andy were to bring peace to the Middle East, or dive into a torrent of freezing water to rescue a cute family of new-born kittens on the eve of the vote, he might still have a squeak.

Kellie Maloney's decision, of course, was courageous, and we must hope she can put the years of torment she has clearly suffered behind her, away from the glare of publicity, in the peace and tranquillity of the, er, *Big Brother* House.

She is favourite to win the contest, with Dee Kelly, known as White Dee from the poverty-porn show *Benefits Street*, second in the betting. I almost backed Dee, having misread her name in the runners and riders as Des Kelly, old chum and *Evening Standard* columnist.

Instead, my money has gone on Gary Busey at 12/1. He was Oscar-nominated for *The Buddy Holly Story* in 1978, which must count as a positive form line, in a field of reality show flotsam and jetsam, and Audley Harrison. The actor seems utterly without malice – or anything else much, quite frankly – rather like Tony Blackburn, a previous winner for me in one of these celeb contests. And please don't worry about my not gambling responsibly. It's only money I would otherwise have tossed away on fripperies, like shoes and food.

❧

Here's a blog post from December 2020. Tim Davie had recently taken over as the BBC's 17th Director-General, setting out new guidelines for the Corporation's staff, stating that they should avoid expressing personal views on current issues of political controversy (which he called 'virtue signalling') on their own private social media accounts.

Some BBC presenters, notably Gary Lineker and Naga Munchetty, had been accused of promoting vaguely leftish views on issues like Trump, Brexit, Covid laxity, and so on.

I have a fairly robust view on this kind of controversy. When I was called into the programme editor's office at BBC Radio Leeds, told we'd had emails from people offended by something I'd said, and asked what I thought we should do, I replied, 'Can't we just tell them to fuck off?'

Clearly, the DG has to take a more nuanced approach, but trying to make the Corporation more right wing, anti-woke or whatever, just because the papers say you should, strikes me as pointless, pusillanimous and possibly counter-productive.

But I knew that in that climate, the panic-stricken Beeb would find some way to keep British sport's top award away from someone who had clashed with the Boris Johnson government over free school meals for poor pupils, and had campaigned strongly on the subject.

Damn them. My mood wasn't helped by the fact that my son David, in a rare fit of acuity, had taken a punt on Rashford a year in advance of the awards and put £25 on him at 150/1 to win the title. The lily-livered BBC cost him the best part of four grand.

The Rashford Scandal.

blog post at martinkelner.com, 4 December 2020

Round about August or September, after Marcus had forced the Government into a U-turn over free school meals, it became apparent that the nation was likely to show its appreciation for his campaign – and more importantly, as a fine representative of Britain's national game on and off the pitch – by voting for him to become Sports Personality Of The Year. He shortened to 8/11 in the betting. There was no-one anywhere near him, it was a near certainty.

Around that time, Tim Davie took over at the BBC amid much talk of whether the Corporation was too woke, too leftish, too remainery and so on. There was, for instance, the row over Emily Maitlis appearing to be editorialising on *Newsnight* about Covid and the Government's missteps.

We also got all those ludicrous statements about employing more 'right wing comedians', like that's a thing.

They'll have had some idiotic *W1A*-style Zoom meeting and decided to give Bob Mills a couple of Nish Kumar's gigs or something. (Bob's a friend and colleague, by the way, and never in a million years is he a 'right wing comedian'. There aren't any. Geoff Norcott is another name mentioned. Not a right wing comedian. He makes funny jokes about his wife; that doesn't make him Jacob Rees Fucking Mogg).

It would have been about then that one of the many otiose managers at the BBC will have spotted that if they were to place Marcus Rashford on the *SPOTY* shortlist, a disobliging public would be likely to damn well vote for him, recognising Rashford as an admirable young man with a social conscience – a rich Premier League and international fooballer who, when he talks about 'giving something back', actually means it.

Many voters might also have wished to support the footballer to send a message to Boris Johnson and his gang of incompetents, but those are the breaks.

At this point, a whole bunch of OMs would have arranged another Zoom meeting, and concluded that the 'personality' element of the award would be ditched this year, and the award for the first time would be about sporting achievement only, and they could fob the Rashford supporting public off with the *SPOTY* equivalent of the J Montgomery Burns award for Excellence in the field of Excellence.

I have no argument with Lewis Hamilton winning in the circumstances. He's a fine driver of motor cars, but Marcus Rashford IS Sports Personality of the Year.

(I should add that I used the expression 'those are the breaks' a full two years before Johnson purloined it for his valedictory address.)

4. The Telly

'Damper than an otter's pocket...'

Here's a piece from my first decade of Screen Breaks. They were frontier days, those, when we'd venture onto the wrong side of the tracks on a Saturday afternoon to a dodgy pub with a satellite dish pointed craftily towards live Premier League football from Scandinavia, meanwhile trying to make sense of all the new stuff chipping away at Sky's dominance; Setanta, BT Vision, ITV Digital, every season something new. And not being a media business expert, all I could do was goggle. By way of compensation, this piece has a punchline.

Not going to the match

Screen Break, The Guardian, *24 August 2007*

A modern reworking of LS Lowry's famous 1953 painting, *Going To The Match,* would require the matchstick figures not to be striding out towards the Bolton Wanderers' ground, but slumped in armchairs with a remote control in one hand and a family-size bag of Doritos in the other. Clearly, they would no longer be matchstick figures. If football was once the people's game – a claim it could make even long after Lowry – there are now new owners.

Confirmation, as if there were still the slightest doubt, that the game belongs to television comes with the launch of the package from the Irish broadcaster Setanta, which consists of 46 live Premiership matches, alongside the 92 to be shown on Sky (which also has tomorrow's Community Shield), the Champions League games on ITV, England home internationals on the BBC, and goodness knows how many fixtures downloadable via BT Vision.

Scarcely a penny of the resultant pantechnicon full of money drawing up outside the Premier League headquarters will, it will hardly startle you to learn, go towards making it easier or more economically viable for spectators to attend live matches. This season, a viewing card, a direct debit to one, other, or all of the sports broadcasters, and a high-speed broadband internet connection will replace scarf, hat and rail ticket in the football fan's armoury.

It used to be that supporters were reluctant to admit to following their team's progress on screen rather than from the terraces; that is not the case now. Listening to callers on football phone-ins quite happy to admit they get their kicks on Channel 406 (MUTV, that's another subscription) will convince you of the primacy of the armchair fan.

In fact, it is almost a working class badge of honour to watch on TV, a sign that though you may not be able to afford a couple of grand for a season ticket, you have not abandoned the beautiful game altogether. There is no shame any more in not being there.

I have even noticed that in football's mythology, epic folk tales about being ambushed by enemy supporters on the streets of Stoke-on-Trent are being joined by stories of extraordinary measures undertaken – illegal downloads from Malaysia, or dodgy satellite feeds from South African or Scandinavian TV channels – to watch your team from a distance in important games.

There is a hilarious and instructive YouTube clip that sums up the current state of football fandom brilliantly. It is simply a recording of the reactions of a West Ham fan as he watches on Sky TV his team's crucial end-of-season fixture at Old Trafford, when Carlos Tevez's winning goal preserved the Hammers' Premiership status.

Nobody watching him burying his head in the sofa cushions, pacing around the room, chewing his fist, alternately muttering imprecations, shouting at the TV, or stunned into temporary silence, would doubt for one moment the viewer's passion. Nor would anyone question his commitment to the cause.

Within a day or two of the match, the YouTube clip had been forwarded to West Ham fans around the world, and has now been viewed by roughly four times as many people as were watching inside the ground. The clip chronicles an experience achingly familiar to Premiership football fans and likely to become more so. To borrow a line from *The Simpsons*: it is funny because it is true.

The clip may be the 2007 equivalent of the Lowry picture. The original, by the way, depicting that bygone age when football truly was the working man's theatre, is safely in the custody of people who could afford the £1.9m it cost. It hangs in the headquarters of the Professional Footballers' Association.

Up until about 2018, Transfer Deadline Day was a big deal for Sky Sports, then still part of Rupert Murdoch's empire. The triple pillars of the day-long broadcast were reporters, often surrounded by the under-employed with nothing better to do than gurn at the camera, stationed in club car parks screaming into the ether, Harry Redknapp or similar giving interviews from the front seat of his SUV, and main presenter, the Scotsman Jim White, in a yellow tie, as the personification of the whole overblown process. Interestingly, most of the names mentioned here have scarcely been heard of since.

How Transfer Deadline Day might go

Screen Break, The Guardian, *30 January 2013*

Some of you may be familiar with the film *The Little Shop Around The Corner*, in which the boss of a Budapest department store calls all his staff together just before Christmas Eve, and delivers a rousing speech about how they're going to have the best Christmas ever.

Well that's what it's like at Sky Sports News on Transfer Deadline Day. For them, it's Christmas, the State Opening of Parliament, and a royal wedding rolled into one. It really ought to be a bank holiday.

Every year they strive to recreate the drama of that very first Deadline Day in the 2002-2003 season, when the football world gathered round TV sets and watched rapt, as Rufus Brevett moved from Fulham to West Ham.

This is how it might go this year:

8.00am: Morning meeting at central command, Isleworth. Troops gather, and Big Cheese – probably not Rupert but someone equally authoritative – lays a huge map of Europe out on the table and begins moving different coloured tokens around with one of those things croupiers use, and you see in old war films; theatre of engagement and all that, he tells them.

The question of star presenter Jim White's entrance is raised. Last year, the screaming king of Deadline Day was filmed getting out of his car and entering the studio. Someone suggests he enters SAS-style this year, crashing through the window in full combat gear. BC looks interested.

9.00am: Toothsome young blonde with glassy stare and her greying uncle – the SSN presenters – cross to Blackpool, where reporter, shouting into the teeth of a force eight gale, or 'a typical summer's day' as it's known round there, says there's been no sign of Tom Ince yet, but he could join any of those interested teams you've been reading about in the papers for the past three weeks.

12 noon: Blonde and uncle replaced by similar, who report that various South American players called Bepé, Pepé, and suchlike, are keen on moving to the Premier League. Meanwhile, Alex Ferguson's signing of Uruguayan Diego Rolan is believed to be because he's a South American with two names.

3.00pm: It's getting frantic in the studio now. Producer phones out for more hair lacquer.

6.00pm: Jim White arrives, and surprises us all by skydiving into the presenter's seat from the royal helicopter, as featured in the Olympic Opening Ceremony.

9.00pm: Norwich City sign Luciano Becchio, and all the other Leeds United players they haven't already got.

11.00pm: In a shock move, White tells viewers he's 'mad as hell and isn't going to take it any more.' He admits Deadline Day is a farce, a desperate and usually pointless last throw of the dice by relegation-threatened teams.

'We're on all day,' he weeps as security drag him from his chair, 'and there's usually only ever one significant move.' This year it's West Ham midfielder Mohamed Diamé to Arsenal, his niece tells us, as White spontaneously combusts.

The anniversary of Sky Sports News; 15 years of groin strains, transfers, and Chris Kamara

The Guardian, *31 October 2013*

There was a time when sports news knew its place; the scores and a couple of minutes of groin strains at the end of the bulletin, before knocking the mud off its boots and shuffling back to its Saturday afternoon ghetto. The idea that the autobiography of the manager of a football club – even the most successful in the country – might dominate the news agenda for two days would have been unthinkable.

While Andy Cairns doesn't take personal responsibility for the hysteria surrounding Alex Ferguson's book, as executive editor of Sky Sports News throughout its 15 years as a stand-alone channel, he has certainly played a part in propelling sport to the centre of the national conversation.

Even if you have never consciously watched Sky Sports News, you will be aware of it, having seen it in bars, with its graphics giving the latest injury news, transfer rumours, and league tables, even through the night, long after games are over and players asleep.

Are groin strains really that important? Twenty-four hours a day? 'It depends on whose groin, and how strained,' says Andy, who is fiercely protective of the news values of his journalists, refuting the idea that any of them would report a below the belt injury, without thoroughly checking it out, as it were, or a transfer story uncorroborated by reliable sources

He can afford himself a glow of pride on his channel's 15th anniversary, celebrating audience figures and approval ratings outpointing its big brother, Sky News; although Andy and I differ on the reasons for this success. He ascribes it to rigorous journalistic standards and technological innovation; I put it down to Chris Kamara.

Not just him, but Chris, a player at Swindon, Stoke, and Leeds among others, and manager at Bradford City and Stoke, epitomises the passion the panel of former players bring to Sky Sports News's flagship show *Soccer Saturday*, which fills those few unforgiving hours on a Saturday afternoon when TV is shut out of the live action.

Chris reports from inside a ground, getting wrapped up in the action we are not permitted to witness. In the studio, a cast of equally committed ex-professionals – most often Matt Le Tissier, Paul Merson, Phil Thompson, and Charlie Nicholas – watch matches on screen, and sort of report back to us on what's going on.

I say 'sort of' because these reports, especially from ex-Liverpool international defender Thompson, are often gabbled, garbled accounts preceded by some kind of ear-piercing noise; what Cairns calls, 'the human touch, emotion and passion, the language of the fan.' It's that human touch that assures him Sky Sports News will survive as TV in the age of instant updates on tablets, smart phones, and newspaper websites.

'We've been growing our audience year on year for the last seven or eight years,' says Andy, 'And things like Twitter just add to the interest. We also constantly survey our audience, and find people trust Sky Sports News. We put a lot of effort in to make sure our output is reliable and accurate.

'Journalism is right at the top of our agenda, with a real focus on training. Our in-house schemes are accredited by the NCTJ (National Council for the Training of Journalists), ensuring everybody working here is trained to a standard comparable with any news organisation anywhere. Even the work experience people have to have 100 words per minute shorthand.'

Shorthand aside, some of us help Sky Sports News towards its impressive figures by staying tuned for those moments when the passion of the pundits spills over into the richly comic.

Kamara, for instance, a man for whom a neat pass is invariably 'unbelievable' and a volley into the top corner prompts something approaching orgasm, often reaches for a simile and finds himself floundering. He spoke of desperate defenders 'fighting like beavers,' while a smooth attacking move 'cut through the defence as easy as ...er ...er ...as easy as anything, Jeff.'

The Jeff is Stelling, described by Cairns as 'masterful' in poking gentle fun at Chris 'while never undermining the authority of the programme.' On one occasion Jeff handed over to Chris at Portsmouth to report on a sending off and found him unaware any player had been dismissed.

'I don't really know what's happening,' Kamara said in a style familiar to anyone who enjoyed the character Peter O'Hanrahanrahan's spectacularly uninformative reports on the spoof news show *The Day Today*.

The format has no right to be a hit. Who in their right mind would want to watch other people watching football? *Esquire* magazine summed up the views of many: 'Imagine a Samuel Beckett play in which a slick circus-master gets four retired clowns to describe a performance to punters stuck outside the Big Top. You will still be nowhere close to the absurdist drama that unfolds for six straight hours each Saturday.'

Retired Sky Sports boss Vic Wakeling invented it in 1992. He told me he got the idea from Bloomberg TV: 'I figured that if people would watch talking heads while share prices scrolled underneath, and graphics updated the big business stories, why not with football?'

The difference is Bloomberg TV never employed Rodney Marsh, whose questionable joke about the tsunami in the Far East (he compared it with Newcastle fans, the Toon army) led to his dismissal in January 2005.

'We now work very closely with the pundits on what they can and can't say,' insisted Cairns. 'We make sure they're aware of Ofcom rules, and we give them legal training. Thankfully, we have had very few problems. Our lawyers are delighted. Our insurance is quite low.'

Sky Sports News's other copper-bottomed hit is Transfer Deadline Day, its round-up of footballers' last-minute moves, which attracted 4.5 million viewers in August this year. The undisputed star is excitable Scotsman Jim White, who has made the day his own. One wag described White meeting Deadline Day as 'like Andrew Ridgeley meeting George Michael.'

He's in his 50s, and usually presents alongside a much younger woman – sort of greying uncle and suspiciously attractive niece – the kind of presenter casting that led Gabby Logan, who worked at Sky for two years in the 1990s, to criticise its policy towards women presenters: 'The girls are basically wearing a leotard while the bloke's in a suit and tie,' she said.

'We never employ anyone on the basis of looks,' countered Andy. 'We get lots of showreels from good looking people, but they have to be solid journalists who know their sport, and they are thoroughly trained.

'Gabby left here 15 years ago. These days, thirty per cent of our staff are women. We're proud of that. Look around the sports desk of *The Guardian* and you won't find that sort of proportion. And recruitment is now running at 50-50.'

Andy added that he speaks regularly to students on journalism courses, where increasing numbers of women are seeing sports journalism as an opportunity, for which he thinks Sky Sports News deserves credit.

And he maintains he can offer these students a career with a future, despite the competition, not just online but from newcomers BT Sport.

'We've faced opposition before,' he said. 'Eurosport set up a sports news service, there was Setanta, ITV Digital, and now BT. It just encourages us to sharpen up our act.'

He's clearly confident that wherever a transfer is mooted or a groin strained, Sky Sports News will remain the messenger of choice.

There's no such thing as a free lunch – BT takes on Sky Sports with free(ish) football

Racing Post, *14 May 2013*

Fact: the average Briton has in his or her cellar / loft / garage between four and twelve obsolete mobile phone chargers, a set-top box or two from now defunct TV services, and several yards of cable with mysterious attachments that look like they were last used when attached to the testicles of an Argentinian dissident at the height of the terror. Not only that, but buried underneath all this redundant electronica is the de-icer that proved so elusive that winter's day when you were running late for work.

In view of this frightening technology mountain, I am often asked (I'm not, but indulge me) if any of it can be redeployed to catch some of the 'free' action currently being trumpeted from the rooftops by BT Sport. The answer is that it cannot. Throw it away, and while you're at it, get rid of some of the other junk too. You're never going to play that *Krypton Factor* board game again.

Several other questions about the new service arise however, so it's as well I am here to help. Here, then, are the answers to your questions about BT Sport:

Is it free?

Yes and no.

You know how you sometimes go into an upmarket restaurant advertising an 'Early Bird' special of two courses for £14.95, and you order a starter of scallops only to be told it's 'not part of the deal', and your choice is the soup or the pate, cheapskate. Well most of the Premier League matches on BT Sport are more minestrone with a crusty roll than escalope de foie gras. Only 18 of their 38 games are 'first picks', which means while there's plenty of Robin van Persie and Gareth Bale on the posters, you'll see rather less of them on your telly. If you want the other 116 fixtures you'll have to order Sky from the main menu.

But it's free, right?

Well, you have to have BT Broadband to get it for nothing, which means you need to change your provider if you are not with BT.

The snag with this is that it will involve telephone calls during which someone may ask you about the 'configuration of your modem', conversations I approach with the joy of a visit to the dentist. I never change any of my providers of anything for this reason. It means I have stuck with BT for all my telecommunication needs, so I at least am tooled up for the revolution.

As luck would have it my latest quarterly bill arrived yesterday, so I can give you an idea of costs. The bill was for £133.83, which seems an excessive phone bill for someone who probably last used the home phone to dial Whitehall 1212, but it includes something called 'Unlimited Weekend Plan' and 'Friends and Family Mobile', bought from some BT snake-oil salesman years ago just to get him off the phone, and BT Total Broadband Option 3, which comes out at £68.25 for the quarter.

So yes, it's free.

But is it reliable?

No complaints. I've only ever had one serious breakdown, involving fraught and lengthy telephone calls to the sub-continent to a chap who insisted on suffixing his every utterance with 'Mr Kelner'. After half a day of 'Mr Kelner' this and 'Mr Kelner' that, and of switching equipment off and back on again, I hoist the white flag, at which BT immediately sent a proper man round, and he sorted it.

(I may have qualified for this special service after I let it slip that I was a BBC broadcaster, and a columnist for a national newspaper. So you might want to get yourself a newspaper column, or at the very least a regular show on one of the larger regional radio stations, before signing.)

BT say their broadcasts will be 'seriously entertaining'. Does this mean anything?

No. It's what we doctors call bollocks. It may be a reference to plans to re-play and analyse moves from the match not on a screen, but on a half-size football pitch in the studio, provided pundit Owen Hargreaves stays fit long enough.

I'm assuming it doesn't refer to main football presenter Jake Humphrey, because I'm not sure relaxed conviviality is his strong suit. I know he earned a decent amount of respect from the cognoscenti when presenting Formula One, but to me he still looks like someone from children's TV who is doing it because he won a competition.

I had a look on the BT Sport website, Martin, and Clare Balding's all over it. Will she be working for them?

Sure. In a dangerous and top-secret operation, the Queen of all Media has been successfully cloned, enabling her to fulfil her duties to Channel 4 Racing, prime time BBC quiz formats, radio shows, chat show guest appearances, *Sports Personality of the Year*, and so on, while the other Clare simultaneously plays a full on-screen role with BT Sport.

Either that, or – and this is me just riffing now – BT sent a Transit van full of money round to Clare's place so she would lend her support.

Given most pundits these days are ex-Liverpool, with Steve McManaman, Michael Owen, and David James now joining the roster, will BT Sport maybe recruit cheeky Scouse comic Jimmy Tarbuck, who used to entertain us on Cup final day with his cheeky Scouseness and Liverpool scarf?

Oh, grow up.

I think we're all familiar with The Apprentice, *so all you need to know to enjoy this piece is Christian Gross was a spectacularly unsuccessful Spurs manager, and former breakfast TV presenter Anne Diamond had put on a little weight. I know, terrible!*

CAPS – The Campaign for Proper Swearing

Screen Break, The Guardian, *13 March 2006*

I am one hundred per cent committed to this column, because that is the kind of guy I am! I am enthusiastic, hard working, and I think you will find that if you give me a chance, you will not be disappointed!

I do apologise, but I have been watching *The Apprentice*, where everyone talks like that most of the time, and it seems to work. In fact, Alan Sugar got rid of the only borderline sane candidate on the programme last week simply because she failed to match her two barking mad rivals for vacuous self-aggrandisement.

The electronics magnate and former Spurs chairman said he was rejecting lawyer Karen Bremner's candidature because she did not stand up for herself; but as far as I could see she approached her appointed task with calm self-assurance and at least as much competence as the others, crucially neglecting however to blub to Sir Alan in the boardroom about how bloody wonderful she was. So he kicked her out. It seems a capricious recruitment policy, but it might explain how Christian Gross ended up at Tottenham.

The Apprentice is, of course, a television programme, so it seems fair to assume discussions take place between Sir Alan and the producers to ensure the fruit loops remain in the game, there being a limited audience, you would think, for sensible people going about their business in a competent manner.

Mind you, Sir Alan gives the impression of a man uneasy around happy, balanced folk anyway. Unlike some rich people, he does not exude contentment. He exudes dyspepsia, sometimes on behalf of Great Ormond Street hospital, and bless him for that, but sometimes he just exudes it. Long-suffering Spurs fans (is there any other sort?) may know more about this than me, but I get the impression that Sir Alan is not a naturally happy man, and if he gets a whiff of joy around him, his inclination is to snuff it out.

Sir Alan is just one of the reasons *The Apprentice* is such compelling television. It is a brilliant production; all the overhead shots of sleek black cars gliding through the City of London, the cutting between the teams as they race to complete their pointless tasks, the shots of Sir Alan's sinister *oberleutnants* taking notes; there is so much going on. It is busier than Anne Diamond's microwave.

That in itself, though, is not reason enough for a denizen of this section of the newspaper to play hooky on the night of two vital European Champions League matches, but I have an excuse; vigilance. Vigilance at all times is something of a cause of mine. I mean, turn your back for five minutes and Leo Sayer is back in the charts.

I do not suppose Sir Alan has any immediate plans to return to football, but I feel we should keep tabs on him. There is also a former Millwall footballer, Ansell Henry, among the contestants, and he is worth keeping an eye on too. So far, Henry has featured mostly as oil on troubled water, especially when the abrasive Syed irks one of his team; which is an interesting irony given that Millwall's normal role is to be the troubled water.

The only reason the former footballer has not made more of an impact is that we are all craning our necks to peer over to the other carriageway at the car crash that is Jo Cameron, the highly strung Charlie Dimmock/Ray Parlour lookalike whom I was startled to learn runs her own management training company. Jo's former husband is quoted as describing her as 'headstrong'. He now lives 3,000 miles away in Florida. I wonder why.

At least Jo swears properly, though, which is refreshing because if there is one thing I am getting naffing fed up with it is the lack of any decent swearing on TV after the nine o'clock watershed. I mean, what is the chuffing point of nominating a time after which it is assumed television programmes are designed for an adult audience, and then treating us like little kiddies for whom exposure to the 'f' word will curdle our milk and make our toes grow crooked.

My colleague Rupert Smith has already pointed out the absurdity of the bizarre usage, 'What the shit is this?' in *Footballers' Wives*; and now we have the dismal new ice skating sit-com *Thin Ice* – described in the *Radio Times* as 'warm', an *RT* synonym for 'not funny' – avoiding the dread word with nonsense like 'well, bugger me blind', which arguably sounds far worse.

But that is not the worst of *Thin Ice*. Here is a joke from the latest episode: Someone steps in some dog muck, and says she would like to 'sew the dogs' arses shut.' 'It's not the dogs you should be blaming, it's the owners,' says someone else, at which she takes off her shoe and sniffs the dog dirt (honest), saying, 'No, it's definitely the dogs.' It is frightening to think there is someone in an executive position at the BBC who actually watched this and then put it on our televisions.

After such unbeatable examples of the genre as *The Royle Family*, *Early Doors*, and *Phoenix Nights*, do we really need another downbeat Northern comedy anyway? The answer from this particular downbeat Northern household is: No, we shitting don't.

Hot enough to boil a monkey's bum – the Malaysian Grand Prix

Screen Break, The Guardian, *26 March 2012*

If you like weather, there was loads of it at the Malaysian Grand Prix yesterday, all in HD, and glorious 5.1 Dolby Surroundsound, as presenter Simon Lazenby never tired of reminding us. That's the 5.1 mind, not your Digital EX or Stereo Creator.

That sort of detail, I expect, is important to Formula One fans, and now Sky has an entire channel dedicated to the sport, you are rarely more than a minute away from some fascinating technical information, much of which this weekend referred to the heat. Even a motor sport agnostic like me could have guessed that it gets pretty hot in Malaysia, making driving a racing car without even a decent cup holder a pretty gruelling business. But what I didn't know was that a brake disc could reach a temperature of 1,100C during a race, a clutch 500C, and the tyres 160C.

The climate can be pretty unforgiving on the humans too. As Martin Brundle and Damon Hill walked round the track with Lazenby on Saturday, the presenter told us: 'The sun is beating down. I'm damper than an otter's pocket, as I think the expression goes.'

It does indeed go rather like that, Simon, although according to that indispensable reference book, the *Viz Profanisaurus,* it is not customarily used as a measurement of humidity. Lazenby's idiomatic audacity may give a clue as to why I feel more at home with Sky's coverage than the BBC's.

I know Jake Humphrey has been a hit with many F1 followers, but I'm afraid – and this is purely an accident related to the age of my progeny – I will always see him as a presenter on children's TV, where references to otters' pockets – and probably hummingbirds' wings and mice's ears as well – are more or less outlawed.

As for my petrolhead friends, the kind who slept in their clothes on the sofa to be ready for the pre-dawn live coverage of the Australian Grand Prix, they tell me they were happy enough with Humphrey, and feel Sky's innovations and day-long full monty HD surroundsound experience, while welcome, do not entirely compensate for having to pay a subscription. But, hey, let's talk about tyres. Thus was the topic introduced – at last, I thought – with the great blank broadcasting canvas of the Formula One channel allowing such discussions to be satisfyingly diffuse.

'The way to keep tyres from degrading is to have more downforce than the next guy so you don't have to scrub so hard,' said Hill, clearly talking in a language I was less than fluent in. 'I was talking to a Pirelli man earlier and he said one of the bigger problems is temperature [as any otter would tell you]. The tyre turns to liquid, and that makes it quite uncomfortable to drive on.'

The good news is that Pirelli have engineered in provisions for tyre degradation, by closing up the compound and softening it all up. I think that's right, but don't try it at home. Mercedes, apparently, have had big problems with tyre degradation. Damon says it's all to do with how the air works around the car, and Brundle added that it's about suspension geometry as well.

There was a deal of chat about good aerobalance, something Hill has achieved in spades with his hair. The long sweeping corners of the purpose-built Sepang track were mirrored in the former champion driver's sleek silvery mane, and precisely trimmed goatee. While Lazenby referenced otters, and reporter Natalie Pinkham jogged through the streets, describing the feeling as 'like sitting in a sauna, wrapped in cling film, with a hair dryer on my face' (a future red button option, possibly), not a hair on Damon's head shifted, nor did a bead of sweat appear.

Later, Natalie spoke to Jenson Button about the heat, and said she felt like 'a jacket potato that's been basted in oil, wrapped in foil, and chucked into the oven at 220.' The *Profanisaurus* could liven up those similes no end.

Happily, Button was able to ease my worries about the lack of cup holders, demonstrating the in-car device that holds a litre and a half of liquid, and has a little motor shooting the liquid straight into his mouth. I might have known these guys would have something like that.

What with the rain, a lot of the prior tyre talk proved irrelevant, with Fernando Alonso's unexpected victory owing much to his wet weather provisions in that area. And if you would like a more learned view on that and allied matters, Sky's F1 channel will doubtless mull them over at excruciating length in the three weeks before the next race.

I would just like to say, to quote Brundle, 'You don't

want to go too soft on the rear roll bar,' which, if not already in the *Viz Profanisaurus*, should be.

Winning – How Does it Feel?

Blog post, 19 March 2016

One of the toughest jobs in sports broadcasting is the immediate post-match interview, the one where the coach or captain is dragged in front of the sponsors' boards, and some poor sap with a hand-held mic seeks instant reaction.

What do you ask? After England's grand slam success in Paris on Saturday, Sonja McLaughlan asked coach Eddie Jones, 'How proud are you?' Jones, being something of a pro with the media, took the wise course of continuing to smile widely and winningly, and answering an entirely different question.

But just once I should like someone on these occasions to take the Q at face value. 'How proud am I? On a scale of one to ten? Well, using the scoring system they use at international ice skating events, probably something like a 6.7, but taking *Strictly Come Dancing* as a template, an 8 or a 9, although obviously if Craig Revel Horwood is judging, a 7 with a withering aside.

'Put it this way, I'm as proud as a the owner of a labrador at Crufts whose animal wins in its category but misses out on Best In Show, but probably just slightly less proud than a university student who manages to get a 2:1 despite doing nothing for three years other than sitting in front of *Pointless* wearing ludicrous trousers, eating microwave egg fried rice (the student, that is, not the trousers).'

The poser Sonja lobbed at Owen Farrell was arguably even tougher: 'Just describe for me your emotions as that final whistle went.' I've tried to write fiction, and describing emotions is something even an effete pinko liberal, white-wine-quaffing wordsmith like me has trouble with, he wrote, feeling preternaturally calm but at the same time strangely enervated.

'Chuffed,' was the word Farrell chose. 'I'm just chuffed for the boys,' he said. 'I'm chuffed for everyone.' Which sounded about right in the flat vowel sounds of the East Lancs Road. We don't do emotions in a big way in that part of the world. We're more about tea and Eccles cakes.

She also asked Farrell, 'How special is this?' and despite encouragement from my sofa, he disappointingly failed to answer: 'Compared to what?'

Not only do I find it difficult to describe emotions, even feeling them can be a problem at times.

Take the programme *Famous, Rich, and Homeless* on BBC One, about people living rough on the streets of London. Clearly, it was meant to pull at heartstrings, and foster the feeling, 'There but for the grace of God...' and so on. And initially, that was how I felt.

I mean, there was former TV host Nick Hancock, begging for money for fish and chips – London fish and chips, that is, not even the decent stuff – hunkering down in a sleeping bag in the stairwell of a depressing inner city flat block, the same Nick Hancock who used to present that excellent sports comedy quiz *They Think It's All Over* in the heady days of Britpop and lads' mags in the late 1990s.

My god, I thought, that's shocking. Sure, we've recognised the folly of our ways and put all that laddishness behind us now, but no-one wants to see him reduced to this? Who next, Damon Albarn?

It was only then that I realised Hancock was merely pretending to be homeless for a week, one of four television personalities taking that challenge; because apparently the viewing public is incapable of understanding or feeling anything these days unless experienced through the medium of celebrity.

Alongside Nick was Kim Woodburn, who seemed like she might be Katie Hopkins's mother, someone called Julia Bradbury (no, me neither), and snooker's Willie Thorne, who because of his own well-advertised gambling addiction, bonded quite touchingly with a well-spoken alcoholic. Not that it stopped him bunking off to spend a night in a hotel. That can't be right, I thought, he's got his moustache to keep him warm.

Finally, on the subject of hair, you may recall Screen Break three, in which I poked some mild fun at Steve McClaren's vain attempt to mask his incipient baldness. As a West Ham fan, I have been advised to look closer to home for the Premier League's most ludicrous cover up, in the person of our coach, the sainted Slaven Bilić. What he has is not so much a combover as a comb-under.

Strands of hair are combed directly forward, as Micky Dolenz of the Monkees might have done, circa 1965 (Google images, kids), and then chopped off in a straight line at the front, possibly by his mum using a pudding basin, assuming his mum's eyesight is going.

And I hadn't even noticed until it was pointed out to me. Which proves, Premier League managers, that the best baldness camouflage is an energetic, creative midfield, and a solid central defence.

Wrightie and Slaven, A Love Story – 2016 European Championships

FourFourTwo *website, 20 June 2016*

It was a frustrating night for England fans in front of the TV, but there was the fun, for those of us who love a romcom, of the burgeoning relationship between Slaven Bilić and Ian Wright.

I don't know where the directors are going to take this, but I see the two pundits walking off into the sunset together, possibly on a French beach, to the strains of Charles Trenet's 'La Mer' as the credits roll at the end of the tournament. What a climax that would be for ITV.

At the moment it's mostly a little light touching of legs and finishing each other's sentences, but that's the way these things start, and there's another England match in Nice next Monday.

Movie fans will know how conducive the South of France can be to romance. *To Catch A Thief*, for instance, with Grace Kelly and Cary Grant, and *That Riviera Touch* starring Morecambe and Wise, to name but two films set there. The leading characters in both ended up in bed together.

For the Slovakia – England match Slaven and Wrightie sat in the middle of a four, flanked by Lee Dixon and Peter Crouch who barely got a look in, apart from Crouchie's whinge about Roy changing the fullbacks and disrupting England's rhythm, which prompted your correspondent to shout 'What rhythm?' at the TV (I've never really accepted television as a one-way thing).

I've never played football at the highest level – or even at the lowest level to be brutally honest – but England seem to me to have played pretty similarly in all three group games, battering gamely at a packed defence, playing some pleasing football, but without having anyone capable of the piece of magic that might break the deadlock.

Slaven said as much, and sagely suggested we might have more chance when we meet a higher class of opposition who take the game to us and allow opportunities for counter attack. Wrightie demurred slightly, but I took that as no more than a lovers' tiff, although there could be trouble down the line if he keeps referring to Glenn Hoddle as 'the gaffer'.

The former England international is fond of picking up on Hoddle's comments in the commentary box and beginning his sentences, 'Like the gaffer says...' despite the fact that much of the gaffer's analysis consists of telling us what we've just seen.

Despite that, one piece of wisdom issuing from the g – which I just about caught over the unholy racket the England fans in the stadium were making – echoed something I have been saying to anyone who will listen (my wife, basically, who has no choice), namely that Hodgson should have taken Andy Carroll with him to give him a different option.

Had he been able to throw the West Ham striker into the fray in those desperate final moments, we might have been able to shake up the previously immovable Martin Škrtel for once.

Škrtel wasn't the only source of frustration, though. That constant drone issuing from the England fans was a distraction. It robbed one of involvement in the match, almost like the dreaded Mexican wave.

'England are being serenaded, but are they being serenaded to victory?' asked Clive Tyldesley, but sometimes I think he just says things for the sake of saying things. It didn't sound like a serenade to me.

Clive also went through the possibilities of England's next round opponents. 'Finish third, and it could be Spain or

Germany; finish fourth, it could be hell or high water.' I have subjected that sentence to forensic analysis and I can reveal it means precisely nothing. Come hell or high water, as I understand it, means you will overcome any obstacle to achieve something. As I'm hoping Wrightie might, finding his way over ITV's Eiffel table to get to Slaven.

Rarely – by which I mean never – has anything I have written in 40-odd years of journalism changed anything, but in 2017, I wrote a piece for The Guardian*'s lost, lamented Media section, supporting Media Minister Karen Bradley, who felt Channel 4 ought to move out of London.*

The piece had such impact that here we are, just six years later, with 250 of the staff settled in the repurposed Majestyk night club in the heart of the beautiful garden city of Leeds. I'm claiming it. The article is also, three years pre-Covid, pretty prescient about what working from home would look like.

Taking telly to the regions

Guardian Media, *30 March 2017*

Sometimes I get on the morning train from Leeds to London and wonder what happened to conference calls, to Skype, the internet, and that vision of the future we were once sold of creative types in their ecologically sound homes in Yorkshire or Somerset, skipping off on the school run, and then sitting by their laptops in jeans and casual footwear, gazing out at the mountain greenery while remaining at the nation's media coalface. Judging by the suited and booted on Virgin East Coast's red-eye, it went the way of flying cars and robots doing the vacuuming.

Partly this is down to the well-advertised deficiencies in broadband networks (sometimes you hear radio interviews via Skype that sound as though they might as well have been done using two cocoa tins), but more likely it's thanks to the attitude Karen Bradley, the Culture Secretary, identified in her speech at the Nations and Regions Media Conference – of organisations 'who recoil in horror at the very idea of media jobs being based outside the capital.'

Organisations such as Channel 4, that is.

She is not sympathetic, and her logic is impeccable. If Channel 4 is to remain publicly owned, as the government has now pledged, its benefits, says the minister, ought to be 'spread far and wide, not just in London.' So they should, but as a semi-professional broadcaster and journalist living in the north, I think I understand the channel's reluctance to move.

The most recent example of the benefits of a media base being spread far and wide is the move of some BBC programmes and departments to Salford. 'Dragging and screaming' does not quite cover the attitude of some of the BBC's semi-famous names to being dumped by the Manchester Ship Canal. Some refused to move. Sian Williams, for instance, stayed put in London, and the north of the nation wept. The newspaper stories of eye-watering hotel bills, flights, removal costs and so on weren't entirely helpful either.

But the move has created jobs and undoubtedly boosted media activity up here; and if rather too much of *BBC Breakfast* is taken up by interviews with 'experts' from the University of Heckmondwike and Little Hulton Technology Campus (made up, but you know what I mean), that seems a small price to pay.

Sure, it would be foolish to deny that some of the BBC's Manchester output is a little underpowered, but if Gary Lineker is happy to sit by the canal and present *Match of the*

Day, still the best football programme on TV, clearly fine broadcasting can emanate from outside London.

Channel 4, of course, cannot be compared directly to the BBC, as it commissions programmes rather than making them itself, and it argues that it already buys in more than half its output from outside London, including the long-running *Hollyoaks*, and Caitlin Moran's *Raised By Wolves*, made in Birmingham. But only 30 of its 800 staff are based outside central London, and arguably it views the provinces through London goggles. If you are pitching a programme from the north or any of the regions, you will certainly have to go to London and attend plenty of stultifying meetings, not unlike those satirised in the comedy *W1A*.

Maybe if Channel 4 were to move, say, another 200 of its people out of London – and persuade them not to live in Didsbury, which is really Crouch End with a little more rain – they would get a view of the regions from the regions, and might understand better what programme-makers up here were trying to say. It's easy to imagine the benefits. Too late now, but I'm sure I'm not alone in thinking if more journalists and broadcasters had been based outside the London media bubble, there might have been a better understanding of what was going on in the EU referendum campaign.

When Channel 4 launched 35 years ago, diversity was its watchword. But it was only really a slogan, best illustrated by a friend of mine who failed to get a job there and was told (I'm not making this up): 'We're really looking for somebody from a disadvantaged background, maybe somebody disabled.' To which she replied, 'I'm from Leicester; how disadvantaged do you want?'

Now might be an ideal opportunity for Channel 4 to go along with Karen Bradley, to prove you can genuinely embrace the rest of the nation.

All Our Yesterdays

No 51: **Celebrity Squares** (1975–1979),
The Independent, 13 June 2002

Interesting list of celebrities, all gone, largely forgotten. As media commentator Victor Lewis-Smith liked to say, at the end of it all, we're all worm food.

● What a stroke of genius it was to put William Rushton in the centre square. Without the doyen of the satire boom, stalwart of *That Was The Week That Was* and *Private Eye*, this would have been standard ATV Sunday afternoon dross. Rushton's presence, though, attracted an audience that would normally hesitate to approach this kind of entertainment with a very long bargepole, as he fired off jokes and topical barbs that flew like Exocets over the heads of the studio crowd.

It was a kind of noughts and crosses game with the squares occupied by celebrities, who answered, in a light-hearted way, general knowledge questions posed by host Bob Monkhouse. Two contestants had to guess if the answers were correct to get their cross or nought on the board. It would take a more dedicated nostalgist than me to remember the kind of 'celebrities' who occupied the squares, most of whom I expect would be nothing but names challenging you to remember why on earth they were famous.

The indispensable *Penguin TV Companion*, though, lists an uncommonly strong line-up for the first show: Diana Dors, Leslie Crowther, Aimi MacDonald, Alfred Marks, Vincent Price, Hermione Gingold, Terry Wogan, Arthur Mullard, and the incomparable Rushton.

5. The Presenters

'The only circumstance in which we [men] will remain on one channel for any length of time is if the remote has slipped down the back of the sofa...'

It's getting near Christmas and I'm up late for SPOTY. *It's a tough gig, especially when everyone looks so young and well-scrubbed.*

Oh, for the grizzled dyspeptic veterans of the press box
Screen Break, The Guardian, *15 December 2008*

It is a late finish for Screen Break, but you would not expect Britain's premier sport-on-TV column to allow last night's *Sports Personality of the Year* show to pass without comment, so hearty congratulations, worthy winner, glittering evening,

Rebecca, eh, shoes, what is she like, nation's sweetheart – take that Cheryl Cole – sports people in evening wear, Gary Lineker, Sue Barker, weak jokes, etc. etc. Oh, and Jake Humphrey.

Jake, third banana on last night's programme, came to mind, when I was watching Craig Doyle hosting Champions League highlights on ITV last week – stay with me, I promise you this is going somewhere – and I began to wonder if one of the problems with sport on TV these days is that some of the presenters are just too young and good looking? Is that not tampering with the natural order of things?

Surely, these fresh-faced kiddies – let us throw Manish Bhasin into the mix – belong on *Blue Peter* or regional news programmes, leaving sports presentation to more mature, comfortably upholstered chaps, usually with a face like a bag of spanners, and occasionally with a troubled or faintly lurid private life.

Any of us over about 35 grew up watching that kind of character on sports shows. It is no accident that when Steve Coogan first launched Alan Partridge – gauche, indiscreet, with a rocky marriage – he made him a sports reporter. Similarly, the bald, insensitive, politically incorrect Bob 'Bulldog' Briscoe on the *Frasier* show was the radio station's sports anchor.

Another classic of the genre was the *Fast Show*'s Ron Manager routine when Mark Williams and Paul Whitehouse's soccer chat with a nervy Simon Day invariably spilled over into homoeroticism. There is clearly a great comic tradition here, in danger of dying. Can anybody imagine Craig Doyle being nicknamed 'Bulldog' or 'Moose'? Where is the fun in Manish Bhasin?

When I was growing up, a well-fed Scottish journalist called Sam Leitch presented the football preview each

Saturday lunchtime. The camera was no friend of his, but he derived a certain authority from the fact that he was manifestly our-man-in-the-press-box squeezed into a slightly grubby cardigan and an ill-fitting overcoat. His place in my pantheon was assured when someone told me he used to turn up to matches with a big shopping bag full of apples and work his way through them.

The rot set in, I think, with the substitution of moustachioed *boulevardier* Des Lynam with clean cut Gary Lineker, respected for his feats in an England shirt, but suspiciously careful about his appearance, and not a man who looks like he knows his way around a big bag of apples. Crisps, maybe.

Leitch or the equally grizzled Geordie journo Ken Jones, who also did the Saturday preview gig sometimes, were never in danger of being asked to do commercials, whereas Craig, Jake, and Manish give the impression they are merely doing a little light sports presenting on the way to celebrity dancing, or some of that lucrative corporate work. Not that any of them is a particularly bad presenter. They just feel a little too practised and smooth, insipid compared to Saint and Greavsie, say, or the inky-fingered figures of my youth.

Frankly, I like my sport less Gabby Logan, more Jimmy Logan; although if I could choose a Scottish entertainer on whose lines I would most want my sports presenter to be built, it would be Chic Murray (kids, try Google images, or ask your granddad).

That said, Gabby did a creditable job on *Inside Sport* in her interview with sports favourite fruit loop – and I mean that in a caring way – Ronnie O'Sullivan. The troubled snooker star (copyright: everything that has ever been written about him) has spent time in the Priory and flirted with religious gurus, so he seemed quite comfortable with *Inside*

Sport's self-conscious getting-under-the-skin-of-the-subject psychobabble style.

When Gabby asks, 'Are you in a good place right now?' the temptation to reply, 'Yeah, Dartford, it's OK,' must be overwhelming, but Ronnie went along with it, although he winked to camera at one point giving the impression he might have been sending the interview up slightly. His wackiest answer came when Gabby asked him about the incident in 1996 when he was accused of disrespecting his opponent by playing left-handed.

'I first played with my left hand when I was 17. Things weren't going well, I needed to find a way through, and it felt good,' said the TSS. 'My left hand is like my mistress. My wife is my right hand and my mistress is my left. It's been good to me, and you don't want to let it go [do feel free to write your own jokes].'

Ronnie certainly gives good interview when he is in the mood, and Gabby got the best out of him; but I should still prefer it if her hair were a little less perfectly straightened, and she were to develop an alcohol dependency, or at least a serious apple habit.

Glamour has its place, of course, and it is on the *X-Factor*, which saw the coronation of Cheryl Cole, who has apparently replaced Princess Diana in the hearts of the nation. A documentary on Five pointed to the parallels between the two, even down to their choice of unpopular husband. One married a man cloistered in a privileged moneyed world, unaware of real life outside, whereas the other (punch line available in Screen Break special edition Christmas crackers).

Those of you keeping a close watch on timelines will know I was recovering from a debilitating illness in September 2013, which may account for a little extra waspishness in this Racing Post *piece about a short-lived BT Sport chat show presented by Clare Balding. It did not play to her undoubted strengths.*

About cobblers

Racing Post, *23 September 2013*

A fellow is telling his friend a story about how he was walking through town when across the other side of the road he saw six guys beating up his mother-in-law. 'Blimey,' his mate says, 'Didn't you go over and help?' 'No,' he answers. 'They seemed to be doing OK without me.'

Now I realise that old joke is wrong on a number of levels. I feel ashamed for committing it to print and in the unlikely event of your repeating it, please don't say you heard it from me.

Back in the 1970s, though, you could switch on Saturday night telly and regularly hear similar material from much-loved family entertainers. Les Dawson more or less built a career on it – 'I knew it was the mother-in-law at the door, the mice were throwing themselves on the traps,' that kind of thing.

Well, thank goodness we've evolved, and our entertainers these days are careful not to say or do anything that might unduly offend readers of *The Guardian*.

Apparently all comedy now has to be approved by a committee chaired by Stephen Fry before being aired in public, for which TV viewers should be eternally grateful. Because Miranda Hart falling over for half an hour is so very much funnier than *Rising Damp*.

It is nevertheless bracing from time to time to encounter

one of those great acts of the 1970s you don't see on TV nearly enough nowadays. Rodney Marsh, for instance, who wasn't strictly speaking a variety act – although you might find supporters of Manchester City and Queens Park Rangers who would disagree – cropped up on BT Sport's *Life's A Pitch*, the best of the new breed of sport chat shows.

Rodders, of course, lost his punditry gig on Sky because of a dumb, ill-advised joke following the tsunami in the Far East, but far from licking his wounds, he's moved to Florida, and returned as cheerfully insouciant as ever in conversation with Des Kelly.

We're currently either living through a golden age of sport chat shows or in danger of drowning in a sea of blather. The launch of BT Sport, the revamp of talkSPORT radio, plus the BBC raising its punditry game now Alan Hansen has said he'll hang up his gob after the World Cup, all mean our contribution to the European bullshit mountain – sorry, but it really is *le mot juste* – is at an all-time high.

Not that I'm complaining. Were I not ill, I should be an enthusiastic contributor – Brian Moore and Paddy Barclay can't do every programme – but probably not to the Clare Balding Show. Certainly not after asking what the heck dear Clare is playing at.

Some of you may remember *Larry Sanders*, a brilliant American show of the 1990s satirising the conventions of the chat show. One episode concerned a new producer arriving, with a mission to make Larry more showbiz. He suggests the host bounds onto the set high-fiving the audience, the joke being that this was about the corniest thing you could do on a chat show.

It was, therefore, with open-mouthed disbelief that I witnessed La Balding on her BT Sport show last Friday bound onto the set high-fiving the audience. And that was just the start of the horror. She did a little dance on stage a la Alan Partridge (I'm not making this up), greeted by the crowd with a chant of 'Balding, Balding' in the style of the *Jerry Springer* audience.

And don't even get me started on the monologue. On Chelsea's Champions League defeat by Basel, she mentioned José Mourinho's convoluted egg metaphor leading to headlines like 'Shell Shocked' and 'Scrambled Eggs'. 'I'm quite worried about where this whole thing is going,' said Clare. 'Does he realise that eggs turn into chickens?' We waited in vain for a punch line, as our host ploughed on with a terminally weak 'joke' about Manu Tuilagi serving David Cameron rabbit stew for dinner, and a routine about Gareth Bale carrying his things in a plastic bag.

'He's wiser than you think,' quipped the Bob Hope *de nos jours*, 'Because he was probably given it for free, and you have to pay 5p for them in Wales, and you have done for some time.' I find it difficult to believe somebody actually wrote this stuff down, and some other poor drone had to type it into the autocue.

The consolation for Clare is that few people, apart from the bored, drunk, and heavily medicated like me, will be witnessing her painful foray into showbiz, so she should be able to put the whole thing down to experience.

The stuff she is good at, she's clearly still good at. The interviews with Joey Barton and Usain Bolt, both chat show gifts, were fine; and as we know, Clare is horse racing royalty, whose occasional turns on Channel 4's coverage undeniably lift the show. A cobbler, as the old saying goes, should stick to his or her last – and maybe leave the other cobblers behind.

Finally, after a hot run, I find the gambling gods have deserted me. I had St Helens and Harlequins in a rugby double on Friday, and was five minutes away from a decent win. And then on Saturday I was five yards or so away – I am not an expert – with my big bet, York Glory at Newbury. I am in a hole and no mistake, and would welcome any help in getting out of it.

Hmmm, the wiseacres who proclaimed Roger Federer's powers were waning got it spot on. In September 2022 he retired.

The not particularly surreal world of Roger Federer

Screen Break, The Guardian, *6 April 2009*

Funny old business, surrealism. Very few of us, I dare say, have subjected the 1924 Surrealist Manifesto to a close reading – it is not a page turner, quite frankly, and you might find Dan Brown more *gemütlich* for the beach – and yet we go around branding all sorts of things 'surreal' purely on the basis that they confound expectations, or feature a bowler hat or a fish in some sort of unlikely circumstance.

Roger Federer's semi-final against Novak Djokovic in the Miami Masters featured neither, but that did not stop Marcus Buckland on Sky calling it 'tense and surreal'. In fairness to the presenter, when Federer smashed his racket on the ground in frustration, the head did end up looking like one of Salvador Dalí's melting clocks.

The World Number Two really whacked his axe into the deck, like one of Pete Townshend's guitars, in one of the most unexpected – not surreal – moments of the week. Federer has been such an unshifting paragon of cool self-control in a sporting landscape of tears, tantrums, and two-fingered gestures that his sudden loss of equilibrium reminded me of that *Simpsons* episode where Ned Flanders turns on the Springfield townsfolk and gives them a piece of his diddly-iddly mind.

Buckland, who is something of an unruffled presence himself, was clearly shaken. 'No handshake for umpire Fergus Murphy afterwards either,' he gasped. And blow me, if Federer did not display a hitherto well-hidden penchant for sarcasm in the post-match press conference. 'I've been winning twenty tournaments in a row, so nobody expects me to win really,' was his response to a question we did not hear, but was probably about media speculation that his powers are waning.

'It's the end of the hard court season and I don't care any more,' he said, with a hint of a bitter and twisted smile. 'Thank God the hard court season is over.' When asked if he had 'lost it,' he countered, 'Just because I smashed a racket doesn't mean I lose it. You write what you want.'

Molly from Wimbledon did, emailing the studio to say Federer had gone down in her estimation. 'He's a bad loser,' she wrote, which could be awkward if Roger is looking for digs in the area in the Summer.

Studio pundit Peter Fleming, John McEnroe's former doubles partner, was more indulgent. 'We all have to get a grip here,' he said. 'People have been telling him he is over the hill for the past year, he's lost confidence, and it's a scary place to be. As a super human athlete, suddenly to lose your powers, if ever so slightly, you think, "Is this the beginning of the end?" That can be scary, and it all just bubbled to the surface.' Not that surreal, then, but possibly ironic, because just as Federer is shown to have feet of clay, he is looking forward to playing on clay. Geddit?

Also not surreal was Mick Fitzgerald's return to Aintree after his terrifying fall on L'Ami last year. 'It's surreal being back here,' he told Clare Balding after one of the several reruns of the footage of last year's accident. Lucky, I think, was the word he wanted.

Another Fitzgerald clip on heavy rotation was the one where he says winning the National is better than sex. This was showing more or less on the hour every hour, and was included in a fine montage marking fifty years of TV coverage of the race, featuring all the great presenters of the past, and prompting the question, '*Ou sont les Frank Boughs d'antan*?' Not that Clare, who did a creditable job as always, would be out of place in the pantheon.

But if it is surreal you want, how about this? I am half awake on Saturday morning, listening to a news bulletin on the radio. What they are saying, I suspect, is, 'Poor weather may have stopped the Koreans from launching a rocket,' but what I hear, clear as you like, is: 'Paul Weller may have stopped the Koreans from launching a rocket.'

Fair play, I thought. The Style Council back catalogue probably does not mean much in North Korea, the local version of *Top Of The Pops* preferring songs like 'Long Life and Good Health to the Leader', and 'We Sing of His Benevolent Love', so it must take real courage for the dad rock icon, who has not previously been notably politically engaged, to take on the Axis of Evil, which is not surreal in the strictest sense, but closer than Roger Federer smashing his racket.

Swearing: It's not big and it's not clever

Screen Break, The Guardian, *23 September 2007*

Warning: some strong language follows. On the other hand, there is very little in the way of explicit sexual content, and virtually no projectile vomiting, so unless you are likely to be unduly upset by a few of Britain's most widely used expletives, it is fairly safe to read on.

The scene is Manchester Town Hall, and, after a week-long tour spanning two continents, creating a carbon footprint the size of Stoke-on-Trent, Ricky Hatton arrives home for the final press conference promoting his fight against Floyd Mayweather on December 8th. It is an opportunity for Sky to drum up customers for its pay-per-view coverage of the contest. That, in fact, is the entire point of the event, and Sky Sports News broadcasts it live on Friday lunchtime. Or at least it would have done, had coverage not been summarily curtailed when Ricky went all potty mouthed on them.

I have to say I found this not only funny, but also rather encouraging. I know swearing is neither big nor clever – remember, kids! – but there are times when it makes a point. Boxing's history is so littered with fighters being owned body and soul by The Man, as the vernacular has it, that when one of them, maybe unintentionally, sticks it back to The Man – in this case, Sky, HBO, and the promoters – it raises the spirits. It was not exactly Muhammad Ali and Vietnam, but you know what I mean.

These pre-fight shindigs, of course, are not 'press conferences' as we understand them. Nothing is being announced or explained. We already know the fight is going to take place. At this stage, Hatton and Mayweather are more or less performing monkeys. Their job is to create spurious prior cause for their fight by conjuring up some sort of grudge, which they have been doing rather well.

Pretty Boy Floyd has been dismissive of his opponent's past triumphs, while Hatton has been mocking Mayweather's participation in a TV dancing show. Ricky opened his address to the nation – live on Sky – by saying: 'If he dances like that on *Dancing With The Stars,* he's fucking no chance, has he?'

Presenters Simon Thomas and Jim White let that one go, although you could feel a twitchiness in the air. Mayweather danced and pranced around the stage, as Hatton continued: 'It's great to be back in Manchester. We've had a long tour, very tiring. Floyd, will you stop touching my dick, you poof?'

At this point, Hatton was faded down, and an audibly rattled Thomas took over. 'We apologise for the language at the moment ... er ... Hatton being put under a lot of pressure by Mayweather ... er ... taunting that's gone on for the last week, but we do apologise for the language that's gone on so far at this press conference.'

They obviously felt it safe to return to Hatton's keynote speech when he started talking about his family, and they were just in time to hear him say, 'I've missed my six-year-old son, but I haven't missed him as much as you might think, because I've been able to spend the week with another fucking six-year-old.'

That was when The Man pulled the plug, and we returned to Thomas in the studio.

'Well, once again, er, we apologise for the language, er, the pressure, er, certainly upon Ricky Hatton in this, er, at the moment, Mayweather such a difficult character to deal with, but, er, we do apologise for the language from Ricky Hatton at the moment, er, but once again we apologise for the language we have whored.' Whored. I promise you that was what he said.

Thomas turned to his co-presenter for a little assistance: 'Well Jim, when you take an event like that live when the pressure's on...' 'Very much so, Simon.' I felt they might have switched to Chelsea's training ground at that point to report on which player's Bentley had just swept past the Sky reporter, but Simon felt obliged to add to his already copious apology: 'Unfortunately, a bit of bad language ... some unfortunate language.'

Enough, already. The point about Hatton is that it is almost impossible to take offence. He has such a cherubic face, and is such an uberManc, with his devotion to City, and his amusing fried breakfasts. That is why we love him. The other point is that Hatton's timing was impeccable. I have never seen anyone seem under less pressure. If they had billed his speech the Bernard Manning Memorial Lecture, it would have been hailed as a triumph.

The people under pressure at the moment appear to be our broadcasters. What with the rows over rigged competitions, ITV's Alzheimer's documentary (the broadcaster, I should say, denies the sufferer's actual death was filmed, meaning nobody has been seen dying on camera since Danny Baker's late night chat show), and bizarrely the *Blue Peter* cat, an atmosphere of hypersensitivity is infecting TV.

I remain fairly neutral about most of these issues, never having trusted television that much anyway, but catgate does intrigue me.

As I understand it, the name Cookie, chosen by viewers in an online poll, was rejected because it is occasionally employed as a euphemism for female genitalia. Well, I have consulted the definitive reference work on such matters, the *Viz Profanisaurus*, which, despite many colourful euphemisms in that area, makes no mention of this one. Intriguing. Apparently, Ricky Hatton's suggestion, Fuckface, was never even considered.

Wrestling in Honey

Here I am, very much in 2006 mode. Need to know: Davina McCall had a phenomenally unsuccessful chat show, which I seem to be obsessed with for some reason, and England manager Sven-Göran Eriksson enjoyed reportedly carnal encounters with TV weather presenter Ulrika Jonsson, and somebody else whose name escapes me.

It's For Charity! That's No Excuse

Screen Break, The Guardian, *17 July 2006*

The best thing about *Only Fools On Horses* was its title, just a hoof beat away from the most mystifyingly popular sitcom in British television history. Genius, although I think the producers should also have considered some of the many similar suggestions with which I have been bombarding them – or at least have sent me a letter of acknowledgement before going down the court injunction route.

I mean, Men Bee-hiving Badly? Where is the problem? You take a celebrity chef or two, a girl who reads the weather on breakfast television, someone who has slept with the former England manager, and a Will Self or David Aaronovitch for the sex appeal, and plunge them into the world of hard-core bee-keeping. Sainsbury's or one of our big arms dealers could sponsor the bees, with each sting helping provide clean drinking water for a parched village in the Sudan.

Or how about Who Wants To Be A Milliner? Celebrity hat making with a couple of property gurus, a girl who once slept with the former England manager, and Alain de Botton?

Rejected out of hand. I do not know why I bother. It is not even as if I am a fan of the genre. Frankly, I find the suggestion that the only way I will consider contributing money to a worthy cause is if I see Paul Nicholas on a horse, slightly insulting.

I do not wish to be curmudgeonly about *Sport Relief*, which is a very effective profile ... er ... sorry, money-raising exercise (there I go, can't stop myself), and its heart is clearly in the right place. Those little films they show, of the starving boy in Northern Ghana literally singing for his supper and so on, do not half tug at the heart strings.

Someone, though, has to let some of those TV personalities know our love for them is not as all-consuming as they seem to believe, or television will morph into a 24-hour-a-day telethon, with nothing demanded of the viewers other than that, in between handfuls of tortilla chips, we telephone to say which of all the celebrities blessing us with their presence on our screens we absolutely adore the most.

Charity, I should say, is not an entirely alien concept to me – with four children in Catholic education, how could it be? – but I made a conscious decision on Saturday not to ring up for fear of giving encouragement to Chris Evans and Davina McCall. Instead I gave ten pounds to a *Big Issue* seller, and told him to buy himself some nice drugs, or a hot meal, whichever need was more pressing (I take the Bill Hicks view that, if you are giving money to someone for necessities, and the recipient is an addict, then drugs are very much a necessity).

I think it was the footage of Evans giving high fives to two young victims of the Tsunami – almost beyond parody – that persuaded me to make my charitable contributions away from the telethon's glare. The presenters tend to put on a special solemn face for these segments, roll heart-rending VT, and say: 'Let us remind ourselves what this is all about...'

Well, up to a point it is, although I got the impression there was a certain amount of rehabilitation work going on for the presenters as well, with prime time family television giving a timely paint job to recently pranged careers.

Davina, of course, is recovering from her epically unsuccessful chat show, while Angus Deayton, host of *Only Fools*, was in some trouble recently (I forget the details, I think he may have slept with the former England manager), and neither will have suffered from the exposure.

Evans, meanwhile, once considered dangerous and cutting edge, is in the process of the most dramatic transformation since Cat Stevens. Before our very eyes, he is reinventing himself as Terry Wogan, and Saturday night's non-threatening fun will have effectively spilled another shovelful of earth over the corpse of the wild and crazy Evans.

Of course, if one presenter wants to use a telethon to hoist himself up a notch or two on the celebrity golf circuit, and another wishes to resurrect a career as the sardonic host of mildly satirical comedy shows, and in the process millions of pounds is raised for charity that surely is a crime without victims.

True, but *Only Fools* went on all week. I know riding a horse is a very difficult thing to do, and well done to those novices who mastered it, but with all the peripheral self-regarding celebrity blubbing, the show occupied about as much screen time as the World Cup. On the BBC Three coverage, they even had a horse whisperer ('You're going to win the 3.30 at Kempton.' 'Sorry, you'll have to speak up, I can't hear a word you're saying.'), prompting the thought that if all the people who work as horse whisperers or personal shoppers – yes, yes, I know, or as semi-humorous newspaper columnists – were to go and drill water holes in Africa...

In the meantime, I suppose charity telethons will continue. So how about Guantanamo Baywatch; four celebrities in swimming costumes lined up against a wall in the searing heat with bags over their heads, and see which one cracks first? I am no expert, but it sounds like a winner to me.

The BBC had clearly come up with a new meaningless slogan in 2011, as pointless as all the ones before and since, 'Delivering Quality First.' Anyone promising to deliver anything, unless it's Royal Mail or a takeaway food outlet, is to be viewed with the utmost suspicion. Like most BBC mission statements, 'Delivering Quality First' was probably about cutting costs, appealing to a younger audience, or crawling round the Government of the day to ensure the licence fee and trebles all round.

Oh bop, fashion, as David Bowie said, not particularly about *Match Of The Day*

Screen Break, The Guardian, *17 October 2011*

Suddenly the shirts are getting interesting on *Match Of The Day*. Gary Lineker was wearing a dark blue number with a black collar on Saturday, a combination I have never seen before, while Alan Shearer wore grey (what else?), with black piping around the breast pocket and the button-holes, carrying definite echoes of the teddy boy era of the 1950s. Alan Hansen, who must not have got the memo about jazzing up the shirts, stuck with his traditional plain black.

I am no Gok Wan, but I had not realised that two-tone shirts were making a comeback. The stripy shirt with the stiff white collar has never lost its popularity among lawyers, and small-town estate agents wishing to cut a dash at the Junior Chamber of Commerce, but Lineker's blue/black combo, and Shearer's Showaddywaddy-esque chemise – he eschewed the crepe-soled brothel creepers the Leicester rock 'n' roll revivalists used to favour, sticking with plain black shoes – were something of a departure in the Saturday night football highlights world, and I am wondering whether they are part of the BBC's exciting new commitment to 'delivering quality first'.

Certainly, if *MOTD* can add some sort of male fashion element – maybe by parading the presenters naked and then showing them how lovely they look in their flattering shirts – to its already popular mixture of football highlights, pointless post-match interviews, so-so analysis, and golf buddy banter, the future of the programme is assured. And if they could only find a way of bringing some competitive cookery or baking into it as well, there is a whole bucket-load of quality, just waiting for delivery.

On the other hand, maybe the pretty shirts are as far as BBC One will want to go in mucking about with a format that still has four million people sticking with the channel till late Saturday night, even after all the celebrity dancing, and the acting-by-numbers in *Casualty*.

I am one of the four million, and as the BBC looks for ways to cut costs – sorry, to deliver quality first – I hope the funds will be found to extend the life of *MOTD* beyond the end of next season, when its current deal expires. I assume cutting back on the Formula One coverage was in that very cause.

Match Of The Day remains important to the BBC, and Gary Lineker is a fine presenter in my view, if only he were not so damned pleased with his little jokes that he feels obliged to bludgeon them to death in the course of the show. He was particularly amused this week by Sir Alex Ferguson's description of the Liverpool – Manchester United fixture as 'the biggest club game in world football,' which he referred back to in his 'comedy material' at least four times.

And, yes, I know I am on dangerous ground criticising anyone for the re-use of jokes. Screen Break archivists, of whom there are a surprising number, frequently email me complaining that a line that made an appearance in the column circa 1997 has resurfaced – for what I like to think of as a whole new generation of readers.

Well, be warned archivists, nit-pickers, and those of you with nothing better to do than criticise hard-working columnists on message boards, I have a line – which has so far only appeared once – about dog-lover Clare Balding being so excited about presenting the Crufts coverage that she travelled all the way up to Birmingham with her head hanging out of the car window, which I love so much I am planning to dust down and use again the very next time I write about Crufts. Think of it not so much as a repeat, more as delivering quality first.

Meanwhile, in case you doubted *MOTD*'s new role as fashion leader, Francois Pienaar, pitch-side pundit for ITV at yesterday's rugby union World Cup semi-final between Australia and New Zealand, followed Gary and Alan's lead in a lilac-coloured shirt with contrasting white collar.

Pienaar, Michael Lynagh, and Sean Fitzpatrick were sure-footed, as they have been throughout the tournament, under the stewardship of Steve (half man, half desk) Rider surgically removed from his desk and flown to New Zealand for the knock-out stages. A welcome tactical switch for ITV saw Lawrence Dallaglio replacing Phil Vickery as co-commentator, and matching his former England colleague for enthusiasm while adding a welcoming smidgin of tactical nous, as well.

Nobody was pretending the match was anything other than the de facto Final, and Dallaglio in fact saluted the All Blacks' victory by saying they 'fully deserved their win in this World Cup Final.'

Commentator Nick Mullins described the victory as

'not the all-singing, all-dancing All Blacks we have had glimpses of recently, more the clinical All Blacks,' but Dallaglio said that for a forward, it was 'a thing of beauty,' the first time I suspect that the word has been used in connection with anything at this World Cup, bar possibly Francois Pienaar's shirt.

Never a huge Commonwealth Games enthusiast, the broadcast of the 2010 games from Delhi at least gave me a chance to write about daytime television, and give the egregious Jeremy Kyle a sound kicking. An indication of the influence this column exerted can be gauged by the fact that after this one appeared in 2010, ITV leapt into action and cancelled Jeremy Kyle's show. On 10 May 2019.

Morning TV, a git in a suit

Screen Break, The Guardian, *11 October 2010*

Professionally, I ought to watch some daytime TV, but not being in need of an ambulance-chasing lawyer, or an online bingo account, I choose not to. All right, *Aerobics Oz Style* occasionally when I need a work-out, and sometimes an old episode of *Frasier* with breakfast, but that is more or less it.

The Commonwealth Games, however, have driven me back to the TV before the sun is over the yard-arm, and I note the *Jeremy Kyle Show* is still on. I read somewhere that Kyle was cashing in on the trend on American TV for odious Englishmen and taking his show over there, which some would say serves them right, and others that it is a terrible trick to play on the nation that gave us *The Simpsons* and Tamla-Motown music. But no, he is still with us, a git in a suit haranguing people in economy-priced leisure wear.

Kyle has two get-out clauses. Number one is to snarl into the face of whichever hapless inadequate he is strafing, 'Listen, sweetheart, there is a child involved here. I don't care about you, but...' And so on, because that is really what Kyle is all about, protector of the nation's children. His second is to say, 'Go off and join our after care team. They'll look after you.' Will they? Is there any evidence that anyone's messed-up life has ever benefited from an appearance on Kyle's show? Call me an old cynic, but I do wonder how long-lasting that 'after care' commitment is. Anyway, one of the victims threw something at Kyle last week. Unfortunately, it was only an envelope containing DNA results, but it is a start.

If you are puzzled over why I'm watching Kyle instead of the Games, it is because he is on ITV2 in the afternoon, and I flip. This is a male thing. I think there may be a synapse connecting the penis in some way with the digit that operates the remote control, but if you have a man around the house, you will know that the only circumstances in which we will remain on one channel for any length of time is if the remote has slipped down the back of the sofa and needs mining from deep.

That said, the restlessness of my flipper finger provides an opportunity to compare and contrast the bright, healthy, highly motivated young people competing in the games with the shiftless specimens misguided enough to participate in Kyle's horror show. The first thing that distinguishes the Commonwealth Games crowd from the Kyle mob is that these young folk are sensible enough to use condoms, if the latest plumbing reports from Delhi are to be believed. More importantly, they display a *joie de vivre* notably absent on the other side.

Regular readers of this column will know I consider swimming to be not so much a sport, more a highly efficient method of not drowning, and there has been an awful lot of it in the Commonwealth Games, but watching the unalloyed joy and pride in achievement of swimmers like Ellen Gandy and Jemma Lowe, after winning medals in one of the swimming races, was quite uplifting. Almost without exception, the athletes give lovely interviews, acting as a kind of mouthwash after ten minutes with Kyle.

I like the BBC's coverage of the games, too. If you are tired of the Sky Sports News format of an attractive young blonde woman with a rather older man, try young Jake Humphrey alongside Sue Barker at the Games, which more than reverses the trend. I think Humphrey may have had a haircut because he is looking younger than ever, so, with the greatest respect and not wishing to be all AA Gill about it, it does sometimes seem the Games are being presented by a young boy and his nan.

Former world champion sprinter Michael Johnson, an excellent pundit for the BBC – Mark Foster and Ian Thorpe are good on the swimming as well – summed up one of the main appeals of the games when he said, commenting on the absence of Jamaica's top sprinters: 'There is enough quality here – not top quality – but enough quality.' He is spot on. It is a little like watching non-league football.

Because it does not all seem so much of a matter of life and death, presenters and pundits feel free to josh, and the viewer can enjoy it for what it is; which is what I shall continue to do – sometimes maybe for even more than seven minutes at a stretch.

Could it be that it was all so different then, or has time rewritten every line? No, it was all so different. This piece should be buried in a time capsule as a picture of what was happening in the media world in 2009. Justin Lee Collins? No, me neither. Channel Five wanted to be called simply Five, nobody knew how to respond to the nascent social media, and Ian Wright, who is now generally accepted as a 'good thing', was trying way too hard, advertising Chicken Tonight, and hosting a desperate talk show on Five.

Wrightie, looking for a role

Screen Break, The Guardian, *21 September 2009*

It is a little like *Flight Of The Phoenix* in the media world at present. For those of you who do not recall the movie, an aeroplane crashes in the desert, the survivors emerge blinking into the light, some wander one way looking for salvation, some another, there are arguments and tragedies, until eventually (spoiler alert, if the film features in your future entertainment plans) someone with the requisite expertise re-builds the 'plane and it flies again.

At present, we are at the blinking into the light stage. Nobody in the traditional media seems entirely sure where to go next. Google Wave? Twitter? Mobile 'phone applications? People, I hear from the back of the wreckage, want information, entertainment, and opinions delivered to them instantly while on the move. Why? Where is everybody going? Moreover – and this is a key question for me – will you customers pointlessly scurrying about want finely crafted semi-humorous light entertainment of the kind you are currently enjoying, or just random noise?

Five have plumped for the latter option in *Live From Studio Five,* Ian 'Wrightie' Wright's new teatime topical chat show and, in what we are contractually obliged to call the current climate, who dares cast the first stone? Michael Parkinson, that is who. Parky has called the show the worst television programme ever, which prompts the thought that he should get out less; and also leads one to take a more benign view of the enterprise than would otherwise be the case.

The programme is not *Newsnight Review*, that is for sure. Its purpose, as far as I can gather, seems to be to discuss the issues everybody is talking about; the future of the planet, the death throes of capitalism, the silence of God. Ho, ho, not really. That would be some programme, though; Wrightie and Richard Dawkins. Come on Five, what are you waiting for? No, sadly by 'everybody' they mean everybody who is tweeting and blogging and leaving comments on Internet forums.

So they show us some widely viewed clip from You Tube, like Kanye West disrupting an awards ceremony, and Wrightie and co-hosts Melinda Messenger and Kate Walsh from *The Apprentice* tell us what they think, replicating for the viewer the experience of surfing the net while three fairly annoying people shout in your ear.

I exempt Kate Walsh, though, who is not half bad. She narrowly avoided working for Lord Sugar, taking the coveted second place on *The Apprentice*, confirming that all contestants on that show really want is to get out of whatever corporate nightmare or dead-end business project they are currently trapped in, and get on the telly. She delivers the odd sharp one-liner, and looks remarkably at ease for someone new to live TV. Surprisingly, it is Wrightie who looks most uncomfortable, mugging to camera like a youth club leader trying to give the impression the Christmas disco is going really well, and shifting around in his seat too much. Not that live TV holds any particular terrors for Wrightie, he is probably just on edge hoping the SAS will mount a rescue mission.

How much does that man want to be on TV? He left a successful and well-rewarded radio show, where every second caller prefaced his thoughts with 'Wrightie, you're a legend,' for a TV show where he gets to discuss whether women should wear high heels for work. For those of you who have lives and may have missed his thoughts on this key topic, here is a brief *précis*: 'Keep 'em on girls. It accentuates everyfink.'

While in time-wasting mode I hopped over to Sky for Justin *Lee Collins – Ten Pin Bowler*, a documentary / travelogue following the presenter as he tried to make it as a professional in America. This could have been a great deal worse, but JLC is quite likeable in these gonzo shows, and producer Will Yapp, who made that very dark Louis Theroux programme with Jimmy Savile, has a fine acerbic eye, and spent a satisfying amount of time on the problems of customising a bowling ball for Collins's unfeasibly slender 'lady's fingers'.

Collins was mentored by Carmen Silvino, a founding member of the Professional Bowling Association, who stripped his game down, and tried to give him a hook shot. Predictably, as anyone who has had a spot of tennis or golf coaching will confirm, Collins's game suffered initially, and the schedule did not allow for it to be built back up again, so what we were left with was a show about a TV presenter not being very good at ten-pin bowling.

It filled an hour, though, as did Wrightie, irresistibly bringing to mind Seinfeld pitching his 'show about nothing' to NBC. 'Why would anyone watch it?' asks the NBC executive. 'Because it's on TV,' says George. Unfortunately, there is nobody around these days sure enough of the new media environment to echo the NBC exec's acid response: 'Not yet, it isn't.'

Hoop nightmares and colourful Keaton

Screen Break, The Guardian, *5 November 2001*

We are all very wary these days of using words such as 'disaster' when writing about a mere television programme, which presents me with something of a problem in trying to convey the full wretchedness of the BBC's coverage of Michael Jordan's NBA comeback game. I am not accustomed to resorting to the thesaurus – at least not this early in a piece – but, in these special circumstances, how about dreadful, dire, calamitous?

Quite simply, *America – A Sporting Tribute*, which is what the BBC called its ludicrously attenuated broadcast of the basketball game between the New York Knicks and the Washington Wizards on Tuesday, may have been the worst live television programme I have ever seen; and I watched David Frost and Angela Rippon on the opening morning of TV-am.

It was one of those rare occasions when every word in the section of *Roget's Thesaurus* marked Adversity fitted perfectly. Unfortunate, ill-starred, inglorious; pick where you like. Why not try out one of those lovely archaic expressions you find in *Roget*: lame dog, planet-struck, cup of sorrows? This was not so much a cup of sorrows as a bloody bucketful.

Actually, the actor Michael Keaton, looking further than the thesaurus for his sources, summed up the programme perfectly. 'What do you think of the game?' asked Garry Richardson, doomed for ever more to be BBC Sport's man with the roving mike, and for once surely wishing fervently this was not the case. 'Dull,' Keaton answered with commendable accuracy. 'Dull?' countered a disbelieving Richardson. How could this be, when the BBC had spent what felt like half a lifetime building it up? 'Yeah,' said the actor, clearly wondering if 'dull' was a word we didn't have over here. 'It's fucking boring.'

'Well, that's one of the problems with live television,' said Richardson, becoming more Partridge-esque by the minute. What he meant, I think, was not that live television could be fucking boring, but that there was always a danger someone might come on and say as much.

The unfortunate, ill-starred presenter of this terminally lame mutt of a programme, whose work I have admired in the past (round the business end of a horse, there's no one better), and whose identity I shall therefore protect by calling her simply CB, back-announced this timeless moment with 'Michael Keaton, there, with some colourful...' before being interrupted by the off-screen voice of Richardson lamenting, 'Couldn't get through with the cameras.'

Ah yes, the cameras. The idea, I think, was that the cameras would follow Garry around Madison Square Garden while he spoke to what CB described as 'celebrities from all walks of life.' Michael Keaton, Richard Dreyfuss, Kevin Bacon, Kevin Kline. You know, all walks of life.

Problem was, as Richardson did his paparazzo act, the cameras frequently remained sniffily aloof and refused to follow. So you got moments like this: CB throws to GR, GR says, 'Well, we're going to keep wandering around. There's all sorts of celebrities.' Camera, meanwhile gives us not Garry but general views of basketball court and people milling around.

The general hubbub is then interrupted by an unidentified female voice saying, 'There's Richard Dreyfuss in a green hat,' the signal for GR, still adrift from his camera, to take over, announcing excitedly, 'There's Richard Dreyfuss,' at which point any viewers still awake either chorus, 'Where's Richard Dreyfuss?' or sensibly switch off and take advantage of the government's recent liberalisation of the laws on Class B drugs. 'Let's go and talk to him,' says GR. 'I think the camera's following us.'

I've got news for you, Garry...

For the Kevin Kline piece, unusually, both actor and interviewer were in shot from the start. Mind you, Garry was always in shot if there was a camera handy, thanks to his practice of positioning himself one inch from the face of his victim.

'Do you come here often?' was his opening question to Kline (I promise you I am making none of this up. I have the tape, which I might agree to destroy should BBC Sport leave an agreed sum of money in a hollow tree somewhere), who charitably declined to chin him when GR rounded off the interview by saying, in case Kline was wondering why he had been chosen for the honour of a Richardson interview, 'We remember you from *A Fish Called Wanda*.' That's *A Fish Called Wanda*, released in 1988, since when Kline has made 26 films including Ang Lee's brilliant evocation of 1970s amorality, *The Ice Storm*, and the 1993 political satire *Dave*.

The 'interview' was followed by another of those gloriously inadvertent off-mic moments, which became such a trademark of the programme, Clare (damn, what a giveaway) saying mysteriously, 'Has anyone got a tissue?,' which must surely now be the title of her autobiography.

6. The Pengest Munch

'A man who dedicated his life to fried chicken went around in a white suit, the least appropriate outfit imaginable when eating a food that claims to be finger-lickin' good...'

A world of chicken

Memoir, Previously unpublished

Everybody, I believe, goes through a KFC phase at some time. It might only last for a week or two, but there's something in that secret blend of herbs and spices that makes you want to return for more.

I had a short-lived addiction to the food in the late 1980s when I was presenting a late night radio show in Manchester, and staying with my mum. I was always ravenous after broadcasting – adrenalin or something, or the effect of Simon and Garfunkel (this was Radio 2) – and the post-midnight food options were either a slice of toast at mum's, or a takeaway.

Driving home along Cheetham Hill Road – kosher butcher shops long gone, replaced by Asian mini-markets, doner kebab joints, and slot machine arcades – I decided Kentucky Fried Chicken, as it then still was (the name was changed in 1980), an international brand, might be the least toxic choice. It was the first time in my life I'd ever eaten it.

I'm not sure it was quite as crisp and delicious as it was in the Colonel's day (he sold the business in 1964 anyway), in fact I thought it was a little greasy. Nevertheless, for the next few weeks, I dropped in late each Saturday night, got myself a couple of pieces and some fries, and sat in a plastic chair munching joylessly.

Others, I knew, had experienced similar cravings.

I remembered being shocked a few years earlier when I visited a friend of mine, something of a hypochondriac and the fussiest eater I knew, and opened his bin to find several of the Colonel's distinctive red boxes in there. His explanation was that he had bought a small portion in extremis to quell an attack of the munchies – he was an enthusiastic smoker of cannabis* – and found the shop well situated when similar circumstances recurred.

My theory, which I shared with anyone who would listen, was that the secret blend included some kind of mildly addictive drug, and that was why it was such a closely guarded secret.

Even after the company was sold, franchisees still had to get the coating directly from the Colonel, and the recipe remained a mystery until after the death of Harland's widow, Claudia, in 1997, when it was found in a scrapbook, according to nephew Joe Ledington in an interview in the *Chicago Tribune*. It's all over the Internet now anyway.

Looking down the list of ingredients, the only real surprise is 'one tablespoon ground ginger', but that means I can cleave to my theory, imagining someone in the organisation tapping the side of his or her nose, saying, 'Let's just call it "ground ginger". Nudge, nudge. Wink, wink'

The KFC people would probably take a different view, namely that the fanatical attention to detail the Colonel exercised over his product, even after he'd sold the company, is an ethos the company has retained, meaning their fried chicken, above all their many rivals, remains the ultimate comfort food.

Colonel Sanders – the title is honorary, bestowed on him by his friend Governor Lawrence Wetherby around 1950, though some versions of Sanders's life place it earlier – was appointed a brand ambassador for his company after its sale, and was not above making flying visits to check standards were being maintained. His story is a remarkable one to which I intend to return after I've finished reading his autobiography, *Life As I Have Known It Has Been Finger Lickin' Good*.

I'm hoping it will be a delicious blend of nouns, verbs, and adjectives, and maybe even answer the question of why a man who dedicated his life to fried chicken went around in a white suit, the least appropriate outfit imaginable when eating a food that claims to be finger-lickin' good.

The book was published in 1974 when Kentucky Fried Chicken was already a big deal, but not the multi-national phenomenon it is now, with around 18,875 outlets in 118 countries, proving, in case there was any doubt, that fried chicken truly is the international language.

I mentioned earlier the short, brutish lives led by the

chickens that are fried, spiced, and salted on our high streets, to which KFC has an answer which is not really an answer: 'We buy our British chicken from the same poultry suppliers and farms that supply the major UK supermarkets,' they say. 'The rest comes from high-quality suppliers in the EU, Brazil and Thailand. When we source from overseas, our minimum starting point is strict compliance with UK and EU welfare requirements, which our suppliers should aim to exceed.'

OK, but not pecking around in the dirt behind a shop in Cheetham Hill.

Meanwhile, the many KFC copyists, the fried chicken shops without a global brand to protect, we must assume – and this may be an unfair assumption – are maybe less fussy about the provenance of what goes into the polystyrene boxes they fill for the post-pub and club crowd.

I use the word 'copyist', but maybe 'tribute' is more current for the KFC lookalikes that crowd the not-so-good bits of our major towns and cities.

'Tribute', as you will know if you have ever had a night out in a Spanish seaside resort favoured by Brits, is the modern word for taking somebody else's act and replicating it in a way that if enough alcohol has been taken on board, the effect will be roughly the same. We have reached a point where are no imitations any more, everything is a 'tribute'.

I wrote a book in 2003 about small-time showbiz acts – don't bother looking for it; it's 1p on Amazon, and I don't see any of that cash – in which I interview a London duo called AbbaGirls, a tribute to the distaff side of the Swedish hit makers. At the time they were competing with dozens of similar acts. Now there are hundreds. The sale of sequinned jumpsuits, platform-heeled shoes, and tinsel wigs is one of Britain's few growth industries. Beyond the costumes, the chief battleground for these Abbalikes seems to be puns on

Abba song lyrics; 'Swede Dreams' (geddit?), 'Abba Dream' (geddit, again?), 'Gimme Abba' (enough already).

And how does this relate to chicken?

Well, I was stuck in a traffic jam in the mean streets of Wembley after a football match one Saturday, and couldn't help noticing the preponderance of budget fried chicken outlets, imitations of, or 'tributes' to, if you prefer, the Colonel's outlets, down to the cardboard boxes and buckets, meal deals, red and white colour schemes, and the names of the shops, heavily favouring US place names.

In an idle moment the next morning, I tweeted my followers, asking for examples of chicken shops in the UK named after places across the Atlantic, hoping to compile a map of the US in chicken. We almost did it.

How about Nantucket Fried Chicken in South London; Maryland Fried Chicken in Leicester; Kansas, New Jersey, Carolina and Boston, in various UK towns; and my favourite, Alaska Fried Chicken, in the Greater Manchester suburb of Cheadle Hulme (I like to think somewhere in Anchorage there's a Cheadle Hulme Fried Chicken)?

And then there are the cheeky rip-offs; Golden Fried Chicken in Manchester, or GFC, easy to mistake for the real thing when sourcing competitively-priced poultry after a night out; various Tennessee and Texas Fried Chickens calling themselves TFC; and Kennedy Fried Chicken in Stoke Newington, yes, actual KFC! I'm guessing it has little to do with the late US president.

There will be an area of pretty well every town in Britain – a wing, if you like – where these chicken shops congregate, and had I not had some serious intestinal issues, I might have eaten in one on your behalf. Fortunately I do not have to, because there's a 24-year-old from Tottenham in north London who has eaten in hundreds.

He's Elijah Quashie, self-styled Chicken Connoisseur, creator of an Internet series called *The Pengest Munch,* in which he visits chicken shops in some of London's less well-heeled suburbs ... Thornton Heath ... Walthamstow ... East Croydon ... and rates wings, chips, and chicken burgers out of five.

In his way, he gives these places the kind of treatment the posh papers might give Le Gavroche or some hot new Michelin-starred joint where they make their own kimchi.

He rates chips on absorption, their ability to soak up salt, pepper, and barbecue sauce; wings on whether the coating adheres to the meat retaining crunch; the burger on its moistness and pepper quotient; and the whole experience on price – wings and chips were £2.49 in one place – and the attitude of 'Bossman', his name for shop proprietors.

At the last count, he had 597,000 subscribers to his YouTube channel, and 34,939,246 views of his programmes. One episode alone, reviewing Chick King in Tottenham, has apparently been watched a remarkable 4.3 million times.

There's clearly huge public interest in chicken – at least I hope there is – but it's Quashie himself who is the main attraction. He's personable, funny and intelligent, and has now been picked up for a Channel 4 series in which he will review fashion and other 'street' items as well as chicken. He also reportedly has a book deal.

I have to admit to not entirely following all of Elijah's commentary. According to the Urban Dictionary, 'pengest' means awesome/nice/OK but, confusingly, it defines 'munch' as a 'low pressure social gathering for people into BDSM'. That's bondage, discipline, sado-masochism.

(How might that social gathering work, I wondered? 'Hello, lovely weather we're having lately, and could you see your way to wrapping me up in cellophane and setting about my private parts with a claw hammer?'). One assumes Elijah is using the word in its more conventional sense.

Mostly you can kind of guess what he means. In one episode he picks up his chicken burger, which he declares is hench (big, good value) but is not impressed by its taste and texture, so dismisses it as 'not peng, just hench'.

Elijah's reviews are mystifyingly entertaining.

But according to website londonist.com, the Chicken Connoisseur's ratings are for more than amusement only. 'People Flocking To Pengest Munch Reviewed Chicken Shops' is a headline on their site. The piece says some shops have actually raised their ridiculously low prices by 50p following a decent review from Elijah.

A less favourable review of the KFC 'tribute' shops was delivered by restaurant critic Jay Rayner, in a piece from Newham in East London, where there are several, much favoured by local pupils after school's out. Jay points to the obesity rates for schoolchildren in the area – above average – notes the standard chicken-shop meal contains 70 per cent of daily calories, and half your daily salt and fat, and then his zinger: 'These chickens lead short, bitter lives of cramped, ammonia-drenched darkness.'

That's a truth more or less universally acknowledged (happy to join the millions of lazy journos who've never read a word of Jane Austen, but are happy to nick her gags. Think of it as a tribute).

There are those trying to improve production of the world's favourite protein, by gentrifying the fried chicken business, and others who want the trade to stop altogether.

But in Elijah's reviews the cramped darkness isn't even a sub-text. He's having too much fun. He reviews as he eats with his chums, mostly young, urban, impoverished, as I suppose Elijah himself was before the book deal and all that.

* *Cannabis, also known as marijuana among other names, is a psychoactive drug from the Cannabis plant intended for medical or recreational use. It is a mildly euphorogenic and hallucinogenic drug.*

7. The Old Days

'Scotland's favourite soft drink can also be used as a tanning agent, "every shade, from summer tangerine to char-grilled and deepest mahogany..."'

At this point in 2016, Screen Break was sponsored by the UK Concrete Show, and appearing on the Sporting Intelligence *website, set up by the fine investigative sports reporter Nick Harris. The British concrete industry should be proud of itself assisting the re-telling of one of the great sports stories of the 20th Century.*

Mary Decker and Zola Budd Meet Again

Screen Break, Sporting Intelligence *website, 1 August 2016*

Few of the stories emerging from the Olympics over the next few weeks, I suspect, will be as compelling as the Mary Decker – Zola Budd imbroglio at the 1984 Los Angeles games. Or maybe it's distance that lends enchantment. Caught up in the cut and thrust of the daily action, perhaps we fail to appreciate every little narrative.

Thinking back to '84, Zola Budd, running for Britain, even barefoot, was no hero to pinko liberal *Guardian* readers like me, as we sat around fulminating against apartheid, and waiting for quinoa to be invented. When she finished in seventh place in the ladies' 3,000 metres, I don't recall being heartbroken.

Budd's story, of how she broke records in her native South Africa – barred from world sport at the time – was bought up by the *Daily Mail* and, fast-tracked to British citizenship, before her fateful clash with Decker, was told in a terrific documentary, *The Fall*, on Sky Atlantic. It was a tale to make even the pinkiest pinko think again about our reaction to the runner with no shoes.

I remember London at the time being quite a bolthole for young white politically conscious South Africans, fleeing their decadently luxurious lives for bed-sits in Camden Town. What struck me most about their stories was the total isolation of their leper state; the banned rock music, the emasculated television service, the censored press. It clearly would have been quite possible for a teenager like Zola growing up in a strict Calvinist home in Bloemfontein, with a controlling father, to be ignorant of the South African reality.

As she says in the documentary: 'The church preached that apartheid was fine. It was talked of as "separate development".'

Thrust by her grasping father and the *Mail*'s nose for a good story into the flash-bulb popping frenzy of Britain's apartheid protests, the poor bewildered girl looked like a small frightened animal. English was her third language. She didn't want to be here. She had never even heard of Nelson

Mandela. But her father, who pocketed 80 of the 100 thousand pounds the *Mail* paid, insisted she stayed. Some impressive archive archaeology unearthed press conferences from obscure athletics meetings, as Zola won a series of Olympic qualifiers and was faced afterwards with a pretty relentless grilling.

Athletics commentator nonpareil David Coleman caught Zola best. 'What a tiny figure in this vast Olympic arena,' he said, expressing what we all thought watching the sad runner line up for the biggest race of her life.

Neither was Mary Decker's progress – in life, as in that fateful race – untroubled. In fact, there were parallels between the two rivals, notably difficult, unhappy childhoods, Decker's father having left home when she was quite young. She trained fanatically, partly to run off her anger.

The programme unearthed several interviews Mary underwent in the 1970s, with American sports reporters in unfeasibly loud checked jackets. A flashing white smile, well-lacquered hair, and an hilarious jacket may have been the law for sportscasters at the time. How American TV survived the decade without succumbing to some mass strobing disaster remains a mystery.

Mary missed the 1972 Olympics because she was too young, the 1976 games through injury, the Moscow games in 1980 were boycotted by the Americans, so 1984 was her big chance.

Just over half way through the race, Mary and Zola clashed, without intent on either side, putting America's sweetheart out of the race. The crowd began to boo Zola and she deliberately slowed down fearing redoubled booing should she ascend the podium. Mary was less than gracious afterwards.

The two runners' stories were told separately, flipping

from one to the other, so clearly the money shot was going to be their reunion. The film kept us waiting over an hour for that, making it all the more moving when both arrived at the Olympic stadium together, hugged, and jogged round the track chatting like chums of old. I must confess I almost lost it.

Thank goodness not watching *The One Show* is part of my daily routine, which meant I missed Zola and Mary on the sofa together plugging the film. Although I suspected there would be some sort of rapprochement between the two, it still would have been a spoiler. Sure, it might have been interesting to hear what the girls had to say about the film, but it's really not worth taking the risk of Gyles Brandreth turning up.

***

In a week replete with nostalgia – '66 World Cup and all that – I watched a short programme on Sky Sports called *Darts Legends,* about Jocky Wilson.

The late lamented Sid Waddell was one of the talking heads, describing the early days of the world darts' championship, when Jocky turned up 'in a Danish army anorak, with a half-eaten cheese sandwich in his pocket.'

Jocky was one of darts' great characters, said Sid, 'a crooked smile with no teeth.' People spoke in similar terms of World Cup winner Nobby Stiles's toothless jig of joy round Wembley Stadium.

I may be worrying unnecessarily, but I just hope recent advances in dentistry don't rob British sport of its characters.

Football in the Old Days, and the first Lionesses

Screen Break, The Guardian, *17 December 2007*

One of the best jobs you could have in the 1950s, better even than lamplighter or muffin monger, was football referee. Your main responsibilities were to keep a neatly trimmed moustache, and look to the Royal Box for the signal to start the FA Cup Final. This became clear watching *A Game of Two Eras,* a hugely entertaining *Time Shift* programme on BBC Four.

In the 'Fifties, when Manchester United, according to the newsreels, were managed by someone called Mett Busbeh, it was apparently not unheard of for a bustling, combative, classically English centre forward to attack an opposition goalkeeper with a machete he had concealed down his voluminous shorts, hacking off limbs *Monty Python*-style. Commentator Ken Wolstenholme would invariably describe this as 'an unfortunate collision', and the ref might even administer a ticking orf.

Peter McParland, to his credit, playing for Aston Villa against Manchester United in the 1957 Cup Final, did little more than launch himself at United goalkeeper Ray Wood from about twenty yards away, and break the goalie's jaw, the defining moment in a match *Time Shift* promised to compare 'scientifically' with last year's final between United and Chelsea.

'This is the first time this kind of comparison has been made,' said narrator John Inverdale, which was palpable nonsense. Get three old geezers together and pour enough rough cider into them, and conversation will inevitably turn to the question of whether Bobby Moore could have adapted to the modern game, or how Cristiano Ronaldo would have reacted to 90 minutes of being scythed down by Peter Storey, and at what point Chopper Harris might have kicked Carlos Tevez into Row Z.

Where *Time Shift* differed from the cider-fuelled OGs is that a serious-looking young chap from Delta Tre, a football data company, sat behind a bank of screens, counting free kicks. Thankfully, though, nerdish analysis was jettisoned in favour of talking heads and carefully selected clips, illustrating LP Hartley's famous gag about the past being a foreign country, where they do things differently.

'Football then was of the working class, by the working class, and for the working class, but it was not a golden passport out of it,' said Gary Imlach, who wrote a terrific book on the subject. His point was underlined by fascinating footage of crafty inside forwards and rugged centre halves shyly displaying toothy grins for the camera, as they ground metal and welded bits of copper pipe together, and did all those things young men used to do before we became a nation of hairdressers.

After one of these 14-hour shifts hammering dirty great lumps of metal about, your 1957 footballer would prepare for the big match with a steak and kidney pie, a side order of lard, and 20 Woodbines; which the programme contrasted with the present regime at Preston North End, where chef Hayley McDonald feeds the players on 'low-fat lean meats'. 'Then before match day,' said Hayley, 'we start carbohydrate loading, with lots of pasta and rice.' (I am not sure this approach works, by the way. I have been carb loading since the early Eighties, and still my professional football career refuses to take off.)

What Hayley's testimony did prove was that while the game may have got smarter, not all the players have. 'I have difficulty getting them to eat fish,' she said. 'But if I tell them it's chicken, they'll eat it. It might be a prawn.'

If *Time Shift* told us nothing we did not already know, the programme that followed on BBC Four, *Nation On Film*, was a revelation. It was a documentary about 'one of the most extraordinary sports teams Britain has ever seen,' and for once the hyperbole was merited.

The story of the Dick Kerr Ladies, a women's football team formed by Preston munitions workers to raise money for soldiers injured in the 1914-18 war, was remarkable. On Boxing Day 1920, 53,000 spectators turned up to watch one of their matches at Goodison Park, with an estimated 15,000 more locked out. Their crowds rarely dipped below 20,000, and they became an unofficial England international team, playing the French, and touring Canada and the USA, where they competed against men.

What was particularly noteworthy was the apparent lack of condescension among the flat caps in the crowd. As far as you could tell, admittedly from limited evidence, women's football was treated as a perfectly credible outdoor entertainment.

The Dick Kerr ladies raised the equivalent of a couple of million pounds for ex-servicemen in today's values until, in December 1921, the FA Council stepped in and banned women's football. All football league grounds and grounds affiliated to the FA were forbidden from staging any women's matches, on the grounds that they were 'unsuitable'. The FA's action, displaying all the wisdom, sensitivity, and far-sightedness for which the organisation has become known, was not reversed until 50 years later, although the team battled on. There was a lovely sequence in which Edna Broughton, Dick Kerr's outside left from 1945-1960, watched recently unearthed footage of herself, playing – and looking quite handy, too – at Belle Vue, Manchester, before a packed crowd in the late 1940s.

Historians of the women's game were still bitter about the 50 years lost to their sport, suspecting that the motive for the ban was the amount of money being diverted from the professional game to veterans of the Great War – or the 'unfortunate collision', as I believe the ruling classes called it at the time.

This piece is given added piquancy by BBC Five Live's decision in 2022 to drop the classified football results. Soon we'll have to explain to our children and grandchildren exactly what a central place the pools used to play in our sporting life. They probably won't believe us.

The football pools towns of Scotland

Screen Break, The Guardian, *28 September 2009*

Nasty, brutish, and short is how Thomas Hobbes described the life of man. It is also how a friend of mine described Noel Edmonds, but that need not detain us now.

The complete Hobbes gag is actually even darker, mentioning such joys as 'continuall feare and danger of violent death', building up to the punch line where life is labelled 'solitary, poor, nasty, brutish, and short.'*

Good stuff, Tom, but I wouldn't open with it.

I am not sure Hobbes was thinking of Scotland particularly when he came up with his n, b, and s schtick, but if he was he would have found a kindred spirit in Jonathan Meades. For the final part of his BBC Four series *Jonathan Meades Off Kilter*, the food and architecture critic and noted humanist toured what he called Scotland's football pool towns – Cowdenbeath, Dunfermline, and the ones that do not even exist like St Mirren (Paisley) and Raith (Kircaldy) – and came up with a stunning film, but one unlikely to be streamed on visitscotland.com.

Where there was a choice between focusing on a row of wheelie bins in an urban wasteland or a troupe of bonnie tartan-clad Scottish lassies skipping through a field of bluebells, guess which Meades chose? In fact, the only tartan that appeared anywhere in the film illustrated a typical Meades diatribe against the 50 million Scots who live elsewhere, whom he called 'lachrymose believers in this land of tartan shortbread, mail order cabers, and bagpipe glens.' Their beef with the English he dismissed as 'a 200 year-old PR stunt, the world's longest running exercise in victimhood.'

Yet you sensed he was on the side of the people of Coatbridge, Falkirk, and Fife, although as a famously acerbic critic of food and architecture he was not about to turn cartwheels of joy at what he found. The grey pebble-dashed houses you see on estates around small Scottish towns he described as 'neo-vernacular hutches', while he suggested the Scottish chip shop as an alternative to Dignitas.

And if the saturated fats do not get you, a wee chib or a Kilmarnock kiss might, said Meades, quoting a United Nations report saying you are more likely to be assaulted in Scotland than anywhere else in the world. Having lived at Partick Cross for a year – admittedly some time ago – while studying in Glasgow, and returning South with nothing worse than a little carpet burn, this sounded bonkers to me, but the report is on the Internet for all to read.

So I assume we can also trust Meades on Irn Bru, which he says is not made from girders, but contains instead 'an exciting cocktail of three dozen flavouring agents and food colourings which cause such grave stains a product has been specially formulated to remove them.' Scotland's favourite soft drink, says Meades, can also be used as a tanning agent, 'every shade, from summer tangerine, through char-grilled and deepest mahogany, to Stuart Hall.'

The bleakness of football pools Scotland, the 'towns that have no existence other than as part of the Saturday afternoon rite, chips in a game of chance', was matched only by the face of Meades himself, the most doleful presence on TV since the late Clement Freud did that dog food commercial (kids, ask your parents).

Where Meades apportioned blame for the desperation and ugliness he found, it went not to the 432 diehards huddling on the terraces at Berwick Rangers ('Irn Bru third division; next year maybe in the prestigious Irn Bru second division'), or the 1,800 faithfully following Raith Rovers, but to their lords and masters.

He meant this literally, pointing to a feudalism still extant north of the border. 'Ninety-three per cent of the people measure their property in square feet, seven per cent in acres,' he said, driving past a seemingly never-ending grey stone wall surrounding one of Scotland's many landed estates. But it was also a reference to Margaret Thatcher and Arthur Scargill, named as twin destroyers of industry in Fife.

Over archive footage of fierce pit-head picketing, Meades talked of 'the human cost of efficiency, and adherence to the bottom line', and 'tens of thousands rationalised into involuntary idleness'. Fife, he said, was where we see 'the social and environmental effects of the initially attritional and consequently violent coiffeur clash between the free-trading ideological helmet modelled by iron steel girder Margaret from Finchley and the smug warm-over worn by King Arthur of Stalindale, South Yorkshire.'

The programme was full of fine fancy writing like this – like Michael Moore with wit. Comparing Scotland's part-time footballers with their counterparts in England's top division, he characterised the Premier Leaguers as 'a bespoke cast of gladiatorial yob-gods, wag-roasting Croesus kids, who once a week descend from their Parnassian blingsteads to run around for 90 golden minutes of bravura vanity.' I cannot remember when I have enjoyed a TV programme more, but I doubt there will be much dancing in the streets of Raith.

* (*Five of the less successful Spice Girls. This is a gag I only introduced into my repertoire in the 2020s*)

Also back in 2009, we were hoping Andy Murray would solve the economic crisis.

Andy Murray – damn him – fails to save the economy

Screen Break, The Guardian, *2009*

It was as if someone had appeared on TV on December 22nd to tell us Christmas was cancelled this year. No daytime schedules packed with Hollywood blockbusters, variety spectaculars, and heart-warming outside broadcasts from hospitals making sick children's dreams come true – as long as those dreams include a *Blue Peter* annual, and meeting Noel Edmonds. Instead, just *Bargain Hunt* and *Loose Women* same as usual.

That was how it felt when we realised yesterday's Wimbledon's men's singles title was to be contested not by Andy Murray, but by two other guys, as it has been every other year in our lifetime. Despite the fact that last year's final, which also featured two other guys, was some of the best sport ever seen on TV, what we wanted yesterday, really,

really wanted, to quote my good friends The Spice Girls, was a match between Britain's Andy Murray – or the Scots bottler, as he will henceforth be known, until the US Open next month – and another guy on Centre Court.

Such was the disappointment at Murray's non-appearance that, according to no less authoritative a source than Saturday's *Guardian*, experts predicted it could cost the economy £150m.

Like me, you may be wondering who these 'experts' are, and how they make such precise calculations. If they are based predominantly on sales of snacks and beverages, I should like to tell them that I am writing this while watching the match between the two guys who are not Murray, and have just cracked open a reassuringly expensive lager and a bag of top-of-the-range nacho cheese flavoured tortilla chips. I do not anticipate the lack of a Scotsman in the final causing significant diminution in my snack or alcohol consumption and, what the hell, I may even make myself a toasted ham and cheese sandwich later on, so that might be something else for the experts to consider.

Is this kind of calculation, I wonder, their sole area of expertise, and if so is it a full-time job? Are they perhaps making similar predictions all year round, but failing to make the newspapers? On a routine Saturday, might they, for instance, work out that defeat for Charlton Athletic could cost the economy £575, while a run of four victories for Liverpool would enable us to resurface the hard shoulder of the M6 near Stafford and keep the war in Afghanistan going for another fortnight? The really frightening thought, of course, is that if the British economy is dependant on a British finalist at Wimbledon, we are in more trouble than any of us thought.

Alongside what is left of the British economy, the BBC were the big losers yesterday, with a large proportion of the

12-million plus audience who tuned in for Andy Murray's matches choosing not to be among those present. Presenter Sue Barker gave it her best shot in a contrived intro linking one of the guys' bid for an historic record-breaking 15th grand slam success with Usain Bolt, Shergar, Torville and Dean, the 1966 World Cup winners, and all sorts of other things that are not tennis. But even the dimmest amongst the Sunday afternoon crowd will have cottoned on within the first half hour or so that what they were watching was a tennis match between two guys playing great tennis, but failing dismally to be British.

I like the sport, and actually watch other tournaments apart from Wimbledon, but far more typical in Britain is the attitude of Arthur Smith's dad. I heard Arthur on the radio yesterday saying his father reckoned Wimbledon was sport for people who are not really interested in sport. 'They just want to put on a hat, squeak, and eat strawberries,' said Arthur.

It should be said the BBC never fail to put on a decent show for the strawberry-eating squeakers during Wimbledon with lots of shots of stuff not featuring tennis balls in any way. During yesterday's final we were treated to a 30-second sequence of Federer's feet displaying, full-screen, the huge gold Nike trademark tick, which in product placement terms would be worth about a thousand licence fees, and acted as supporting material to Serena Williams thanking Nike in her victory speech on Saturday.

There were regular cutaways, too, of stars of stage and screen on Centre Court; Cliff, of course, Richard Branson, and others too annoying to mention, including Michael Parkinson, who emerges mostly these days to have a go at reality TV stars, lightweight chat show hosts, and all the young, pretty, airheads who are taking the place of experienced authoritative figures (mentioning no names) in the increasingly vacuous world of TV.

Look mate, thought this particular viewer, why don't you just trouser your Centre Court tickets, be grateful, and shut the flip up about the toothsome blondes doing your gigs?

While the rest of us, Parky, are pinning our hopes on Ashes success to revive the economy, for some of you it is Christmas every day.

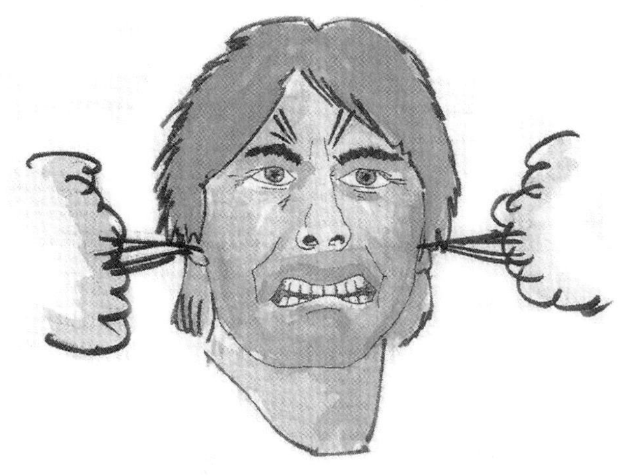

8. The Gaffers

'If you're looking for close-up reaction shots of someone hopping up and down, seemingly quite literally trying to tear his hair out, Conte is your man...'

I was getting desperate. Screen Break was clearly not returning to The Guardian *any time soon, so I started just putting it straight on to my website accompanied by increasingly desperate appeals for people to read it online, as if that might magically make money. Which, ironically, soon became* The Guardian*'s business plan.*

Managers, what *are* they like?

Blog post, 11 September 2016

You may be familiar with Shakespeare's line from *Macbeth* about something or other being 'full of sound and fury, signifying nothing.' It's a gag that I recall every time I see a football manager in his technical area, taking time off from haranguing the fourth official to gesticulate wildly at his players; in what I'm sure must be a doomed attempt to convey tactical information to them.

The Scottish king's words certainly came to mind watching Swansea versus Chelsea on Sky yesterday. Chelsea manager Antonio Conte was unmistakeably full of S and F, as he ran through the gamut of emotions, from teeth-grinding frustration to semi-orgasmic joy.

Actually, no, forget the gamut. There was no gamut. Conte tends to bypass the in-between emotions. He doesn't do thoughtful, troubled, amused, mildly annoyed, or any of those. You never see him looking like he's wondering if he might have left the gas on at home, or whether to pick up a takeaway on the drive back.

What he resembles more is someone emerging from his vehicle after a road traffic accident to confront the driver who has just shunted him from behind.

He's a gift to the cameras. I mean, Jürgen Klopp can be fun, but if what you're looking for are close-up reaction shots of someone hopping up and down, seemingly quite literally trying to tear his hair out, Conte is your man.

I know racial stereotypes are not exactly *comme il faut* these days, but as the BBC is running a season celebrating its hit sitcoms of the 1960s and 1970s, I think I'm allowed to say Antonio is just so gloriously Italian. Short of wiping the Bolognese sauce off his meat cleaver and belabouring the opposition manager with it, to a soundtrack of grand opera, he could not conform more fully to the popular image.

And he does re-open the question of how much influence a manager can have on a game once his players have, as football people like to say, 'crossed the white line'. I suppose continually letting the officials know he is unhappy with decisions could arguably tip the balance in his favour later in the match – it's a technique Sir Alex Ferguson was often accused of employing – but that weird thing where you thrust both arms out in front of you, as if holding an invisible ball of wool, move them in a piston-like motion, and then furiously hold up three or four fingers to your team, is that communicating anything to the players?

I should think it's more likely to muddy the waters. I've never played football at the highest level – or even at the lowest level, to be brutally honest – but I'm sure that if I were to catch sight of the gaffer on the touchline waving his arms about, in some visible distress, I should lose focus, trying to decode the message. 'What the hell's he on about?' I should ask myself. 'Clearly something has got in amongst him, but what does he want me to do about it?' I might find myself pondering, as the tough-tackling opposition midfielder robbed me of the ball.

Within the game, as you may have noticed, my view is not universally supported. Players, we are often told, respond to those managers described as 'demonstrative'. Managers certainly believe their pitch-side mimes have an effect.

Stoke boss Mark Hughes, for instance, who outdid Conte in fury to the extent that he was banished to the stands, was so insistent on getting his thoughts through to his struggling charges, that he insisted on being connected electronically to his coaching team down below.

The pictures on the BBC's *Match Of The Day* showed a still fuming Hughes struggling with some primitive device, which looked disturbingly similar to the toy walkie-talkie set my dad bought me for Christmas when I was ten years old, so I could play secret agents with Ian Goldberg over the road.

Once Hughes got the hang of it, I expect he was passing all sorts of important instructions to his assistants: 'Right, hold up three fingers now. No, hang on, four, move your arm backwards and forwards. No, the other arm. OK, that's right, now go to the other end of the technical area and point to your eyes with both fingers, look angry; touch the side of your head.'

It's possible the Bard was thinking of this kind of pantomime when he wrote of a 'poor player that struts and frets his hour upon the stage' (or an hour-and-a-half with time added on, in the case of the gaffers).

But then again, Macbeth was only under siege in his castle. Hughes had just gone 3-0 down at home to Spurs.

André Villas-Boas, learning quickly

Screen Break, The Guardian, *29 August 2011*

Britain's great gift to the world is undoubtedly sarcasm – that, and Marmite – so congratulations to Chelsea's new coach, André Villas-Boas, on picking up the lingua franca so quickly, alongside everything else he has had to deal with in his new life here; Roman Abramovich, a suddenly wobbly defence, and finding anything on TV that isn't *Come Dine With Me*.

When it was suggested to Villas-Boas on *Match Of The Day* that Ramires seemed to go down too easily for the penalty which saw Norwich goalkeeper John Ruddy sent off, he responded, with what I took to be an ironic smile: 'Yes, that's right, all our players seem to go down. Others don't go down. It's going to be aware of this difference of opinion.'

All right, he lost it a little at the end, but here clearly was a man who, before taking the job at Chelsea, had not only done his homework on English Premier League football, but had put in the hard yards studying the collected post-match interviews of Messrs Dalglish and Ferguson. Mind you, his compatriot José Mourinho was also not averse to giving earnest *Match Of The Day* interviewers the bum's rush in this style, so maybe the biting put-down is yet another area in which our belief that we lead the world is little more than a sad delusion.

This is not a situation we intend to accept meekly here at Screen Break headquarters, where a permanent sneer is the minimum requirement of new recruits, and a ready supply of rainwater is always on hand lest we should see a parade. So, imagine our delight on receiving a call from old friend Will Buckley, former fellow sneerer of this parish, now just doing a spot of sneering in his spare time, with the information that John Fashanu is hosting *Deal Or No Deal Nigeria*, available here on The Africa Channel on Sky.

I will run that by you one more time; the former Wimbledon striker and co-host of *Gladiators* is the black Noel Edmonds. This seemed such an open goal that I gave the job to one of my work experience chaps, who reports back that the warmth and humanity of Edmonds that made him such a well-loved figure in the TV world – quick learner, this lad – has been largely jettisoned by Fash in favour of leering at the young women they enlist to carry the suitcases of money.

'*Deal Or No Deal* is all about glamour,' announces our host at the start of the show, 'and we couldn't have glamour without our twenty-six beautiful models. Please welcome twenty-six of the most beautiful, gorgeous, wonderful True Love models. Ladies come on down. Hello ladies. Wow, do you see what I mean?'

My keen young trainee also brought to my attention some interesting ads during the show, including one for Christianmingle.com, where you can find 'God's match for you.' 'Isn't God rather supposed to be in charge of that sort of thing himself?' the cheeky young scamp asked, 'And if not, what did he do before the internet?' You do not want to stifle enthusiasm, but I had to warn him to leave that sort of material to more experienced sneerers.

Still, his sterling work did free me to address more general questions such as; is anyone still watching *Daybreak* on ITV? I have barely seen the programme since it started but was unfortunate enough to witness half an hour or so of it on Friday. I assume regular male host Adrian Chiles was taking what folk in broadcasting call, without a trace of irony, 'a well-earned break,' because a chap called Dan was squiring Christine Bleakley.

After a cursory news bulletin, in which the public health implications of the 'obesity epidemic' were illustrated by footage of a woman with a fat behind walking down a street, they showed a funny clip of two cats playing pat-a-cake, a useful public service for anyone not among the 11,468,922 people who have already viewed the sequence on YouTube. (A quick tip for you: if you like watching funny clips of pussy cats and you wish to avoid breakfast television, there are quite a few on the internet).

Sofa guests, John McCririck, Kate Thornton, and money expert Martin Lewis then reviewed the newspapers, by which I mean they read out loud the funnies from *The Sun*, and the lovable racing tipster revealed he had two cats, one called Burlington and another called Bertie.

A story about a planet consisting entirely of diamonds prompted our hosts to read out texts from viewers nominating substances they wished planets could be made of. What I assume were the most entertaining contributions were one asking for a planet made of shoes, and another from a viewer saying she liked the old Marvin Gaye record in which the late soul singer declared the world to be just a great big onion. Note to André Villas-Boas, as he continues to assimilate: none of this was meant ironically.

Mourinho – searching for true happiness

Screen Break, The Guardian, *1 May 2006*

The Chelsea-supporting comedy writer Andy Hamilton once told me that to enjoy fully his team's triumphs he has to block from his mind thoughts of the turf as 'stained red with the blood of Russian peasants.' Similarly, I doubt that the inequities and iniquities of Russian society were paramount in the minds of the rest of us watching the celebrations at Stamford Bridge on Saturday afternoon; but even so, unless you are a Chelsea fan, I warrant your heart failed to sing as the Blues received their unarguably just desserts.

Though you might stop short of the muscular views of Joseph Harker, expressed in the grown-ups section of this newspaper last week, that Chelsea is 'a moral stain on the face of football', and stands for nothing so much as the greed that has disfigured the sport, they are still pretty difficult to love. Suffused with joy on Saturday afternoon? I thought not. Me neither.

It is not envy either. I like nothing more than seeing young people enjoying themselves. Three days earlier I had rejoiced unreservedly alongside the Middlesbrough fans at their team's improbable passage into the UEFA Cup final; or would have done had I not been in a position on the sofa from which any major rejoicing – or anything else much – could have meant serious consequences for a man of my years. Still, I threw those scatter cushions around the room a bit.

On Saturday afternoon, however, my soft furnishings remained unmolested. Interestingly, I was joined by Chelsea manager José Mourinho in finding the whole title-winning business less than thrilling, if his interview on *Match of the Day* is anything to go by. He was asked if he had enjoyed this season's triumph as much as last, given that at times during this campaign his *mien* had been that of a man who has just taken delivery of a brand new sports car, but unwisely chosen to leave it in the street outside George Michael's place (the interviewer, Ivan Gaskell, did not put it exactly like that).

'No, I didn't enjoy so much,' said José, 'I won the fourth consecutive title, I think I should be more happy. You are right. I am not enjoying 100 per cent.'

For goodness sake, the man has – in the words of 'Seventies bar-room rockers Dr Hook – more money than a horse has hairs, has the financial backing from his chairman to buy any player he fancies to adorn his team or warm his bench, and has just won a second championship with Chelsea. Forgive me if I put José Mourinho's happiness deficiency fairly low down on my list of priorities.

The Chelsea manager is not alone, however, in finding himself thus afflicted. It is a fairly common phenomenon, best expressed by Peggy Lee in the Jerry Leiber – Mike Stoller song 'Is That All There Is?' You strive for what you think will make you happy, only to find true happiness and fulfilment reside elsewhere, and if José would like to make a small contribution to my charitable trust, I am sure we can help him further.

Failing that, if he is seeking the real sense of achievement that derives from overcoming almost insurmountable odds to triumph, he might want to try managing Aston Villa for a season or two.

But no. He stays at Chelsea. A concerned Gaskell asked

him when he might start enjoying himself again. 'I will have to think about it,' replied José. 'But I'm staying with Chelsea because I believe I can enjoy it more.' If he thinks a third season of seeing Roman Abramovich exchanging high fives with his henchmen in the stands is where true happiness lies, I should say he is deluding himself.

What with Rooney's injury, Saturday was fairly miserable all round. Motty, as ever, found an interesting way of summing up England fans' Rooney-centred hopes and fears, explaining: 'Having lived through the metatarsal in 2004, when Rooney goes down like that every England fan shivers.'

I have never heard 'the metatarsal' used quite in that way, representing a period in time, as if it were the Renaissance, say, except with more emphasis on the foot.

There was little light relief in the snooker, either. Despite having shed viewers since its golden age, snooker, I think, is still potentially a great television sport but boy, at present it is shorter on personalities than a Davina McCall chat show. Apart from immediate family and those with a financial interest in either player, is there anybody who cares who wins a final between Peter Ebdon and Graeme Dott? They can call them Ebbo and Dotty as much as they like, but these guys are dull, dull, dull, an impression only confirmed by the profiles and interviews intended, no doubt, to make them more box office.

Ebbo, for instance, describes himself as 'a quiet family man, who likes to keep himself to himself,' a cliché normally reserved for the neighbours of serial killers. He would probably have gone into the police force, he says, had he not made it on the green baize, and now lives in Dubai where he has 'a fabulous lifestyle'. 'One of the bonuses,' he says, 'is that it is a tax-free country.' Go on, who would have thought it?

Dott, meanwhile, says his favourite food is Chinese, and his favourite TV shows are *Only Fools And* ... I am sorry, I appear to have dropped off.

❧

Mourinho, Di Canio, and style in the dug out

Screen Break, The Guardian, *9 January 2012*

Not enough thought, in my view, is given to the importance of the overcoat in football management. José Mourinho, for instance, according to an excellent series on Sky, *Football's Greatest Managers,* 'announced himself to the watching world' with his exultant run along the touchline at Old Trafford when Porto knocked Manchester United out of the European Cup. But would he have made half the impact if his dark navy overcoat had not been exactly three-and-a-half inches too long?

The programme, narrated by Gabriel Clarke, declined to bring in a menswear expert to answer this key question, contenting itself with the typically Clarke-esque pun, 'Mourinho's career was off and running.' I remember thinking at the time, though, that the last overcoat I had seen flapping in the breeze quite like the Porto manager's was Clint Eastwood's in the Sergio Leone westerns.

Fascinating footage unearthed by the programme, of José's Man With No Name era, interpreting for Bobby Robson at Sporting Lisbon, Porto, and Barcelona, and taking his own first steps in management in Portugal, underlined parallels between Mourinho and some of the Eastwood characters. Intelligence and clarity of purpose, leavened with a dry sense of humour, shone through. I was particularly impressed with a Mourinho team talk, where he stressed he was not putting pressure on his players to win the game, but quietly made the point that if his tactical plan were followed the game would not be lost. Obviously, though, it all starts with the coat.

Just as some actors build a character from the shoes upwards, my advice to any tyro managers is to get the coat right – by which I mean sometimes slightly wrong, to emphasise your individuality – if you want to make your mark. There was a time when any old camel hair coat or shiny suit would do, but not now. If I were advising Paul Jewell, say, I might recommend a trilby hat at a jaunty angle, not to replace tactical nous or inspirational words, but just to make a statement – although that might be a little late at Ipswich.

Incidentally, I do not write without some expertise in this area. My late father was in the rag trade, so I was delighted to see Paolo Di Canio celebrating his Swindon team's victory over Wigan in the FA Cup wearing an item similar to one my dad used to produce in the 1970s, which he called a shorty car coat.

I am sure Paolo's, which had contrasting lining, a refinement my dad never thought of, was of more expensive provenance than the ones the old man used to turn out for discount clothes shops, but accessorised by Paolo with a retro red-and-white Swindon scarf, it struck exactly the right note on third-round FA Cup day – a day sold to us, by television partners, ITV and ESPN, on what the great philosopher Barbra Streisand called 'misty water-coloured memories.'

The importance of Paolo's style was noted by Paul Ince, pundit on ITV's highlights show. 'He has a pride in what he does, in the way he looks,' said Ince. He fell short of suggesting that the style of football played by Swindon stems directly from the coat, but fellow panellist Gordon Strachan paid tribute to the 'lovely one and two-touch football' contributing to Wigan's defeat.

Presenter Matt Smith reminded his experts quite properly of the widely expressed doubts about Di Canio's suitability for a management job. Clearly, we will only know if the Swindon boss has the requisite tactical sophistication when tested at a higher level, but temperamentally he seems perfectly suited – and booted – for football management, if a new series on Radio 4, *Among The Managers*, is anything to go by.

It is a typically Radio 4 take on football, in which the BBC's business editor, and Arsenal fan, Robert Peston looks for parallels between running a big business and managing a football club. If you can get beyond Peston's insistence ON stressing RANdom syllables, there are some vaguely interesting observations, which may enlighten the odd stray from *Woman's Hour*, but are unlikely to strike the average football fan as news just in. There was much talk of the football manager's charisma, leadership qualities, ability to hold a room, and, as with Mourinho and Di Canio, capacity to embody the spirit of a football club.

Peston's most interesting interviews, though, were with those actually doing the job. Harry Redknapp mentioned the incontrovertible truth that the determining factor in managerial success these days is the money to pay the best players. 'Roberto Martinez could be the greatest coach in the world at Wigan, but he's not going to win the league,' said Harry. Sam Allardyce, meanwhile, felt science could level the playing field.

'I like to start off in the morning with a urine test, testing the nutritional value of breakfast, that kind of thing,' said Big Sam. Every manager has his own style, of course, but my guess is Paolo and José prefer to start the day with a practiced eye over the wardrobe rather than a urine test.

Steve McClaren, fine coach, but not a man you want as your number one. He never really recovered from his umbrella-themed England sacking in 2007, his mock Dutch accent when he managed FC Twente in 2012, and had reached his nadir at Newcastle in 2015. He lasted less than a year, and probably didn't need me pointing out that his efforts to disguise male pattern baldness were somewhat comic. Anyway, he's back assistant coaching at Manchester United, so we can laugh about it now. I hope.

Steve McClaren, the twilight year

Blog post, 2015

I used to live between Chepstow and Monmouth on the B4293 (I didn't actually live on the road, I had a small house). The point is the road was unlit, so when I was out in the car at night I frequently encountered rabbits caught in the headlights, but I never saw one that looked like Steve McClaren.

I only mention it because Martin Keown on *Match Of The Day* on Saturday used the well-worn simile to describe the floundering Newcastle United manager, and I'm not sure it fits.

For a start, I never saw a rabbit that looked like it spent as much money on its hair as Steve McClaren. Unlike his team, the manager's barnet is in exceptional order at the back. The exquisitely clipped hair tapers for the last two-and-a-half inches and concludes at the neck in a slick carefully ordered line. Sculpted, I think, is the word.

I have never been a hairdresser – I was never that interested in people's holiday plans – but I am confident this is no five quid haircut. Forty-five quid minimum, I should say, and if only newspapers these days were prepared to spend money on investigative journalism, somebody would be going through Steve's dustbin right now to find the receipt.

It's an important issue for Newcastle fans, because that 45 quid – 55 possibly, if he was in one of those hipster retro places and went for the hot towels and the wet shave – is pointless expenditure. Nobody, apart from a hard-working old-fashioned newspaperman like me, is looking at the back of Steve's head, given what's going on up top.

Steve has been going bald for a number of years, but by carefully arranging a few strands of hair into what unkind tonsorial commentators have dubbed the McClaren Island – though I would say it is more of a peninsula – he is fooling himself into believing he is beating nature.

Before our very eyes, those of us who have been watching *Match Of The Day* for the past decade, the peninsula is shrinking, like one of those tiny islands in the Pacific, where sea levels rise and destroy the islanders' natural habitat, though in Steve's case scientists are unable to prove it's anything to do with climate change.

Your man on the Jesmond omnibus, therefore, must be wondering, if the boss is prepared to throw so much good money after bad down the barbers, does the same kind of policy apply to transfers? Also if Steve has so little luck in preventing or even delaying the inevitable, how is he going to prevent the Geordies going down?

Keown played under McClaren for England and took the view that while he's a perfectly good coach he is not a manager, an opinion for which there is no shortage of supporting evidence.

McClaren, of course, may well have been defenestrated

by the time you read this and replaced by a manager with a full head of hair, in which case feel free to ignore the above and go elsewhere on the Internet where I am pretty sure you will find adorable pictures of a cat that looks like Hitler.

Meanwhile, we turn to another, er, Newcastle legend, Jermaine Jenas, this week's comedy booking on *Question Time*. His was a less than commanding presence, and I suspect some of you tuning in to the programme for enlightened political discourse – a vain quest at the best of times, I should have said – might have asked yourself what he was doing there.

I assume it's some sort of exchange scheme under which Iain Duncan Smith will get a go as a pundit on *Match Of The Day*. Either that, or they've run out of stand-up comedians to fill the left-of-field seat on the show, and Jermaine being young, non-white, and not a politician, ticks a satisfying number of boxes.

It may not startle you to discover he had nothing to say. No, less than nothing. The first question, about Europe, he answered with some complicated analogy, which involved Wayne Rooney's agent falsely telling Manchester United he was wanted by Real Madrid, in order to bump up his wages. Apart from the fact Madrid happens to be in Europe, it stumped me.

Not that I'm likely to be swayed on the Europe issue by Jermaine Jenas, fine box-to-box midfielder though he was. I'd really need to hear what Kieron Dyer and Scotty Parker have to say on the subject first.

How soon we forget these characters. Richard Keys and Andy Gray were Sky Sports's main football broadcasters from the start of the Premier League 1992, but were sacked/resigned in January 2011 after they were recorded when they thought they were off mic, making disparaging remarks about female officials, notably referee's assistant Sian Massey. They went off to the Middle East, where great wads of money were stuffed into their every orifice, and are currently lead presenters on the BeIN Sports Channel.

Christian Purslow was managing director of Liverpool from June 2009 to October 2010, his main task being to sell the club. His history in money included co-founding private equity firm MidOcean Partners. I've no idea what they do. I'm better informed about his next job as an executive with Burton, home if I'm not mistaken of the thirty-bob suit. After leaving Liverpool, he was in charge at Chelsea, and at time of press, is stewarding Aston Villa, having moved his old chum Steven Gerrard into the manager's seat.

After a disappointing 2009-10 season in which Liverpool finished 7th in the league, left the Champions League in the group stages, and the Europa League in the semi-final, Rafa Benítez's position became as untenable as Geoff Shreeves had suggested it might. Benítez went on to manage Inter Milan, Chelsea, Napoli, Real Madrid, Newcastle United, Dalian Professional in China, and Everton. Such is the European management merry-go-round. Carlo Ancelotti, Louis van Gaal, Fabio Capello, Pep Guardiola... for most of the 1990s and 2000s they just followed each other around.

That's the problem with a weekly sports column. The circus moves on, and characters that seem significant one week are barely worth joking about a few weeks later.

Geoff Shreeves is still Sky Sports's man below stairs

Taxi for Rafa

Screen Break, The Guardian, *30 November 2009*

It comes to something when Andy Gray is the voice of sweet reason. But that was his role in Sky's post-match analysis/blood lust after Liverpool's pyrrhic victory in Budapest. As the curtain fell on the Reds' Champions League season, presenter Richard Keys clearly sensed vultures shuffling into their dinner jackets, and giving their shoes a last-minute shine, ready to feast on the still twitching corpse of Rafa Benítez, and was not about to be diverted from this scenario.

Geoff Shreeves, Sky's man below stairs with the hand-held microphone, was duly despatched to witness the ravaging of the Spaniard's bones, but sadly for Shreeves no-one seemed inclined to tuck in, least of all Liverpool's suave managing director Christian Purslow.

Purslow strikes one as the sort of chap for whom the word 'urbane' was invented, someone who would know exactly how to send back a bottle of Chablis Premier Cru if it was not up to snuff. I imagine if several close family members were to be wiped out by a meteor falling to earth, you might catch him with his tie slightly askew, but elimination from the Champions League appeared to leave him neither shaken nor much stirred.

'What are the financial ramifications?' Shreeves asked him. 'Limited actually, Geoff,' was the unruffled response. 'If we play two or three games in the Europa League, it should be financially neutral,' which seemed to contradict the conventional wisdom, but did not stop Geoff from cutting to the chase: 'In terms of the manager's position, though,' – ah, the manager's position – 'Would it have been a minimum requirement that you reach the knockout stages?'

'We don't run our business in that respect,' explained Purslow patiently. 'We don't make managerial and strategic decisions around results in the short run. You can never predict last minute goals. Two goals have cost us dear in the Champions League, and that's no basis on which to make managerial decisions.'

'So going out of the Champions League at this stage, would that not induce the owners to review the manager's position at the moment?' countered Sky's rottweiler, with his teeth firmly clamped on the manager's position.

'Absolutely not,' said Purslow, leaving Shreeves with no option but – with apologies to Quentin Tarantino – to get hypothetical on his ass: 'What about this season, though, if Rafa Benítez was unable to finish in the top four and qualify for the Champions League next season?'

'Rafa has just signed a new 5-year contract, we're about four months into it. He has signed up, and we are very happy he has done so.'

Keys somehow found equivocation in this, and the return to the studio found him with furrowed brow: 'Does that leave us with some doubt whether he will be there in six months time or not?' he asked his pundits. 'What's he saying?'

'I think he is saying he WILL be there in six months time,' deconstructed Gray. 'That's the impression I got from the interview.'

Purslow's interview made for an interesting contrast with the press conference from Portsmouth announcing Avram Grant's assumption of managerial duties, broadcast live on Sky Sports News.

Chief executive Peter Storrie, acknowledging Paul Hart's achievements in difficult circumstances, said of the decision to sack Hart: 'Unfortunately, this is a results industry,' which is something he might want to discuss with his counterpart on Merseyside.

It was a relief to turn to the less opaque business of chess boxing. As hybrid sports go, it is a peach. Could they have picked two less compatible disciplines to combine? For a start, how are you expected to pick up the chess pieces wearing boxing gloves? And what if you are concentrating on the chess game, and someone wallops you in the middle of your Benko's Opening?

Fortunately, these and other questions were answered in a typically thorough Transworld Sport feature. The sport is the invention of a French-born but Serbia-based cartoonist Enki Bilal, who used it as a plot device in his graphic novel *Froid Équateur*. A Dutch fan of the book, Iepe Rubingh, started organising real matches, and now there are 150 professional competitors.

A match consists of alternating rounds of boxing, and 12-minute chess sessions, with a short pause between rounds for the guys to take off their gloves, spit in a bucket, and possibly receive confusing advice like, 'He's leaving his bishop exposed, keep jabbing away.' As far as I know it is the only sport you can win by knockout or checkmate.

In the tournament from Berlin shown on the programme, Nikolay Sazhin, a 19-year-old Siberian neo-physicist, beat German Frank Stoldt, an experienced riot cop, described as the 'godfather of chess boxing'.

'It is extremely challenging,' says Sazhin. 'The chess part is even harder than real chess. You come out of the ring, your heart's racing, you are still breathing heavily, and suddenly you have to calm yourself down,' which I guess is how Rafa feels when he walks off after a match and finds Geoff Shreeves in the tunnel.

All Our Yesterdays

No 48: **Rising Damp** (1974–1978),
The Independent, 10 June 2002

Interesting list of celebrities, all gone, largely forgotten. As media commentator Victor Lewis-Smith liked to say, at the end of it all, we're all worm food.

● It was old-fashioned British seaside postcard humour – some of landlord Rigsby's (Leonard Rossiter) exchanges with his tenant Philip, supposedly the son of an African tribal chief, certainly belonged in a bygone age even then – lifted out of the rut by Rossiter's masterly timing.

With his grubby sleeveless cardigan, flea-bitten cat Vienna, and rich vocabulary of twitches and sneers, Rigsby slunk around his seedy boarding house constantly dropping in on his tenants; long-haired student Alan (Richard Beckinsale), Alan's room-mate Philip (Don Warrington), and shy spinster Miss Jones (Frances de la Tour), after whom Rigsby naturally lusted. The humour derived from Rigsby's tight-fistedness which often caused him to fall prey to conmen and the like; his pretensions – like Hancock and Steptoe, he constantly claimed to be a cut above those around him – but above all, from his disastrously incompetent efforts to sweep Miss Jones off her feet.

The series grew out of writer Eric Chappell's 1973 stage play *The Banana Box* about a shabby boarding house presided over by a landlord called Rooksby, in which most of the origninal cast appeared. While the supporting players all had their own little turns – Beckinsale's shy charm, Warrington's effortless superiority, and de la Tour's quivering concupiscence – it was Rossiter you paid the rent to see.

9. Mammon

'There's an awful lot of spiking, gelling and careful vertical arrangement to cover up – a sort of high definition version of what Bobby Charlton used to do...'

Important notes; 2008 was very much a year of financial crisis, which, as detailed in the film The Big Short, *stemmed in part from sub-prime mortgages being handed out in America to bad risks. Gary Glitter was under investigation, but not yet arrested, charged, and jailed. Not Leader of the Gang, but not yet persona non grata.*

The Ryder Cup in the midst of financial meltdown

Screen Break, The Guardian, *22 September 2008*

My main thought watching Sky Sport's coverage of the Ryder Cup, sponsored by the Royal Bank of Scotland, was that I hope they got the money up front.

What I had failed to register was the important difference between the plain Bank of Scotland, which is in a similar position to James Stewart's Building and Loan in *It's A Wonderful Life* after Uncle Billy left all the cash on the bank counter, and the Royal version which, like Lionel Barrymore, is steering a steady course through the crisis, as nervous investors north of the border flock to it as a safe haven for their beautiful and exotic five pound notes.

On which topic, we might have to take a revisionist view of *Wonderful Life* when it resurfaces this Christmas. The saintly Stewart, you may recall, lent money to the poor people of Bedford Falls, with no real guarantees the money would ever be paid back, while the villainous Barrymore said it was madness granting loans to every redneck hick from the sticks (I am paraphrasing) who could write his name on a piece of paper. Turns out Barrymore was right, and the whole movie is based on a flawed premise. Into the water with you James Stewart.

You will gather I am not entirely engaged with the golf. It is this way every two years. I take an interest in it; the captain's picks, the pairings, and all that – it is more or less unavoidable down this end of the newspaper – but when it comes to the golf itself, I constantly fail to get as excited as the BBC's Ken Brown.

Brown, who was the man at the first tee for the BBC's highlights programme, wore the rapt expression of a child on Christmas morning or Russell Brand at the fellatist's annual dinner. 'The atmosphere's electric,' he whispered. 'Nervy moments, but you can't believe it. The thirty-seventh Ryder Cup is about to begin. Ding, ding. Match one.'

He paused for the first two balls to whoosh past his admiring gaze, before burbling on: 'Let the matches begin. I just can't wait. What do you think Peter?' And Alliss made that gurgling sound that indicates excitement and anticipation in his corner.

I am sure the more measured Tony Jacklin, a former Ryder Cup captain, on Sky, was equally excited, but he was managing to keep a lid on it. Jacklin seemed distinctly unimpressed, for instance, by a feature in which the players made mild fun of their team-mates, answering questions about which one they would least like to sing karaoke with, which one has the worst fashion sense, and so on. 'What about humour?' presenter David Livingstone asked him. 'Did you encourage it, or let it develop naturally?' 'They weren't out there to have fun,' said Jacklin. 'They were there to play their best golf.'

Livingstone credited Jacklin with ushering in the Golden Age of the Ryder Cup in the 1980s, helping turn it into the ultra-professional, highly successful media event it is now. 'You gave them cashmere and Concorde,' Livingstone said, but all I could think of was John Cleese in an episode of *Monty Python*, ranting about the middle classes 'with your lousy colour TV sets, and your Tony Jacklin golf clubs, and your bleeding Masonic secret handshakes.'

Golf is much more classless now, of course, but looking at the paradisiacal pictures from the appropriately named Valhalla in Louisville, I could not help thinking, in a very *Guardian* sort of way, that just a few miles away from these Elysian Fields people were being chucked out of their homes.

In fact, was this not where the trouble started: when America's city slickers stopped making jokes about rednecks (you know you're a redneck, goes my favourite, when you read the *Auto Trader* with a highlighter pen) and started giving them money.

I blame the remote for my inability to focus on the greatest team tournament in sport, or whatever the hell it is.

Flipping channels is just too tempting, especially with Davis Cup tennis on, bucketloads of football, rugby league play-offs – now, there's a game – and such diverting spectacles as Ann Widdecombe trying to show a gang of teenage girls in Birmingham the error of their ways. Remember that Woody Allen film where he was pursued by a giant tit? It helps you understand how those Brummie girls must have felt.

I had also forgotten how indecently entertaining the early stages of *The X Factor* are. Who wants to watch golf when you can see a 66-year-old woman singing 'We're Having A Gang Bang?' Shame on Simon Cowell, though, for failing to eliminate the cutesy Welsh kid, the reincarnation of Little Jimmy Osmond, who announced himself as from 'Pontypridd, the home of Tom Jones' and proceeded to wink and grimace his way through The Zutons' 'Valerie'. I know he was only 15, but you are never to young to be discouraged from that sort of caper.

Finally, good news for Gary Glitter. I will run that past you one more time because it is not something you see in the papers every day: good news for Gary Glitter. When the Bulgarian team PFK Litex Lovech scored the opening goal in the UEFA Cup tie against Aston Villa, their celebration included a good twenty seconds of Glitter's anthemic 'Rock 'n' Roll', broadcast on Five and possibly on the radio as well. So there may be some royalties there for Glitter to claim. On the other hand, he may prefer to keep a low profile.

Not so long ago, Guinness was running a vaguely surreal ad for their beer, all monochrome, strange expressions, and horses charging into the waves. The advert may have reinforced your feeling that Guinness is a damn cool thing. No-one thinks that about banks, and their ads just make us feel it even less. Stop spending money on pointless adverts. Give us all a five pound note and a Cadbury's selection box at Christmas instead.

The desperation of banks to make us love them

Any Other Business, Forty20 Magazine, *March 2017*

We are what we do. Hang on; let's just subject that wisdom to closer analysis. Yes, you're right. It's bollocks.

But don't tell me, tell the National Westminster bank, currently selling its services via a TV advertising campaign using that meaningless slogan. We are what we do, we are who we are, I am what I am, I think therefore I am, don't forget the fruit gums mum (kids, ask your grandparents). All make equally as much sense.

The commercial, shot in gritty black and white (no cliché overlooked), begins with two children sitting in the street sharing an ice cream, establishing I assume a caring, sharing motif. Because obviously, as we've learnt, sharing is what banks are all about, chiefly in the form of dividends for shareholders and bonuses for executives.

More gritty monochrome images follow; dog fighting, suffragettes, a woman with tattoos, soldiers returning from a war, Charlie Chaplin for some reason, the Polar ice cap melting, Alvin Stardust gutting a mackerel, and someone feeding a new-born lamb with a baby's milk bottle (all right, I made up the Alvin Stardust). 'We are all what we have done, and what we will do,' intones the honeyed voiceover.

And what? That's supposed to encourage me to switch my account from Lloyds to the Nat West? I happen to like the black horse trotting through the hospital where all the doctors and nurses are frozen in mannequin pose.

Actually, I couldn't give a fig for the black horse, or the bank's promise to be 'by my side for the next step'. My account's at Lloyds because when I started work and had some money to bank for the first time, I was in Bristol, and Lloyds seemed to have a lot of branches round there.

I've only switched once, and that's because I could do it with one click. I moved my current account to Lloyds Club, because they were giving away free cinema tickets, enabling me to snooze through *La La Land* with the family at no cost – disregarding the sixteen quid for refreshments – but that's as far as I'm prepared to take it for now.

There's a similarly arty ad running on TV at the moment for the Nationwide, trading on its foundation (in black and white, obviously) in 1884, using poets Jo Bell and Heather Wastie to laud the cuddly caring, sharing thing finance houses are so keen on.

In Heather's ad she's sitting, wrapped in well-worn outdoor wear, in some windswept allotment by a tumbledown shed lamenting the departure from the family home of her son, who now has a home of his own (thanks to the Nationwide, I assume, though nobody says as much. That would be just too literal). She and her old man have made a life-size cardboard cut-out of the lad which they prop up while they're eating their dinner. He still won't eat his carrots, says Heather.

The phrase 'mad as a mongoose' immediately springs to mind, followed by the thought that the effort of moving her son out of the house, and the costs involved have possibly tipped her over the edge.

'The currency of kindness' is Nationwide's slogan, negated somewhat by the caption on screen reminding viewers that 'your home may be repossessed if you do not keep up with mortgage repayments.' Way to destroy a warm glow.

And thank you by the way for your concern over my watching too many commercials.

Those of you collecting these columns in the limited edition, leather-look, luxuriously embossed 'Any Other Business' binder will have noted that my last piece fulminated against Rob Brydon's cruise ship adverts, and I am guessing there might be a general feeling that someone ought to take me to one side and explain how the fast forward button works.

Well, I should point out that I do watch some of the programmes that interrupt the commercial messages but very few of them have had similar amounts of time and money lavished on them, and when you have just sat through the fourteenth re-imagining of the *Bake Off* or *Antiques Roadshow* format, the urge to put pen to paper tends to leave you.

(My god, he can't work the remote, and he's still using pen and paper).

Goochie and Warney unstumped by hair in the plughole

Screen Break, The Guardian, *8 November 2010*

Sometimes I forget to watch programmes in high definition. Having become accustomed to viewing sport on what you might call old-fashioned Sky, I sit there peering through the gloom at footballers booting a casey around a paddy field while consumptive types painted by LS Lowry huddle for warmth on the terraces, until one of my children comes in and reminds me how much more vibrant and 21st Century the pictures will look if I re-tune to an HD channel.

And my goodness, they are right. For instance, without the remarkable clarity of HD, I should not be aware of the fine work currently going on at the Advanced Hair Studio.

My interest in hair replacement technology, I should stress, is purely academic. I have a full and, if I say so myself, rather impressive head of hair – although these days sadly it serves more as a cruel reminder of carefree youth than anything else – but on behalf of my friends in the bald community I like to keep an eye on the latest advances.

I am particularly interested in the state of play up top for Shane Warne and Graham Gooch, who I had the pleasure of interviewing a few years back when the advanced hair people opened a place – I suppose they would like me to call it a laboratory – in Leeds. In the course of a full and frank discussion about the likely destination of the Ashes, the subject of hair loss arose. I cannot remember who raised it, but it appears that many a time, when showering after a hard day with bat or ball at the Oval or the Gabba, our heroes would notice strands of hair blocking plugholes or nestling reproachfully between the bristles of the styling brush.

Thanks to this early diagnosis, W and G told me they were able to embark on evasive action, as a result of which to look at them now you would not know they had a hair loss problem at all – unless, of course, you had read about it in all the ads in the papers, or seen them talking about it on the telly commercials.

The latest highly defined TV spot features Warney and Vaughanie (England's Michael Vaughan) in a kind of Top Trumps game in which they deal cards with pictures on them of cricketing colleagues who, by implication, have benefited from the 'strand by strand procedure' offered by Advanced

Hair Studio. The cricketers on the cards are Greg Matthews, Goochie, and Michael Crowe, looking 'spectacular' according to Warne, but to me looking like a bunch of guys going a little thin on top and doing an awful lot of spiking, gelling, and careful vertical arrangement to cover it up – a sort of high definition version of what Bobby Charlton used to do.

The aim, I suppose, unless going for the full Bart Simpson, is to get the cricketer's style du jour, the Kevin Pietersen look, which could be studied closely on Sky One HD, where KP was a guest on *A League Of Their Own*.

Tragically, this is now into a second series despite the critical mauling the first one received, showing how little notice anyone takes of what we write.

Which is liberating in a way, since it means I can say what I think with no danger of harming anyone's livelihood; and what I think is that if you look up the word 'crass' in the dictionary, you will find a picture of this show.

Amanda Holden, for instance, one of this week's guests, had to look at waxwork dummies (feel free to insert own joke here) of José Mourinho, Jonny Wilkinson, and Cristiano Ronaldo, and decide which might have been most visited at Madame Tussauds, so she walked over to them and massaged each model in the groin area, to paroxysms of mirth from the rest of the cast, and especially host James Corden, who continues to look about six times as pleased with himself as he has any right to be.

But Corden is not even the main problem. For a show on which money has clearly been lavished, the writing is unutterably poor. The waxworks schtick was followed by a joke I have mercifully forgotten about Ronaldo possibly being gay, and then the following from Corden: ...José Mourinho, one of only two managers set in wax. The other is Avram Grant, on one of his kinkier visits to the brothel.'

That joke is so bad, it is difficult to know where to start. Had there actually been any sado-masochism in Grant's background – apart, obviously, from taking the West Ham job – allowing the joke to end on the words 'Avram Grant', it would still have been hackneyed, but at least it would have had the structure of a joke. The addition of the explanation, 'on one of his kinkier visits to the brothel,' crushes the last scintilla of humour from a joke no decent writer would have let near the page. At least Bernard Manning and his old-school low-def crowd knew what a joke should sound like.

10. Just About Me

'This conjures up a nightmarish vision of safe sex warnings having to be printed on packets of Werther's Originals...'

A peek behind the scenes at Screen Break. In which I get a new sofa, and try and watch the Masters from Augusta courtesy of Sky's new 3D technology (how did that go, by the way?)

Screen Break, The Guardian, *11 April 2011*

The most common query we receive in our huge weekly mailbag here – apart from 'What is this email thing everyone is talking about?' – simply asks how we go about composing the column/blog you are about to enjoy. From time to time, therefore, we like to grant you a peek behind the scenes at Screen Break's international headquarters.

Wrestling in Honey

The first thing to say is that there is no substitute for experience. I have been doing this column, or one very like it, for nearly 14 years now. In much the same way as TS Eliot's J. Alfred Prufrock measured out his life in coffee spoons, I have measured mine out in Matches Of The Day and Grand Nationals. So familiar am I with the language of televised sport that I am probably one of the few people in Britain who can perform the death scene from *Camille* in the style of Eddie and Stevo from the Super League show.

In my years of selfless devotion to the cause I have worn out two chain store sofas – clearly not up to the job – which I have now replaced with a more substantial piece of furniture I am hoping will see me through until either I peg it or the public appetite for jokes about Clare Balding's hair style is finally sated. This new sofa is called a Mitford, 'custom made and hand crafted' according to the manufacturers, 'with joints triple and double doweled,' and augmented by cushions described as 'Oriental duck feather pads' (something I am sure I ordered once in a Chinese restaurant).

Alongside the toll the punishing Screen Break routine has taken on the furniture, my eyesight has paid a price too. I can never quite remember whether it is near-sighted or far-sighted that I am, but if I wished to read this piece in the newspaper without spectacles I should need someone to stand in the next street and hold it up for me.

So what I normally do is position the Mitford at a distance from the screen comfortable for the naked eye, and then take advantage of the triple doweled arm rests by placing scrap paper and reading glasses on them to note down important hairstyle changes and commentator absurdities.

Unfortunately, this long-standing routine has been thrown into disarray this week by the arrival of a 3D television set, on which I have been watching the Masters from Augusta, which I must say looked pretty spectacular. The problem is I have not yet found a way to co-ordinate 3D glasses and reading glasses, often forgetting to swap them round when making notes, which leaves me writing in the dark, something I failed to master years ago as a film reviewer (with much younger eyes) making notes in dark preview theatres. Believe me, it is not easy writing a considered piece about *Schindler's List* based on notes beginning 'incendiary halibut cloak'.

Watching the Masters, it was tempting just to sink into the Mitford (students of 1930s gossip, write your own joke) and let it wash over you, which the commentators on the 3D coverage, Terry Gannon and Paul Azinger, gave you every encouragement to do. 'The familiar images of tall pines, dogwoods, and azaleas frame the Augusta National Golf Club on an absolutely pristine day,' cooed Terry, as the velvet voice of Nina Simone (or similar) singing 'Georgia On My Mind' signalled a break.

At one point, to my delight, a colourful little songbird flew across my screen in a suspiciously three dimensional fashion, prompting the unworthy thought that Sky had maybe hired someone to stand at the side of the camera with a box of little birds – endangered species probably – and instructions to release them at propitious times to emphasise the depth of field.

Sky only had two hours of 3D pictures a night, limited, one assumes, by host broadcaster ESPN's agreement with the Augusta National, but I suspect the Augusta coverage presages more golf in 3D, as golf clearly benefits from the innovation more than other sports, as the commentators never forgot to point out. 'See the difference in elevation between the tee and the green,' marvelled Terry. 'You can pick it out so well.'

As a non-golfer, the trees, the bridge, and the

shimmering water impressed me more. This was nature not so much red in tooth and claw, as manicured to within an inch of its life. 'The very fabric of spring,' said Terry, now close to orgasm.

I also liked the way the 3D helped you pick out individual crowd members at the front of the stand, adding interest for us golf agnostics. I could not help noticing, for instance, that the generally chubby but tanned legs of some of the overweight American spectators seemed, rather unfairly, to suit shorts rather better than my own slimmer, pale pins. As I noted at the time, 'pork diagnostic Cumberbatch.'

❧

By Christmas 2016, I was clearly suffering from advanced withdrawal symptoms after my departure from The Guardian, *so I started writing elaborate letters to car parking companies.*

Email to Athena, which I remembered as a shop selling prints of tennis players who had neglected to attend to underwear requirements, but seems to have branched out into the car park business.

To: Athena Car Parks
December 14, 2016

Re: Notice No. 0 002 635 750

Thank you for your invoice for the 23 minutes extra parking I enjoyed in the Lidl car park at Chapel Allerton in Leeds at the back end of November 2016. Apologies for being somewhat tardy in my response, but what with Christmas and Brexit and everything, the invoice sort of remained on the back burner.

Believe me, I am sorry for overstaying the 23 minutes, but I was under the impression one was allowed to stay in the car park for two hours, giving one sufficient time to do a little shopping and visit one's son, who has recently left home and is sharing a house in Methley Drive adjacent to the car park (he's doing very nicely thank you, thanks to the scouring pads and other cleaning materials I was able to source for him in your store).

I hope you will accept my sincere apologies without prejudice, in view of the fact that your car park was far from full, as can be seen from the lovely picture of my car. You will not, therefore, have suffered any financial damage through my thoughtlessness.

I accept there are notices in your car park stating your rules, including the 90-minute limit, but, what can I say, I didn't read them. What with the approaching festive season, Brexit, Donald Trump's election victory, Channel 4 losing the racing, and so on, my mind was probably elsewhere.

In light of that, I'm not sure how valid is the contract I have entered into. It seems to me that in any other sphere of life, a contract has to be fully understood and agreed by both parties.

From my own experience and from reading social network postings on the issue, there seems to be a divergence of opinions on the subject. A lot of people say that one should just ignore the notices from firms such as yourself, but I think that's rude.

I realise that your normal *modus operandum* now is to ignore this letter, and merely follow up with a letter or two full of red ink and banner headlines demanding £90 for the 23 minutes, and then to sell the alleged debt on to a debt recovery agency, who will send out a few threatening letters, often rather badly written, implying I might be subject to court costs, unable ever to get a loan again, and might have my property seized, and my first born slaughtered (he'll be easy to find, he's only in Methley Drive).

Well, I can probably save you some time.

In the spirit of the approaching festive season, and given that there's every chance that after the excesses of Yuletide, the New Year will see me taking advantage of the very reasonable prices in your store when I want to combine a visit to my progeny with a little discount shopping, why don't we just forget about the 23 minutes, and part friends.

(I know it's not your shop, you're just in charge of taking pictures of the car park, but clearly without the shop, you'd have nothing to take pictures of and as the Prime Minister likes to say, we're all in this together, so my custom helps us all. Keeps the wheels of the retail trade turning, as it were.)

I do hope we can avoid any further unpleasantness.

Happy Christmas.

(I never heard from them again. My son has now moved.)

Listeners to my various shows on a bewildering array of radio stations will be all too familiar with my encounter with Coronation Street*'s Ken Barlow. It's in the top five of my accidental encounters with famous people.*

Ken Barlow, Johnny Vegas and the wonder of Sue Barker

Screen Break, The Guardian, *10 April 2006*

A well-known television newscaster once told me how he hailed a cab in the suburbs of London, and climbed into the back of the vehicle apparently unrecognised by the driver.

On checking the rear view mirror, however, the cabbie registered his passenger's celebrity, and did a swift double take, before spluttering, ''Ere, 'ere... do you know who you are?'

I only tell the story because I had a similar moment when I shared a pee at Aintree on Saturday with William Roache, TV's Ken Barlow. For the benefit of female readers, who may be unfamiliar with the etiquette of such urinal encounters, I should explain that there isn't any.

There really is no universally recognised code of behaviour to consult on those occasions when you find yourself standing next to a star of stage and screen with your penis in your hand. Unless the encounter has been pre-arranged – as a leisure time activity as it were – possibly with money changing hands, in a style that will be familiar to readers of the more lurid newspapers, a certain awkwardness is inevitable. It is unwise to spark up a conversation lest you lose concentration and wet his shoes, or even worse your own; and a nod or smile of recognition could easily be misinterpreted, especially if your eyes were inadvertently to stray downwards.

Not that I would have had much to contribute to any conversation anyway, as I do not watch *Coronation Street,* and all I know of Mr Roache is that he once sued somebody for saying he was boring, and at a recent election, he campaigned, I believe, for one of the fringe political parties; UKIP or the Conservatives, or someone.

It seemed therefore that our meeting was destined to fizzle out in silence, possibly with one of us saying, 'I'll phone you,' or 'We must have lunch some time,' as we washed hands and parted company, but nothing more significant than that. However, as my new friend removed his hands from the hot air drier with something of a flourish, he flashed me a brilliant smile, delivered a cheery actor's 'Hello,' turned on his heel and left.

This, I expect, is William Roache's coping strategy. It must be awfully difficult to walk around doing normal things, like shopping and micturating (not simultaneously, obviously) when your face is on TV every night and you are constantly being bearded by gibbering starstruck idiots blathering at you. Mr Roache was clearly demonstrating the famous person's version of getting your retaliation in first.

Aintree on Grand National day is uncommonly fertile ground for the starstruck. I saw Cliff Richard as well, although not in the toilets – I expect he has some sort of private arrangement like the royal family – and the comedian Johnny Vegas, whose coping strategy is to talk to anyone and everyone; and you try getting rid of him. He was on Aintree's closed circuit TV, taking the mickey out of the sponsors John Smith's, grabbing the microphone, and bellowing for some reason: 'I am a horse.'

I can never decide whether the wayward Vegas is a comedy genius, or some kind of roly-poly simpleton taking us all for a ride, which I reckon probably makes him a comedy genius. At his best, he always seems on the verge of going completely out of control, and that is why we laugh. It is uncomfortable laughter to begin with, but somehow Vegas draws you into his madness, and eventually it is impossible not to surrender to him.

That is what Sue Barker discovered on *Grandstand* when she found herself on something of a runaway train, interviewing the eccentric comic, who – unusually for a young man from St Helens – was wearing a sand-coloured hunting jacket and brown trilby hat.

'Sue, I have sometimes given my life over to drink,' Vegas said, somewhat unnecessarily, before commenting on some footage from a previous year of him in jockey's silks mounting a racehorse. 'My gentle man breasts encourage the horse to run faster,' said Vegas. 'The horse feels younger, like it was being fed, by a mother sat aloft.'

A lesser woman might have been tempted to curtail the interview at this point, but Sue is a veteran of thousands of editions of *Question Of Sport* through which she has had to surrender herself to paroxysms of laughter at Ally McCoist and John Parrott's desperate japery; Sue has carried the mantle of 'golden girl of British tennis'; she has done All Bran adverts; she was reported as being romantically involved with Cliff Richard for goodness sake. If there is anybody in Britain whom it is impossible to embarrass, it is Sue Barker.

Vegas ploughed on. Over a shot of the jockeys' room, he boomed: 'In the Isle of Man, they are breeding people only two feet high. Your days are numbered. Table tennis, table tennis, when will you take on a fat professional. You sit there watching *Seabiscuit*. It's a bad film.'

The pictures of the jockeys enjoying the badinage emphasised the strength of the BBC's National coverage. There is an 'access all areas' quality to it; a microphone stuck under 'Slippers' Madden's nose at the moment of victory, jockeys wandering round in towels watching the re-run of the race minutes after they have washed off the Aintree mud; the cameras and microphones are everywhere, and everyone is happy to see them.

Well, not absolutely everywhere, as it happens. There has to be somewhere for Ken Barlow and me to share a quiet moment.

Me and my printer

Any Other Business, Forty20 Magazine, *August 2022*

To fully appreciate the following you need to know that my printer is an HP Laser Jet P1006, which I have had for, I don't know, ten, maybe twelve years now, and I am very happy with it. I look back on my inkjet days with disdain. The thought of taking the cartridge out of the machine and shaking it about to liberate the last little bit of ink, the memory of the occasional blots on the paper, those things make me shudder quite frankly.

Fortunately, for much of that dark period I had a proper job working for the BBC and – prepare to be shocked – whenever I could I would use the printer at work, and sometimes for jobs not directly connected with the business of the Corporation (I also used to take paper clips home occasionally).

In fact, I wrote two books while at the BBC, and in the interests of full disclosure, and in preparation for making peace with my maker when the inevitable reckoning arrives, I must confess I may have printed out a chapter or two on the office printers, or – I did say full disclosure – to be scrupulously accurate, a book or two.

So now may be the time to afford yourselves a glow of pride in the knowledge that your licence fees in some way funded what I laughingly call my literary career. But at the same time, they also funded *Two Pints of Lager and a Packet of Crisps*, *BBC Breakfast*, and the career of Claudia Winkleman so, you know, swings and roundabouts.

Since I have no longer had Auntie's skirts to cling to for protection from inkjet horror, the HP Laser Jet P1006 has been doing a fine job, with the bonus that it's unlikely to get rid of me because it's looking for someone younger/older/slimmer

/fatter/less male/more diverse or, possibly, just a little less heavy on printer paper.

To my eternal shame, I rarely give the benefits of the P1006 a second thought. It sits there quietly on my desk. I cannot remember having a paper jam, the toner cartridges seem to last forever, and when I do need replacements I buy them in packs of two and get on with my life.

Recently, though, I have been doing an inordinate amount of printing. One of my daughters is buying a house, which has involved moving some money around, and for some reason the legal profession requires hard copies of every pertinent document, something to do with money laundering regulations I believe.

(Apparently, it's fine for the Prince of Wales, now King Charles III, to accept bundles of bank notes from Arab potentates in Fortnum & Mason carrier bags, but if my daughter wants a house in Leeds with a bathtub and a spare bedroom, everything has to be printed out in triplicate to prove we're not linchpins in some international criminal enterprise).

Anyway, she's temporarily printerless so I've been doing the necessary, and noted the characters on the documents becoming just a little pale and decided to treat the P1006 to the fresh cartridge that had been sitting on my shelf for goodness knows how long and order replacements..

Normally, as I say, I should not give this procedure a second thought, but this morning I received the following letter:

> 'Dear Martin, Thank you for your recent purchase from Cartridgesave.co.uk. In order to improve our service, we have partnered with the independent review site Trustpilot to collect customer reviews. Please click on

the link below to give us your feedback. All reviews, good, bad or indifferent will be visible immediately.'

I received a further copy of this a few hours later, closely followed by this opportunity: 'Tell us what you think. Rate and review your recent purchase. As a thank you for leaving a review, you'll be entered into our monthly prize draw for a chance to win a £100 Amazon voucher.'

Wow, they really really want to know my thoughts on these printer cartridges. I'm feeling quite guilty now, having accepted what the P1006 has done in smoothing over the divorce from the BBC and restoring equilibrium in my life, not to mention the fine work of the Compatible HP 35A Black Toner Cartridge, about which there's been not a word from me. It's time I showed proper appreciation to the joys of laser printing

So here's my review: 'I ordered the cartridges. They arrived. They're intact. The chap from Royal Mail smiled, said 'how do,' swiped the barcode. The cartridges are sitting on the shelf. I'll use them one day.'

I'm not sure that's worth a hundred quid, even of Jeff Bezos's billions.

Here I am in the outer suburbs of the Sky remote, attempting to provide fun for the ageing Guardian *audience in the only way I know how. All you need to know is the nation at the time was dealing with the scandal of comedian Russell Brand's unpleasant prank telephone calls to the much-loved* Fawlty Towers *legend Andrew Sachs.*

Honey, Fighting and the Disturbing Topic of My Libido

The Guardian, *3 November 2008*

I was called by a researcher from *Woman's Hour* last week – although these days you can never be entirely sure a call is genuine and not just Russell Brand mucking about – and asked about my libido. Apparently, some scientists have discovered that the older male is prone to tiredness, moodiness and loss of libido. These boffins, presumably from the department of No Shit Sherlock at the University of Please Yourself, have concluded that this is down to a testosterone deficiency.

Fortunately I was recording the call for training purposes, or I might have been tempted to camouflage a rapidly waning libido by making suggestive remarks to the young woman, in the manner of Tony Booth out on a window-cleaning job.

Instead, I was forced to admit that science was right, and what was once a going concern is now more like one of those fireworks that fizzes a little and which, were it not for the safety code, you might be inclined to go over and try and reignite, or else put out of its misery. As to this being a problem, I take a similar view to Kingsley Amis, who said he found his diminished sex drive rather a relief, likening the possession of a full and functioning libido to being chained to a mad dog.

As far as being tired and moody goes, guilty as charged, but isn't everybody these days what with the credit crunch, approaching armageddon and West Ham's inability to keep a clean sheet – and without even Jonathan Ross's Saturday morning radio show to cheer us up? Anyway, *Woman's Hour* tells me that a growing number of men are having hormone replacement therapy to counteract all this and give them a more optimistic mien in their latter years – 65 was the age she mentioned – and to re-lead their pencil, as it were.

This conjures up a nightmarish vision of elderly blokes behaving like a cross between Pollyanna and Russe ... well, you know who I mean ... and safe sex warnings having to be printed on packets of Werther's Originals.

I told the researcher I could not see myself raging against the dying of the light in this way. Apart from anything else, it must be humiliating to be constantly having to say 'You what?' when a woman is trying to talk dirty.

It set me wondering, though, whether it is at this generation of seasoned-up hyenas – in the memorable words of the late Ian Dury – that some of the late-night programming on The Fight Network is directed. 'All Fights All The Time' is the channel's almost irresistible proposition, and while during the day this is taken care of by reruns of wrestling matches from *World Of Sport* in the 1970s and 1980s – pasty-faced English doughballs kneading each other's flesh in Dudley Civic Hall before an audience of grim-faced crones and Brylcreem-ed spivs (I know memory plays tricks, but I am sure the 'Seventies were never quite that beige) – in the late evening the network provides what it fondly imagines to be more colourful, racier programming.

By this, of course, it means women fighting each other – sometimes Japanese women, sometimes American, and, for that niche audience with an interest in Lithuanian women wrestling in honey, *Amberlady Honey Wars*.

This is not a great programme, but whatever else you say about it, it does provide a genuine alternative to *Newsnight*. Bikinied Lithuanian women, competing under names like Jungle Girl and Bronze Thumbelina, slide around in an inflatable paddling pool half-full of honey, pretending to fight. They tend to be more lithe than the American girls fighting under the Women's Extreme Wrestling banner, and I think it safe to assume the chief attraction for its somewhat specialist audience is the possibility of one of the combatants losing her top. Do not hold your breath, would be my advice.

The warning that precedes the female fight shows on the network – 'The following programme contains violence, sexuality, nudity and coarse language; viewer discretion is advised' – serves a similar purpose to those newspaper bills you used to see proclaiming 'Famous Film Star Dies', only to discover on buying the paper it was some no-mark who played Robert Mitchum's best friend in a B-movie in the 1940s.

The most shocking thing you are likely to see in *Amberlady Honey Wars* is guys with unfeasibly wide lapels in the audience smoking, although I was more outraged at the criminal waste of honey. At a time when the honeybee is an endangered species, threatening us with ecological disaster, and you can barely find a jar of decent stuff in the shops, to have young women, however lithe, sloshing around in bathtubs of it seems profligate in the extreme. Not at all erotic either. As the Sky commentator Stevo said yesterday morning about England's performance in the Rugby League World Cup, 'We needed fireworks, but so far it has been a bit of a damp squid.'

Finally, on the subject of television turning out to be not as advertised, Dermot O'Leary promised Saturday night's *X Factor* would 'quite literally be murder on the dance floor.'

Disappointingly, it quite literally was not.

Wrestling in Honey

This is a previously unpublished piece, touching on death and television.

The racehorse Red Rum and me

Blog post, January 2018

Some time in the late 1980s I co-presented a TV show called *Living It Up*, whose big idea was to combine the sensibilities of Saturday night light entertainment spectaculars – shiny-floor shows, I think they call them – with journalism.

It was clearly a doomed marriage, of the type that has celebrants muttering behind their hands, 'I give it six months', or in the case of *Living It Up*, six programmes. Or it may have been seven. I honestly don't know. It's more or less been written out of my *cv* in the way one might gloss over the six months spent in Wormwood Scrubs on your application for a post at Barclays Bank.

Strangely, not only have I purposely forgotten the show, the Internet seems to have followed suit. That repository of everything ever is strangely silent on the subject of *Living It Up*.

I spent a good hour searching for even a mention of it, just to check on the exact year, and could not get beyond *Living It Up*, a 1950s British sitcom with vaudevillians Arthur Askey and Richard 'Stinker' Murdoch – one I'll make a point of watching should it ever turn up on Talking Pictures TV – a Dean Martin and Jerry Lewis film of the same title, and a furniture warehouse in Leicester.

In truth, our show was probably a little ahead of its time for the 1980s. The idea was that we would help older people achieve a long-held dream, at the same time celebrating the relatively new phenomenon then of old age being about bungee jumping or hiking up Mont Blanc rather than sitting in bus shelters moaning about how young the policemen are these days.

Our ideal participants would be the handsome silver-haired couple you see in adverts skipping along a beach somewhere because they've invested in the right pension plan.

One of the few episodes I remember involved my driving to Southport to meet a lady horse-racing enthusiast whose dream was to ride a thoroughbred. We took her to where the Grand National winning horse, the late Red Rum – obviously it was alive back then – was stabled, and I interviewed her, while she was allowed a little trot round under the watchful eye of the trainer the late Ginger McCain – also alive then – and I spoke to him about his famous horse. All this was fine, if not hugely exciting, the kind of thing you would still see today on *The One Show* or your local news magazine.

The damage was done in the light entertainment section of the show, when we all got made up and put on our Saturday night suits. The show was recorded in the big studio at Yorkshire Television. We journalists sat on high stools before a live audience – obviously live, dead audiences being less useful for the applause and the whooping and hollering needed for the celebratory atmosphere the show demanded.

We had a proper presenter too, Amanda somebody or other, who was used to this kind of set-up, and the old folk joined us on stage to do a bit of something, the idea being it was their big night, and they would be celebrated / patronised on prime time television.

My horse rider for instance rode into the studio on Red Rum, we both dismounted – her from the horse, me from the nightmare of the big stool – she did a bit of horsey stuff, patted the animal, gave it a sugar lump or something, a bit of chat, and off to music and applause. Sadly, the horse failed to shit on the stage or I'd still be getting repeat fees from those blooper shows.

Unlike me, the horse was a seasoned pro – I'm not saying I defecated on stage, only metaphorically – making a good living out of personal appearances, opening supermarkets, shopping centres and the like, which was still a thing back then. One day I was hanging round the office snooping through what private correspondence I could find relating to the programme when I came across an invoice from the horse's management company – honest! – and found the animal was being paid roughly five times as much as me.

I mean, to qualify for my side of the contract, I'd had to achieve 100 words per minute shorthand and have a working knowledge of local government, according to the National Council for the Training of Journalists, quite apart from the driving to Southport and the sitting on the high stool business, whereas the horse had just had to walk and remember not to void its bowels.

My fellow journalist on the show, John, was a brash, much more self-confident type, to whom the showbiz element of the enterprise came more naturally. He couldn't save the show but he later became quite successful and famous, a fixture on BBC Radio 4 discussion shows, and in the posh papers. He and his wife, a teacher, divorced and he married Nigella Lawson. They were very much the thinking person's celebrity couple, the toast of the London media world. It helped that he wrote and talked brilliantly, and I yield to no-one in my admiration for what his missus does with a chicken on the telly.

And then he got cancer. This was very bad cancer, involving the removal of his tongue, and lengthy, painful and undignified treatment, which he chronicled in a weekly column in *The Times*. It was a riveting read that he kept up until he died in 2001.

In his last column, he addressed the question, 'What the hell is the point of it all?' As he was, like myself, a non-practicing Jew, I know there would be little comfort to be taken there, so John fell back on Philip Larkin's somewhat reductive view that none of us would ever be able to get out of bed in the morning if we had any sense of our own mortality.

John was lavishly obituarised, some of it before he died which may have helped a little, and Nigella might have possibly worked some magic in the blender, but nobody could commute the death sentence, which John was living under, and as the years pass I'm keenly aware we all are.

If nothing else, it has given me a sense of perspective – as people like to say when their football team gets beaten 2-1 on the same day as 16 children drown in a well. It has certainly lessened the pain of the pay disparity between me and the bloody horse, which I was pretty peeved about at the time.

Remember March 2020 when we first heard about Coronavirus? We thought it was all a bit quaint, and probably wouldn't affect us too much here. Unfortunately, the government took a similarly cavalier attitude, and all they could come up with in those early days was advice to wash your hands. You know, like really thoroughly.

And so it starts, Coronavirus

Any Other Business, Forty20 Magazine, *15 March 2020*

I don't know about you, but I'm getting pretty fed up washing my hands. The Government, bless them, have been helpful, suggesting songs we might quietly sing while our hands are immersed in or under hot water to adequately fill the time needed for the process to have the required anti-bacterial effect. But, unless I've got the song wrong, it seems a heck of a long time and you're supposed to do it several times a day, as a result of which the backs of my hands now feel like the underneath of Wilson, Keppel and Betty's trainers.

(Look teenagers, I really don't have the time to explain all these references. It's on YouTube, look it up, and you'll be laughing your socks off in ten minutes unless you've been diverted by a bit of click bait about Piers Morgan).

One other effect, pointed out by my friend Darryl on Twitter, is that there really is no way to scrub your hands repeatedly while quietly singing 'Happy Birthday' to yourself without looking like a serial killer attempting to wash away the blood from his latest slaying.

Point is, we're all going to die. It's hard for me to say exactly where we will be in the progress of the Black Death as you read these words – some of you may be dead already – so I cannot help you with specific medical advice, but what I can do, if you are hanging on in there, is make the experience more palatable.

They say that as you die, your whole life passes in front of your eyes, although I'm not sure this is true.

Around 2013, I spent a few weeks in hospital alongside some rather poorly people, and one afternoon as I shuffled out of the ward to greet some visitors – I am not making this up – I noticed that the chap in the next bed to mine was making guttural noises that sounded suspiciously like the death rattle.

Nurses rushed to his bedside, and he was indeed breathing his last. Not too long earlier, he had been filling in one of those forms they give you in hospital to book your food for the day, so, inasmuch as you can be sure of anything in these tragic circumstances, I believe his final moments were spent not alongside some kind of celestial Davina McCall saying, 'Let's have a look back now at some of your best bits,' but choosing between the shepherd's pie and the fish cakes.

But just in case conventional wisdom has got it spot on and our last moments are to be spent in remembrance of things past (*à la recherche de mon temps perdu*, as Marcel Proust put it in one of his famous gags), and you find at the last minute that your time on this planet does not amount to a life well lived, but merely to a life, well, lived, here are a few colourful memories you can borrow (not mine, but I keep them handy because you never know) to ease your way beyond the veil:

April 21st 1963, the *NME* Poll Winners' concert. Do you remember? It was an afternoon gig at the Empire Pool, Wembley. We went to the Lyons Corner House first, and had egg and chips, white bread and butter and a pot of tea for a shilling, immaculately served to us by a clippie in a starched white apron, setting us up nicely for The Beatles and John Lennon belting out their hits, 'Please Please Me' and 'From Me To You', alongside 'Twist And Shout' and 'Long Tall Sally'. 'Those boys are going to go places,' I said to my dad.

Still in the 'sixties, we're in Detroit, Michigan now, and out of respect to Diana Ross and the Supremes, this is a memory I'm not going to share. You're on your own. Suffice to say, Berry Gordy and I still exchange Christmas cards.

1989 now, Tiananmen Square, a flower in my hand, straight down the barrel of the tank facing me, 'Where do you think you're going with that tank matey boy,' and he reverses to the cheers of the gathered thousands.

1990, in San Francisco for a gig by the greatest comedian of the time, Richard Pryor. He's asked me to look over his stuff. 'I wouldn't open with that Dicky Boy,' I say. And he reaches for the blue pencil.

I've got a million of them, but if the whole Proustian thing, as I suspect, turns out to be no more than a strategy to make us feel better as we enter the home strait, and the end is more like a light being switched off, I wouldn't go for the fish cakes.

And so, at the end of 2012 I faced the final curtain. I believe they got rid of me, my friend Harry Pearson, and a few other writers for economic reasons. As freelances, we were easy to get rid of, and sacking people, in whatever industry, is a much prized skill. That's how you cut costs. It's a twenty-first Century speciality.

In the 2009 Ivan Reitman film Up In The Air, *George Clooney plays a professional downsizer who flies across America visiting companies to tell people they are being 'let go', as popular parlance has it. I didn't get a visit, they let me go via a phone call. Clearly the growth of the Internet had made physical newspapers a declining, increasingly unprofitable enterprise.*

I'm not an idiot – actually I am, but let that pass – I knew my days were numbered, so I bore no malice.

I Was Wrong About Everything

Screen Break, The Guardian, *30 December 2012*

In the first sport-on-TV column I wrote for this newspaper, 16 years ago, I described the experience of watching horse racing in a basement betting shop in Soho and the thrilling opportunity it provided to enjoy a lifetime's passive smoking in a single afternoon. *Autres temps, autres mœurs,* as the lads down my local are fond of saying.

To give you an idea of just how *autres* those *temps* were, I wrote about the high street bookies as a place of social interaction with no regard for race, creed, colour, class, or even age difference; where men and the occasional woman would happily bond over a narrowly beaten second-favourite, or historic tales of ante-post derring-do. And if I failed to integrate quite as fully as usual that afternoon down the stairs in Wardour Street, I wrote, it was only because of my lamentable lack of fluency in the major Chinese languages.

At least I think that's what I wrote. A fingertip search of what I laughingly call my archives failed to turn up the original piece, although I did find a receipt for some carpet we had fitted in our old house, and a picture of me with 1980s chanteuse Mari Wilson.

I should say that I do not normally spend holiday weekends seeking out old Screen Breaks, but as this is the last of these columns I was interested to see if there was a unifying theme I could leave you with, some overarching philosophy that would make sense of the last decade and a half of broadcast sport. But all that united those few pieces I was able to find was a determination to appear classy by getting some French into the first few paragraphs. *Plus ça change, plus c'est la même chose.*

No hard feelings, by the way. This newspaper, like the rest of us, is having to embrace austerity. As even middle-class families find it necessary to forgo fripperies like meals out and weekends away – and those less well-fixed do without luxuries like shoes and food – so this newspaper trims its sails too. Think of me as a spring break in a lovely spa resort we can no longer stump up for. In any case, I'm told there's a factory in Indonesia that turns out these columns at a price I could never match. Harsh economics, I'm afraid.

And bless the newspaper for allowing me the chance to bid you farewell, ignoring the lesson of the chap in the Blackpool rock factory who gave a sacked employee a month's notice, and now has a mile-and-a-half of rock with 'Fuck you' written through it.

Frankly, though, I never contemplated a Danny Baker-style valediction. I thought his recent sign-off from BBC London, while unerring in its analysis, was in rather poor taste. Coming as Comet announced imminent closure and local councils in the north faced massive, possibly irreparable, cuts in budget, his protracted burble about the axing of his radio show was *de trop* (enough already). Danny is undoubtedly a fine broadcaster and writer but that day he came across as a self-regarding arsehole.

So, I'll go quietly guv. I was wrong about almost everything anyway, certainly about betting shops. If you believe in LP Hartley's famous gag about the past being a foreign country, that piece is Kyrgyzstan.

No one peers at screens through a tobacco fug any more and as for passing the time exchanging pleasantries with the fellow delusional, no time for that these days with fixed-odds betting terminals – gambling machines basically – whirring and clanking in every corner, and computer-generated races from fake venues like Sprint Valley and Canterberry Hill filling the unforgiving three-and-a-half seconds between real events.

Betting shops were probably changing almost as I wrote the piece. There is still a community of what I like to think of as social gamblers but, much like readers of this newspaper, we gather on the net now.

As for the rest of the Screen Breaks I uncovered, they

were mostly from the past decade – I could, I suppose, have subscribed to *The Guardian* archive but, you know, fripperies and all that – and merely served to underline my dismal record in spotting trends.

There was a piece from 2009, for instance, about an edition of the *Football League Show* covering a Nottingham Forest versus Derby County match that ended in a brawl, described by presenter Manish Bhasin as 'sadly, another unsavoury incident on a football pitch'. Indeed, so sad was the programme about the incident, it showed it only four times and invited viewer comments.

One viewer suggested a Derby midfielder started all the trouble during the warm-up by 'waving various parts of his anatomy at Forest fans'. How could I have missed the fact that the midfielder would go on to become a respected sports broadcaster without whom no football show on the BBC is complete? I should have warned you about Robbie Savage.

I'm sorry. It's time for me to go. *Adieu*.

UK Press Gazette Website

2 January 2013

Axed Guardian columnist Martin Kelner has been signed up by the *Racing Post*. Kelner's last weekly Screen Break column appeared in *The Guardian* on 30 December after 16 years writing about sport on TV for the paper.

His new column (again writing about sport on TV) will appear on Tuesdays in the *Racing Post,* with the first instalment appearing tomorrow.

In his last *Guardian* column, Kelner wrote: 'This newspaper, like the rest of us, is having to embrace austerity.

As even middle-class families find it necessary to forgo fripperies like meals out and weekends away – and those less well-fixed do without luxuries like shoes and food – so this newspaper trims its sails too.

'Think of me as a spring break in a lovely spa resort we can no longer stump up for. In any case, I'm told there's a factory in Indonesia that turns out these columns at a price I could never match. Harsh economics, I'm afraid.'

Guardian News and Media is currently trying to make cuts to the annual editorial budget totalling £7m. The company plans to make 100 editorial staff redundant. Kelner is not included in this total because he was on a freelance contract which was not renewed.

The Racing Post said in a statement: 'The former *Guardian* journalist will continue with his lighthearted and witty preambles about the world of sport on TV. His first column offers refreshing insight on this year s *Celebrity Big Brother* contestants including Frankie Dettori, along with a closer inspection of the betting for the reality TV show.

Editor Bruce Millington said: 'I've been a huge admirer of Martin's writing for many years so it's tremendous that he's now a columnist for the *Racing Post*. The positive reaction we've had from readers and within the media shows the regard in which Martin is held.'

11. Indoor Fun

'Joey Chestnut, the Lionel Messi of processed pork...'

Early in my tenure at The Guardian, *I was making it known exactly where my area of expertise lay. George Carlin, exceptional stand-up comedian (1937-2008)*

Chess and the Comfort Break

Screen Break, The Guardian, *2 October 2006*

I do not know a great deal about sport – if you are bothered about all that, there are some red hot experts elsewhere in this section I can heartily recommend – but I have over the years built up a level of expertise in the area of toilet facilities, so I may be just the man to deconstruct the dispute affecting the championship chess match currently taking place in the

Russian republic of Kalmykia – Toiletgate, as this paper tentatively dubbed it on Saturday (that's the dispute, not the republic, which may not be blessed with the world's most advanced sanitation, but *The Guardian* would never be so rude).

The match, between Vladimir Kramnik and Veselin Topalov, is what boxers would call a unification bout. It is to determine the undisputed world champion (a term, incidentally, that the comedian George Carlin takes issue with: 'If he's the undisputed champion, then what's all the fighting about?' asks Carlin).

Topalov, as I understand it, complained after game four of the 12-game match that his opponent was visiting the loo too often – 50 times, he said, during six hours of chess. He thought Kramnik might be logging on (you should pardon the expression) in the seclusion of the cubicle and using computer aided expertise to plot his next move (on the chess board, that is, not in the toilet, where outside advice is rarely needed).

The committee overseeing the match responded by closing the two toilets in the rest rooms, and designating a third for the use of the chess players only. That is, out of bounds to anyone without a domed forehead, unfashionable glasses held together with sticking plaster, a slight personal freshness problem, wearing a shirt with a frayed collar, and a tweed jacket with a row of ball point pens in the inside pocket. I joke, of course. Do not send emails; I am well aware that using outmoded stereotypes is a facile way to get cheap and easy laughs. In fact, I am rather banking on it.

Anyway, Kramnik refuses to share a toilet with his opponent, and forfeited game five in the series rather than do so. You can see his point. There is nothing worse than settling onto a disconcertingly warm seat when your posterior is conditioned to expect a bracing slight chill, and if Topalov is indeed in there long enough to establish a wireless broadband connection and search authoritative chess sites, well that is even more unsettling than seeing someone disappear into your loo with a copy of the *Daily Mirror*.

In tennis, I believe, players are allowed to leave the court for a toilet break, but are accompanied by an appointed official – the Master of the Water Closets or some such – to ensure there is no jiggery pokery of any kind, but such a system, I suspect, would not work in chess. Whereas your tennis player would probably be used to showering in public and so on, and feel quite comfortable about his bodily functions, enabling the mission to be completed successfully, one imagines that you do not get to be a tournament standard chess player without being a little anally retentive – tight-buttocked if you like – making assisted toilet breaks dispiritingly unfulfilling occasions. I should feel uneasy myself, being monitored in this way, and my chess never reached championship levels.

A possible solution would be to restrict players' toilet breaks to those periods when no game is in progress, which might mean cutting down thinking time, to bring the span of the game more into line with the capacity of the human bladder. If the sport wishes to go this route, it might consider adopting the methods we have used in our house to make a game of Scrabble pass more quickly – a system of heavy sighs and pointedly picking up the paper and starting to read it.

On the subject of tennis, hands up anybody who knows how the Davis Cup works. It is one of the great mysteries of sport. Sky Sports brought us the exciting news this week of Tim Henman's possible return to Davis Cup action, but failed to clarify in what matches, and against whom he might compete. We constantly seem to be taking part in play-off matches in the Davis Cup without ever reaching any finals or being knocked out. It seems to be a never-ending process, in the course of which we seem always to be pitted against teams like Upper Volta and Kazakhstan, rather than big nations with proper toilet facilities like Sweden or the USA? It may simply be because we are not awfully good at tennis, but I think we should be told.

Rugby league is another sport that could be said to suffer from a surfeit of play-offs, but when the matches are as exciting as the two on Sky at the weekend, one is inclined not to complain. Such was the compelling intensity of the competition I almost failed to notice Stevo's irritating habit of unremittingly referring to teams as 'this Bradford outfit' or 'this Warrington team' rather than simply Bradford or Warrington.

Stevo, of course, has built his reputation on colourful but meaningless commentary – not so much stream of consciousness as puddle – but sometimes you feel he abuses the privilege. 'I said they were tiring, but someone somewhere has given them some plum pudding or something,' he said of Bradford. Don't ask me where plum pudding came from. It is the kind of poser you need a good sit down to ponder.

Filling the unforgiving minute

Screen Break, The Guardian, *7 May 2012*

Pro-celebrity marbles, extreme badminton, power chess, and that old favourite, first pitched by Alan Partridge, monkey tennis, are just a few of the events that as far as we know Barry Hearn has not yet suggested to TV executives to fill the wide open spaces in their schedules. But give him time.

Hearn, the People's Promoter, as he was dubbed in a profile on BBC last night (Sun), 'understands the needs of broadcasters with hours of programming to fill,' according to Barney Francis, managing director of Sky Sports. 'He comes up with a million ideas, some are not for us.' But given that Francis decided *Fish-o-Mania,* a day of blokes sitting by a lake just outside Doncaster trying to catch fish, was for him, I should like to have heard some of the ideas considered too *outré* even for Sky Sports.

Maybe there was another famous Partridge pitch in there, 'Youth Hostelling with Chris Eubank', which Hearn could easily have delivered as it happens, having developed a close relationship with the boxer after inheriting him from rival promoter Frank Maloney.

Maloney explained on the programme how he and Eubank fell out over a cup of tea. 'I put on his first two fights,' said Maloney, whose mildly crumpled face presented an interesting contrast to the sleek tanned Hearn. 'But when he came to see me, and asked for a cup of Earl Grey tea, I only had ordinary, so he walked out, and the next thing I know he's signed with Barry.'

Despite the apparent gazumping, Maloney was full of praise for his rival: 'Everything he says he is going to deliver he does, and that's not always the way in boxing. If he says there's a pound in it for you, there will be a pound. Maybe he's making one pound twenty, and he doesn't tell you about the 20p, but he'll always keep his promise.'

Barry's son Eddie, who has joined Hearn's Matchroom business, says people consider his father 'one of the straightest men in boxing,' which is a little like describing someone as one of the best Dutch ski-jumpers, but 'nice to hear,' said Eddie.

In fact, Eddie and his sister Katie, who both participated in the programme, would have found it all pretty nice to hear. It was hagiography rather than biography. If there were people with a bad word to say for Hearn the programme didn't find them.

The only real voice of dissent, given fleeting recognition, was that of snooker world number twelve, Mark Allen, who says that since Hearn took over the sport in 2009 not all players are happy with his changes, some feeling they are on a kind of treadmill, required to adhere to an overly rigorous tournament schedule.

On behalf of the shift workers of Britain, I should like to add my demurral to Allen's. The early stages of the snooker World Championships used to provide an ideal opportunity to compensate for sleep deprivation elsewhere. The click-clock of cue against ball, the satisfying plop of ball in pocket, and the soothing Caledonian tones of Hazel Irvine, were audio soporific. Eyes became heavy, and rarely was it long before a satisfying job was being done on the ravelled sleeve of care – right through till teatime if you were lucky.

Now, aping the success of darts, which Hearn's alchemy has transformed into a runaway TV hit over the past ten years, the snooker players have walk-on music and nicknames, and just as you are about to drift into a satisfying reverie, announcer Rob Walker is screaming, 'Let's get the boys on the baize.'

Not that Hearn himself needs any TV analgesic to relax. He owns a carp lake in the grounds of his Essex mansion, and, following the obligatory business tycoon's heart attack, suffered by the promoter in 2001, now makes sure he spends plenty of mornings relaxing by his lake, listening to country and western music – if that's your idea of a good time. With the fastidiousness of the chartered accountant he used to be, Hearn keeps detailed records of every one of the fish in his lake, naming them, and recording any weight changes.

His mum suggested he take up accountancy, as a route out of working-class Dagenham, still bearing the scars of the blitz when Hearn was born in 1948.

He changed course after buying Romford snooker hall in 1982 initially for the value of the site, and seeing Steve Davis play, since when it has been an almost uninterrupted record of success in sports promotion and management.

Uninterrupted, that is, save for the time during the recession of the early 1990s when Matchroom almost went bust. 'You find out a lot about yourself in those times,' said Hearn. 'And without being big-headed, I liked what I found.'

I think most of us will have liked what we found out about Hearn last night too, and anyway, who could have anything but admiration for the man who brought us Snooker Loopy, darts from Ally Pally, and the madness of Eubank? But not yet international crazy golf. 'We've had a look at that,' said Hearn. 'Tiger Woods playing one in off the windmill. Why not?'

Once a disc jockey, always a disc jockey.

My Favourite Waste of Time

Screen Break, The Guardian, *29 April 2007*

The snooker has been interesting, hasn't it? Ha, ha, only joking. I am not saying I am not enjoying the coverage of the World Championships, just that in the early stages, it tends to be not so much compelling sporting drama, more a highly effective way of killing an afternoon. In fact, in the words of 'Eighties pop muppet Owen Paul's only chart hit, my favourite waste of time.

See, title and artiste. That is the kind of detail you want when a popular music reference arises. I am becoming increasingly irritated by sports programmes using a vocal track in a montage sequence, and failing to tell you what the heck it is. Am I alone in this? Is there the beginnings of a campaign here?

If there is a child in the house when it happens I can usually get the information I want, although I suspect they sometimes shout out 'Fratellis' or 'Klaxons' just to keep me quiet. (Jo Whiley on Radio 1 often neglects to give details of the records she plays as well, but that is a separate issue.) Only Sky's *Soccer AM* is good enough to provide a caption over their goals compilations to help those of us whose grip on popular culture loosened around the time Gary Glitter was still considered an all-round family entertainer.

Anyway, the snooker on BBC Two (Yes, the snooker. Sorry, I drifted off, but what do you expect, I have been watching the snooker) prefaced the match between John Parrott and Shaun Murphy with footage of the two players on their way to the Crucible, to a backing of 'Run Wild' by New Order (thanks kids), part of the BBC's attempt, I suppose, to make the World Championships just a little sexier.

In this, I think the BBC is missing the whole point of snooker. We do not need it to be more interesting. We are actually perfectly capable of spending seven hours in front of the TV in an afternoon – is it seven hours? It is something like that – watching two young chaps we have never heard of knocking coloured balls into pockets. It is what separates us from the animals.

The very dullness of snooker is the perfect accompaniment, I find, to an indolent afternoon. The clack, clack of the balls, the comforting voices of the ex-players in the commentary box, mellowed by smoky snooker halls and a lifetime of not getting too excited, the safety shots, the endless close-ups of one player slumped in his seat showing no emotion as the other cleans up the frame, showing no emotion. So satisfyingly un-José Mourinho like.

But about the music; who decided the lyrics need not be relevant any more? We knew where we were when the only tunes used in sports shows were 'Simply The Best' and 'We Are The Champions', but that New Order song included a lyric about Jesus which did not seem entirely germane to the best of 25 frames, and, as Parrott and Murphy's cars approached the Crucible, the words, 'Dusty roads to distant places...'

Exactly how dusty are the roads in Sheffield, and is the council doing anything about it? Sheffield, that is, easily accessible from junction 34 of the M1; hardly distant.

And if New Order's song seems to belong elsewhere, how about this year's wacky title sequence, which I am only able to deconstruct for you because of the time I spent in the 1970s in the old Academy Cinema in Oxford Street watching art-house movies?

It starts with a close-up of the cue being thrust forward (phallic symbol?) coming into contact with the perfectly round shiny surface of the cue ball (I am seeing a well-rounded buttock here, but that could be the result of too much Buñuel in my formative years). Just for a micro-second – it is almost subliminal – this mixes into an image of a big, spooky, soulful horse's eye (we are all familiar with *Equus*, further comment unnecessary), and then the horns of a bull, which somehow lock together to form a single horn, at which the horse rears up. A shot of a snorting bull's nose with a ring through it is followed by the white horse galloping through a ring of snooker balls trailing wisps of blue smoke. We then see a pair of gloved hands polishing a ball, before the *pièce de résistance*; the same white-gloved hands apparently massaging the flanks of a horse, conjuring up definite echoes of Catherine Deneuve in *Belle de Jour*. I could not say what happened next, because I went for a cold shower.

Fortunately, presenter Hazel Irvine seems the kind of sensible gal to bring a chap down to earth, and she is doing a bang-up job on the snooker, helped by as fine a selection of good eggs as any sport could muster; the genial Parrott, fast-talking Willie Thorne as the man-most-likely-to-be-mistaken-for-Mr-Potato-Head, and Steve Davis, who gets better with every tournament and is now an official National Treasure.

His style, of course, is to send himself up rotten. In a celebrity challenge match with Sam Torrance, for instance, he allows the golfer to win; just one of many bits of business with which the afternoons are studded, because the BBC, I suspect, feels it has to dress its baby up in pretty clothes to disguise the fact that it is actually a rather dull baby. But hey, on behalf of timewasters everywhere, let me say, we like it that way.

Nothing too complicated for hangover days

Screen Break, The Guardian, *5 January 2009*

Analysis of the highest order from Craig Burley on Setanta last week – or some time during the recent bacchanalia – when an elderly Manchester United fan was seen celebrating a Park Ji-sung strike against Middlesbrough long after it had been ruled out for offside. 'He doesn't know what day of the week it is,' Craig chuckled. Very satirical Craig, except at this time of the year nobody knows what damned day of the week it is.

To minds befuddled by alcohol, lack of sleep, and a surfeit of Quality Street – incidentally, what is the point of the circular gold one, the plain toffee, nobody likes them? – the calendar is just too abstruse a concept to grasp. The folk who schedule sport on TV know this, which is why the period between Christmas and New Year is traditionally home to two of the least complicated competitive activities known to man; strongman contests and darts.

Do not take my word for it. Asked why the strongmen put themselves through all the pain, Kevin Nee, an American competitor in *The World's Strongest Man* on Five, came up with this refreshing analysis: 'We're a bunch of meatheads, I suppose.' The question was particularly pertinent for Kevin, as the year started for him with an injury: 'I tore my bicep tendon off the bone, and had to get it reattached,' he said, in the tones you or I might use to describe a snagged fingernail.

Maybe I lack the commitment for strongman contests, but if bits of my arms were being torn off, I should take it as a sign that the time had come to relax with an improving volume and a comforting drink. You certainly would not catch me racing another big bugger up a sand track in Charleston, West Virginia, carrying a metal keg twice the weight of Pavarotti's Christmas shop.

'You're always hurt, there's always something nagging or something aching,' Nee explained. 'What pushes you on through the pain is knowing that it's going to make you better. The reason we compete is quite primitive. Men from the beginning of time have wanted to know who can throw the furthest, who can lift the heaviest stone.'

Possibly true, Kev, but even those primitive types stopped pulling trucks around once the internal combustion engine was invented. 'Ooh look, we can get inside it now, sit down, and away it goes,' they marvelled.

The big plus for the strongman contest is its simplicity. The bullet-headed chap who lifts the stones onto the pillars, or drags the truck over the finishing line, before the other b-h chap, is the winner; and that is about as complicated as you want life to get in that cloud cuckoo land between Christmas dinner and reacquainting yourself with the grim reality of your online bank account.

The PDC darts championship from Alexandra Palace, which dominates Sky Sports at year's end and beginning, is another seasonal great escape. The mob jigging around to that catchy tune they play after each leg, is so full of *joie de vivre*, you have to check your newspaper to see if we really are all facing financial Armageddon. And then of course there is the joy of Sid, although I fear the doyen of darts commentary may be losing it a little.

I say that because he quoted 'Simon Barnes of *The Guardian*' as writing that darts is the purest sport of all. Not *The Guardian*, Sid, but one of our so-called rivals – as we like to put it. The fact that Waddell could confuse the fine sports writing on this newspaper with the penny-a-line hackery available elsewhere casts doubt on some of his other flights of fancy. When he describes Phil Taylor's emphatic victory over the Dutch contender Co Stompé in the quarter-finals as 'like watching a Roman phalanx crossing the Rhine and ending up in Muscovy,' do we take the geographical and historical accuracy as read, or do we Google to make sure?

There was a real danger Sid might spontaneously combust, as Taylor averaged 116 in the first leg of the match. 'He's on tungsten fire,' screamed Sid. 'It's like watching Titian with a paint roller.' There was some stuff about Genghis Khan I didn't quite catch, which segued effortlessly into an Abba reference. 'Mama Mia, here he goes again. My, my,' marvelled Sid. 'It's grievous bodily tungsten.'

It was wondrous to watch, and if the darts did not make you forget the woes of the world, the advert for the part-work *Tractors and The World of Farming* did. The fact that there might be, in these difficult times, people willing to buy a magazine costing £7.99 every fortnight, in order to acquire a collection of little die-cast models of tractors, I found strangely encouraging.

⚬

God bless whoever it was looking after The Guardian *in Spring 2007, leaving my column untouched by political correctness or any kind of propriety. Also, it's still not OK if it's for charity!*

Crufts, my yearly opportunity for favourite dog jokes

Screen Break, The Guardian, *12 March 2007*

My parents would not let me have a dog when I was a child. They took me to Butlin's in Pwllheli instead, as a consequence of which I have grown up with an abiding love of the North Wales coast, but no real understanding of people's utter dottiness about their dogs. The annual jamboree at Crufts reaches me like a communication from another planet.

It is unmissable TV, though. Twenty-two thousand dogs, 140 thousand people ranging from the mildly eccentric to the totally barking (last pun, I promise), and Clare Balding in a leather coat. What is not to like?

As for Clare's co-presenter, he sets me wondering if, in

the same way as dog owners are said to grow to look like their pets, television presenters might begin to resemble the events they cover; because if ever there was a bright-eyed, bushy-tailed, shiny-coated, eager, panting pedigree puppy of a TV front man it is Ben Fogle, as he bounds onto the sofa alongside Clare to apprise her of the latest developments in the gundog category. He was that close to laying his head in her lap, I swear.

Maybe the BBC is playing it for laughs this year. Just as it is well nigh impossible to take seriously the music of bands like Saxon, Krokus or those with an unnecessary ümlaut or two in their name, after the merciless lampooning of *This Is Spinal Tap*, so the same team's spoof dogumentary (all right, two puns) *Best In Show* must make it difficult to approach Crufts with an entirely straight face.

The crew certainly seemed to be finding it so at times. There was a glorious sequence where Ben, having bought little fluffy facsimiles of some of the dogs from a stall, returned to the studio and presented them to their canine models, who did exactly what dogs tend to do with soft toys.

'Archie, don't eat yourself,' Ben instructed the animal, to the very audible amusement of the boys behind the cameras, who were clearly thinking of dogs eating themselves in the more literal sense occasionally referred to in whiskery old locker-room jokes. I should explain, for those of you who have not spent much time in that bracingly masculine atmosphere, that these jokes usually involve a male watching an act of canine self-fellatio, saying, 'I wish I could do that,' which is hilariously misconstrued by a second spectator, whose response is on the lines of, 'Well, give him a dog biscuit and he might let you.'

That joke, by the way, before you throw down the paper in disgust, was in aid of Comic Relief, under which banner I believe almost any old tat is currently considered acceptable.

Regular listeners to BBC Five Live's hit Saturday morning show *Fighting Talk* will know of my objections to Comic Relief on the principle that comedy should by its very nature be subversive and anti-establishment, and while it is laudable that performers work for charity, it would be preferable if comedians at least were to do this on the quiet, while publicly turning their mocking gaze on self-regarding leviathans like Comic Relief.

Charity begins at home, I say, not on prime time BBC One with repeats and expanded coverage on BBC Three. I am not entirely sure exactly where the comic element comes in either. Though it might be mildly amusing for a nanosecond to hear Ray Stubbs murder The Jam's 'Going Underground', it is not exactly The Marx Brothers. And who decided the event should go on for two weeks? Later this week, God help us, there is a celebrity version of *The Apprentice* under the Comic Relief imprimatur. This is not so much telethon, more fund-raising eternity.

And so, with some relief, back to Crufts, where competitors are going through their paces in the obedience ring, which is not, as you might have imagined, an internet network of like-minded fetishists, but the area where owners demonstrate how damned clever their dogs are.

My favourite bit is where the dog careers around the ring before the judges, with its handler clutching the lead and running behind with what dignity he or she can muster. I particularly enjoyed the work of Miss Jonna Sanden, a statuesque Swede, trailing after her flatcoat retriever Simon, successful in the gundog category. The commentators praised Simon's 'deep girth', and one spoke admiringly – I am not making this up – of his being 'obviously a male dog, but without being overdone anywhere.' I could not say myself, because I was busy watching Miss Sanden. Is that wrong?

There has been some talk this year about this kind of event being tantamount to animal cruelty, but my view is that when an owner spends hours on end following behind his or her animal with a little plastic bag scooping up its waste product and looking for a bin in which to deposit it, it does not seem too much to ask for the mutt to give something back once a year.

I am inclined to accept the assurances of Jessica Holm, one of the BBC's commentary team, that the four-legged competitors find all the fussing, the training, the preening, the pimping, and performing a huge blast. 'They love it. My dogs turn themselves inside out with excitement when they know there is a show in the offing,' she said. 'It's like a big social for them,' and with 21,999 brand new backsides to sniff, who could doubt it?

Christmas 2012, when you could still write 'dancing girls' in The Guardian *without praying for forgiveness from the gods of political rectitude. As I faced my final curtain, so did that kind of sexist malarkey, thank goodness etc. etc. But really it was mainly a piece pointing out what skilled sportsmen darts players are, which Sid Waddell, who died earlier that year, never tired of doing.* Guardian *readers should appreciate that as much as anybody.*

Darts – it's a bloody hard thing to do!

Screen Break, The Guardian, *23 December 2012*

So – as you will be aware if you have been shopping or listened to a radio station in the past couple of weeks –

this is Christmas. And if Christmas is about anything, it is about fat men dancing; in nightclubs, at the office party, but most of all at the World Darts Championship.

Of course, not all the participants are total chubsters (a term I feel liberated to use in the delightfully retro context of the darts), but quite a few do look more corpulent than ever this year. This could be down to the continued commercial success of professional darts enabling more hot dinners, but I think it is a consequence of the introduction to the championships of what I can only describe as dancing girls.

These lissom young performers are a new addition to the pre-match buildup. They wear short shorts and bikini tops, and gyrate their exposed mid-portions on what looks to be a fast-spin cycle as the players progress to the stage, escorted by yet more pulchritudinous young women. If it's true that the portly can appear more trim simply by hanging around with the even-better fed, then what we are seeing is the reverse effect. Placing an Adrian Lewis or a Phil Taylor next to so much lithe glamour is never going to show the boys off to their best advantage.

There is, of course, a Sid-shaped hole at the centre of the world championship this year. The players now compete for the Sid Waddell Trophy, an appropriate tribute to the late broadcaster, but one that somehow serves to emphasise his absence. When organisers considered how to maintain the competition's appeal in a Sid-less world, someone evidently came up with the answer, 'More birds', as these performers would undoubtedly be called.

Frankly, they needn't have bothered because the tournament, televised exhaustively on Sky Sports over the festive season, remains brilliant television. There is never a shortage of colourful stuff to point the camera at; Colin 'Jaws' Lloyd, for instance, quite light on his feet for a big man, and with a highly entertaining dad dance to his 'Is it a Monster?' walk-on music. He does a little mock march, then an outstretched-arm aeroplane move, before jogging to the front of the stage and grinning shyly at the audience.

He beat Mark 'Spider' Webster fairly comfortably, and celebrated by jumping up and down and punching the air, testing not just the sturdiness of the stage but the very foundations of the Alexandra Palace.

These guys hold nothing back in the post-match interviews either, re-living every missed double, keenly aware of turning points in the match. 'I went 3-0 up, and I thought I shouldn't be 3-0 up here, but Lloydy you've got to take it,' Jaws told commentator Stuart Pyke after his win. 'Then he came back at me and I have to say my backside began to flap a bit,' an image which is going to be a tough one to shake off.

I like the fact that the players often appear as a pair after the match, victor and vanquished, rehearsing the game from opposite standpoints, and mostly showing what I believe the young people call maximum respect for each other. Clearly, the success of darts I alluded to earlier means the guys are now more or less a travelling circus, rather like the ATP tour in tennis, and while you would expect some not to get on, there often seems to be a lot of love between darters in the post-match interviews.

Paul Nicholson, beaten by Robert Thornton in a sudden-death leg after what, if I were in Sky's commentary box, I would undoubtedly call a terrific tungsten tussle, was typically gracious in defeat. 'All I wanted was to enter this tournament with dignity and leave with dignity,' he said, although how much dignity there is in performing before a crowd of beery geezers dressed variously as superheroes, the Village People, and Marcel Marceau, holding up placards with scrawled on messages, among them the legend 'I love custard', is open to question.

'Just give me one shot,' Nicholson said. 'That's my mantra.' You tend to think of darts players having lagers rather than mantras but that is to do them an injustice. Amid all the dancers, the silly walk-ons, the daft crowd, these chaps are doing something that is very difficult to do, under immense pressure. And obviously they take it seriously but they do not take themselves seriously and that is half the joy of darts. The couple of weeks at Ally Pally is, in my view, the most reliably entertaining sport on TV.

Now all we have to do is get through three days of Christmas and we are into the final rounds. As the great poet Sir Nodward Holder says this time every year, 'Look to the future now, it's only just begun.'

I'd like to think it was shamefully sexist articles like this one which spurred on the development of women's football in England, paving the way for the Lionesses' triumph at the 2022 Euros. I still don't like seeing women shovelling down huge quantities of sausages, though. Does that make me a bad person?

Hot dog

Screen Break, The Guardian, *11 July 2011*

Emmeline Pankhurst, Germaine Greer, Clare Balding, your struggle is far from over, if Saturday's sports coverage on TV is anything to go by. There I was watching *Nathan's Famous Hot Dog Eating Contest* when, once the men's championship had finished and the female troughers donned the nosebag, ESPN America made a brief announcement about how it was a 'world leader in sport', and switched with indecent haste back to Major League baseball.

If that is the respect world leaders show to women athletes, is it any wonder concerned MPs were addressing the issue last week, before they found a better way to get on the BBC News Channel was to have a view about the *News Of The World*?

Competitive eating, according to ESPN commentators, is 'the fastest growing sport in the world', which surprised me, as I have always thought of competitive eating as less of a sport, more as something that goes on at particularly feisty bar mitzvah buffets, where there is a good chance if you reach out for a chopped and fried fish ball, you will get a fork in the back of your hand. But if competitive eating has joined the sporting pantheon, the least the channel could do is give us an idea of the current standing of the women's game compared to the men's.

Not that I had any particular desire to watch women in the kind of frenzied routine Joey Chestnut, the Lionel Messi of processed pork, went through to retain his title – his fifth championship in a row. These competitive eaters do not so much eat the hot dog as mush it up and cram it down the cakehole with their fist. It is not pretty.

'Look at the bite, look at the gnawing motion,' one of the commentators cooed admiringly of Chestnut's technique. 'When I see Joey eating with this ferocity and determination, I get filled with emotion. I'm more emotional than the last episode of *Oprah*, because this kid brings every bit of his fibre to the contest.'

While I prefer a woman with a healthy appetite to one who pushes a piece of steamed fish and half a cherry tomato around her plate, I am not sure a 'gnawing motion' is ever a particularly admirable quality in a woman, an old-fashioned attitude I know, which these days probably places me about one step from Bluebeard.

Joey managed 62 hot dogs in ten minutes in the traditional July 4th contest in Coney Island, six short of his own record, and celebrated with a bottle of Pepto-Bismol, the stomach medicine, and one of the sponsors of the event – which tells you pretty well all you need to know about it. 'He looks like Djokovic up there kissing the Pepto,' said the commentator. 'It's not the All-England cup, but it's his best friend.'

As it happens, the MPs who wrote to BBC director general Mark Thompson asking for a fair deal for women's sport on the telly, were less concerned with female participation in America's gift to the proprietary brand indigestion remedy business than in live coverage of the women's football World Cup, which the BBC were offering as a digital option, with highlights later on BBC Two.

However, Britain's young ladies are apparently so unfit these days that finding the remote and pressing the red button is beyond them, so the MPs demanded England's quarter-final against France be shown live on proper TV, and the BBC, in the current media climate where policy can be determined by anyone with a few hundred thousand followers on Twitter, of course complied.

I am not sure, though, that showing the match in full did the women's game any favours. Some of the earlier highlights packages have looked impressive, but as players in this game tired visibly in the latter stages of a match that went into extra-time, there were some horribly misplaced passes, and an awful lot of hit-and-hope football, especially from England – not because the players were women, but because they do not have the fitness levels of full-time professionals. In the event, the women's performance mirrored that of our male internationals, failing to progress because of a couple of flaky penalty misses.

If it is indefatigability you are after, try Sky's Super League where commentators Eddie and Stevo never tire of extending metaphors beyond breaking point. As Warrington Wolves faded after building up a 22-point lead over Huddersfield Giants, and the Giants hit back, Eddie noted, 'Warrington have been throwing down the "come in," "come in" calls to Huddersfield, and they've come through the door. The big bad wolf – or the giant – is knocking the door in.'

'Well, will it knock the house down? That's the big question,' countered Stevo, reinforcing the feeling that there are times when a well-placed famous hot dog or two would not go amiss.

Not every joke you made over a decade ago ages well. Ironically and tragically the constantly smiling, heartwarming darts presenter Dave Clark began to lose some control of his facial features when diagnosed with hereditary Parkinson's disease around 2011. He has spoken of his struggles and contributed to understanding of the condition. He retired from broadcasting with Sky in 2020. Jade Goody was a contestant on the Channel 4 reality show Big Brother. *She did not come across as a reader. In 2008, she was diagnosed with cervical cancer. She died in March 2009 at the age of 27.*

Phil 'The Power' Taylor's World of Wellness

Screen Break, The Guardian, *12 February 2007*

I am a little worried that Phil 'The Power' Taylor may have fallen into the hands of a sinister cult; although I have no firm evidence of this, other than his beatific smile after a 7-7 draw against Dennis Priestley in his latest Premier League darts match.

Taylor has now failed to win in his last three televised matches, which by his extraordinary standards is a run as barren as Jade Goody's bookshelf. You might, therefore, expect the Power to carry a careworn, or at least slightly concerned, look. But no, he beamed joyously after Dennis's thrillingly filched point, hugged his opponent, and spoke about how delighted he was to have taken part in such a great match. 'I've made a few changes in my life,' Taylor told Sky's Dave Clark, 'but I'm really, really, really enjoying it.'

Even so, he did not seem to be enjoying it quite as much as Clark, whose constant smile – on his face and in his voice – is one of the wonders of television. Either someone is telling him blisteringly funny jokes just before he goes on air, or he was abandoned as a child and brought up by disc jockeys. I am waiting for one of the players to tell Clark how he has lost all his family members in a bizarre gardening accident and been diagnosed with an incurable disease, just to see if it puts a dent in Clarkey's relentless good cheer.

Not that Phil was ever in danger of wiping the smile off our man's face. His life changes have brought him only joy. He has lost weight and gone teetotal – which puts him out of step with most members of his profession on at least two counts – and is undergoing an intensive training programme, he says, with 'Andy Hamilton in the Skylark.' I did check to see if this Hamilton fellow was a lifestyle guru and the Skylark an ashram of some sort, but it appears it is just a pub, and Hamilton another darts player from Stoke-on-Trent, helping Taylor to run in his new darts.

What rang alarm bells with me was the nature of Phil's smile, rather than the fact of him smiling. It was one of those zealous, slightly pious smiles you get from someone just before they tell you they are 'in a good place now,' which is one of those irritating expressions that somehow insinuates its way into the language and people start slinging about at every opportunity – like 'don't go there' and 'too much information.' I blame the fluoridation of the water supply.

Phil did not actually say he was in a good place now – he was in Wolverhampton, after all – but he promised the new cleaner, healthier Taylor would soon be back on full power. Hallelujah!

The darts Premier League is in its second week of fifteen and, with the possible exception of England's dramatic one-day win over Australia in the cricket and the inter-hemisphere punch up at QPR, which Sky Sports News seemed to be screening every five minutes, was comfortably the most exciting sport on TV last week. This made it roughly four times as entertaining as the England football match, and about a third as thrilling as the commentators, led as always by the peerless Sid Waddell, would have you believe.

Sid was not entirely convinced by Phil's life changes. 'He's lost too much weight too fast,' said the Geordie nutritionist. 'Those big Popeye arms are out of synch with the upper torso.'

Sid reckoned the diet regime was weakening the former champ for the latter stages of matches. Well, he is the expert, but The Power still looked to me to be built very much on the lines of a darts player and not at all on the lines of, say, Rupert Everett; and how strong do you have to be to play darts anyway?

Maybe Sid was comparing the Power to Peter Manley, the 44-year-old well-fed former newsagent from Carlisle, who uses Tony Christie's hit record 'Is This The Way To Amarillo?' as his walk-on music, and almost makes you long for Andrew Neill and Michael Portillo's performance of the same tune. But that is what makes darts so irresistible. What other sport gives middle-aged newsagents the chance to dance on stage in front of what commentator Stuart Pyke described as 'Fourteen hundred darts crazy fans packed into the Wolverhampton Civic Hall?'

The DCFs had made it to the Civic Hall despite the white hell that engulfed the West Midlands on Thursday night, gifting the commentators a range of weather clichés to add to their armoury. 'The Black Country is hotter than Vladivostok on a wet Wednesday,' avowed Sid somewhat mysteriously.

He described the atmosphere in Wolverhampton as like something (I find I am missing every third word Sid utters these days; either his mouth or my ears are giving out through age) 'mixed with the Mardi Gras in New Orleans, and we are in downtown Wolverhampton,' to which co-commentator Pyke responded with some comment about the cold outside compared to the white heat within, which Waddell then trumped with 'Yes, who needs jazz when you've got the music of tungsten?'

The travelling darts circus bashes out its tunes in Nottingham next, so place your bets now on Robin Hood references. I am setting the spread at 12 to 15.

The Bus Pass Bodybuilders and Motty's giant sentence

Screen Break, The Guardian, *5 March 2007*

Old age, I have always felt, is God's way of telling you to move into more voluminous underwear. I do not mind admitting that when I hit 40 I set aside all youthful thoughts of Y-fronts and started wearing briefs, which were substantially more modest in the area we doctors call the upper thighs. Now in my fifties I buy sensible boxer shorts in packets of four from the Bernard Manning range at Marks & Spencer.

I mention this only to explain my vague unease at the sight of 70-year-old Eric's posing pouch, part of his armoury as he prepared for the Natural Universe bodybuilding contest in California, featured in the BBC's *One Life* series last week. Eric seemed a little embarrassed himself as he held up a skimpy piece of shiny black material and explained that that was all that stood between his pension-age genitalia and the spectators.

Not that a Chippendales-style scenario was ever a danger. The question of sexual attraction surfaced only fleetingly and rather unconvincingly in the programme, which followed competitors on the older people's bodybuilding circuit, the Seniors' Tour if you like.

Kathy, a 54-year-old grandmother, said she had taken up the sport to hold age – and particularly the dreaded so-called bingo wings – at bay; and husband Mike suggested the results had been something of a hit in the boudoir department, although he was 'not drooling over the dinner table,' for which relief, I suspect, much thanks.

I do not wish to be ungallant and I am as inclined to drool as the next man – especially if I fall asleep on the sofa after a decently alcoholic dinner – but I am afraid time's wingèd chariot seemed to me not only to have caught up with Kathy but to have pulled up alongside her and be flagging her down. She looked exactly like a lady of 54 or maybe a little older, albeit one with extraordinarily well-developed muscles who would have no trouble holding her place in a Post Office queue. Her enduring allure in the marital home possibly has less to do with her physique than with her temperament, which seemed as sweet as a nut.

Unfortunately she was also the colour of one. Nobody, apparently, can take the stage at one of these bodybuilding shindigs without calling upon a small mahogany lake of fake tan. Linda, wife of 61-year-old Bernie, competing in a championship at Southport, applied her old man's gloss finish with a paint roller and rather sweetly ended up with a smudge of it on her own face when she kissed him after his success.

Alongside the creosote and the tiny cossies, the third element that normally surfaces in programmes about bodybuilding was notably absent. Apart from one mention of Preparation H – 65-year-old Ted uses it in his training routine in some unspecified way – pharmaceuticals were the elephant in the room.

I am sure I was not alone in wondering whether in order to train into your fifties, sixties and seventies, it might not sometimes be necessary to run to the shelter of Grandmother's Little Helper.

Then again, old-age bodybuilding did not appear a fiercely competitive business and the participants we met seemed thoroughly decent folk, so maybe it is only an old cynic like me who would even raise the question. Good luck to them.

And good luck also to another senior pushing himself to the limit as he enters his twilight years. Sixty-one year-old John Motson, commentating on the Reading-Manchester United Cup replay, showed the youngsters a thing or two by attempting the longest sentence ever uttered by a commentator at a live football match.

In the midst of a paean to John Madejski, during which he failed to mention where the Reading chairman currently stands with Cilla Black (there's some senior action we could stand being updated on), Motty provided us with the following (this is just a portion): '...outside there's a conference centre and a luxury hotel and there's an indoor training complex but I think what most of us appreciate – those of us old enough to drive anyway, heh, heh – is the location of the Madejski, just a mazy dribble by Cristiano Ronaldo over a couple of roundabouts onto the junction 11 of the M4 as that westbound motorway roars out of London through the Thames Valley and ...'

Screen Break would like to break into that sentence for a moment and ask if anyone else has noticed how often during a Reading match, commentators will say 'here at the Madejski'. It must be at least twice as often as they would say 'at Villa Park' or 'Stamford Bridge'. I mean, the guy has his name on the stadium, how much more publicity does he need? And now, back to Motty.

'...onwards to Bristol and Cardiff where the Millennium Stadium is still on standby just in case the new Wembley is not ready to stage a final from which these two teams tonight are just three matches away.' I was disappointed there was no mention of the Chippenham turn-off or the Leigh Delamere services but Motty proves once more that, when it comes to stream of consciousness or, more accurately, oozing river of random thought breaking its banks and flooding several small fields, you never lose it.

This piece appeared in the early days of The Guardian *sports blog, which gave the great unwashed, or our valued readers, as they are sometimes known, the opportunity to give valuable feedback to us writers, the main tenor of which was usually 'I can't believe you get paid for this.'*

Wordiness

Screen Break, The Guardian, *6 October 2008*

Did you know that Eric Clapton is an exact anagram of Narcoleptic? Appropriate, I think, with reference to some of his fairly dull recent output, but not really much to do with sport, as I am sure I shall be told in no uncertain terms on the *Guardian*'s sports blog.

But hold on just a doggone minute there, people with computers and nothing better to do on a Monday morning – late Sunday evening in the USA – than tell semi-humorous columnists how much better you could do the job.

My dictionary defines sport as 'competitive activity involving physical exertion or skill, governed by rules, and sometimes engaged in professionally,' on which basis tournament Scrabble and its fiercely competitive participants (whose idea of a good time is rearranging guitar gods' names) definitely qualify. They featured in *Word Wars*, a nifty documentary on the Sky Arts channel.

Yes, Sky Arts. I am afraid I deserted my post again. I know I have the attention span of a goldfish whose wife has just left him, but honestly, the sheer weight of European football on TV last week, just daunted me, leaving me full of *ennui*, *weltschmerz*, and all sorts of other foreign things we British should really not countenance. Faced with a Portsmouth UEFA Cup tie at the end of what seemed like several hours of football played in half-empty stadiums – which man would not hit the remote looking for naked women, car crashes, even cookery programmes?

Word Wars, subtitled 'Tiles and Tribulation' (geddit?) in the *World of Competitive Scrabble*, was better than any of that. It reminded me of one of those Christopher Guest spoof documentaries like *Best In Show*, except its stars, word freaks with an eight games of Scrabble a day habit and an inability to visit Las Vegas without noting it is an anagram of Salvages, were real, and quirkier than anything Guest would dare invent.

In the style of the Guest movies, *Word Wars* focused on a few stalwarts of the circuit as they prepared for the national Championships in San Diego. (Or agonised, as they might say). GI Joel Sherman was the first we met, swallowing pre-tournament chromium picolinate tablets, while noting that picolinate is an anagram of antipolice.

Sherman's flat looked like the aftermath of an explosion in Superdrug, with containers of brain boosting supplements jostling for space with remedies for Joel's various physical ailments. He explained that the GI in his name is not a military thing, but stands for gastro-intestinal, he being something of a martyr to his stomach. I could believe it. He did not strike me as someone who would take the time to cook wholesome food. Not with several dictionaries to memorise.

Actually I am not sure I even saw a kitchen in his flat, the style of which could best be described as classic single-man-in-his-forties-with-an-obsession. Joel himself, were he a creation of Steve Coogan, would be played with shaving cuts and sticking plaster holding his glasses together. His hair was in a combover, and his eyes frequently red and swollen like those of a boxer the morning after, except in his case they were testament to late-night extra-curricular games of Scrabble against fellow word warriors.

What Joel had, which Coogan and Guest characters usually lack, was self-knowledge. At one point he says, 'I have done very little to contribute to society. I don't have a real life,' and then, after a nicely timed pause, 'Even compared to other Scrabble players.'

If GI Joel was exactly what you were expecting, Marlon Hill was not. A big cheerful black man from an area of East Baltimore for which the term urban blight might have been invented, he wore his hair in dreadlocks, his drug of choice a family-sized spliff, and his preparation for a tournament included an encounter with a prostitute, whose generously proportioned rear end he later happily eulogised for the cameras. Marlon was admirable in many ways; not least in giving talks to local black schoolchildren who might not have considered Scrabble as a way out of the ghetto.

Perhaps the biggest surprise in the film, though, was US Number One at time of filming, Joe Edley, who had somehow got himself married and had a child. He meditated before a game, enabling the narrator to say: 'Edley is unblocking his energies, Joel is unblocking his sinuses.' Tension built, and you found yourself rooting for your favourite to win the title. At least, this viewer, who would undoubtedly be known on the Scrabble circuit as Ken Tramliner, did.

After I left The Guardian, *occasionally some veteran of the old days on the sports desk would remember the glory glory days of Screen Break and throw me a crumb or two in terms of the odd commission to write a general piece. By 2014, the Christmas season had very much become the darts season for TV sports viewers*

Spit, sawdust, bullseye! How we all learned to love darts

The Guardian, *3 January 2015*

When the comedian Mel Smith died in 2013, most of the tributes on TV included his famous 'darts sketch', from the 1980s satire show *Not The Nine O'Clock News*. In it Griff Rhys Jones is Dai 'Fat Belly' Gutbucket, competing against Smith, as Tommy 'Even Fatter Belly' Belcher. Puffing away on cigs, they stand by a table groaning with bottles of booze, the joke being that instead of throwing doubles, they're downing doubles; brandy, vodka, and so on.

Oh how we laughed, the young, savvy, *Guardian*-reading – there, I've said it – audience for that show. But in recent years, darts has become much more than a reliable source of cheap laughs for the chattering classes. Its major events sell out fast (Darts historian Patrick Chaplin tells me World Championship tickets were the eighth quickest seller online this year, not far behind Kate Bush and Fleetwood Mac), while TV audiences approach a million on Sky, and top two million for a rival tournament (of which, more later) on the BBC.

You'd like to think that's because viewers have lost the taste for feeling superior, that sneering has somehow become unfashionable, but in a TV world where *The Only Way Is Essex* flourishes, a second season of *Benefits Street* beckons, and Jeremy Kyle's circus rolls relentlessly on, that can't be the case.

My view is that with regular exposure to the sport, the sport-loving public, especially sofa-sprawlers like me, has come to recognise the truth of my colleague Sean Ingle's view on darts: 'Its pleasures come from its purity. Dart and board, eye and nerve.'

In a recent TV documentary, Martin Amis, a darts fan of long standing – Keith Talent, a character in Amis's *London Fields* is a darts professional, and Amis spent some time hanging around with former World Champion Keith Deller for research – described the sport as 'elemental'.

How did I miss that? I've been looking back at the

many pieces I wrote about it in my fourteen years as sport-on-TV columnist for this paper, and it's clear darts was one of those programmes, like truck racing, strongman contests, or *Mrs Brown's Boys*, I've been watching ironically.

The shame of it. Distracted by fat men with inadvisable haircuts, gangs of spectators dressed as penguins, and the late Sid Waddell's sublimely nonsensical commentary, I somehow failed to give credit to the players for the steely nerve it takes to hit a match-winning double in the rumbustious atmosphere of a packed Alexandra Palace, where the Professional Darts Corporation world championships climax this weekend. 'Like tiddlywinks in a bearpit,' Amis said.

And it's the frequency with which they have to throw the big dart that makes the skill even more admirable. As Stuart Pyke, commentator on darts for 12 years, told me: 'They're always finishing; a leg, a set, or a match. They have to be fully focused for every second.' (Roughly every 90 seconds, a double needs to be thrown for some kind of finish). 'You can never relax into a game, and coast,' says Pyke. 'If you do that, before you know it, the game will have gone.'

It can be heartbreaking – trust me, I sometimes bet on darts – but thrilling. I know of no other sport where fortunes change in a trice like that. It's like a constant penalty shoot-out, the kind of pressure under which our top footballers might – and often do – go to pieces. And there's another clue to the growing popularity of darts.

For some, it's blessed relief from the vainglory of Premier League football. As clubs become the playthings of rich owners, and more and more we find ourselves just cheering on a set of shirts, darts brings us chaps we can identify with, sportsmen who don't need a 'community initiative' to mix with the common people, because you might meet them doing their shopping in Asda.

Eric Bristow, of Stoke Newington, five times world champion, and one of the undisputed stars of darts' first wave of popularity in the late 1970s and early 1980s, was like that, always approachable, as demonstrated in a cracking documentary, *Arrows*, from 1979, recently re-run on BBC Four, which showed him playing exhibition matches in pubs, and smoking his way through a long, frank, radio interview of a kind you'd never hear from a star of any other sport.

Bristow, who later suffered dartitis – like yips in golf, an inability to perform the routine he'd spent a lifetime perfecting – discovered and mentored darts' greatest ever player Phil Taylor, only for Taylor to beat him in a *Star Is Born* scenario in a championship semi-final in 1997. For sport as soap opera, you could not better it. Meanwhile the debate over whether darts is a sport or merely a pastime continues.

Andy 'The Viking' Fordham, former British Darts Organisation champion (one of the two world titles), who ballooned to around 31 stones at one time, defused it best when asked how he could call himself an athlete. 'Sure I'm an athlete,' he responded/ 'I wear trainers and I've been on *Grandstand*.'

Fordham is substantially slimmer these days, and Phil Taylor, 16 times world champion, has been talking about his new-found love of fruit juice. He says he's been in consultation with 'a qualified juice therapist', (who knew you could qualify in juice?) and even spent three weeks on a retreat in Portugal with his juicemaster. His favourite, he said, is apple, avocado, and ginger.

But still the image of Mel Smith with a cushion up his front and a pint in his hand refuses to fade. Not that anyone in the PDC championships seems too worried. Phil, I feel, is out on his own with the ginger grater. Certainly Michael Smith and Stephen Bunting, who met in a last-16 match the other night, did not look to me like the sort of chaps guilty of intimacy with either cross-trainer or juice bar.

The PDC is one of two championships bestriding the festive marathon, running from mid-December, culminating in tomorrow's final, after which the BDO tournament starts. The BDO was formed in 1973, and according to Patrick Chaplin, did fine work in organising tournaments and getting the sport onto TV. But by 1990 ITV had abandoned darts, fearing its 'Fat Belly Gutbucket' image too downmarket for its advertisers.

The top players found their prize money much diminished, and in 1993, sixteen of them set up their own organisation, first called the World Darts Council, later the PDC, and signed up with Sky TV. Ollie Croft, the autocrat who runs the BDO from his home in Muswell Hill, banned the 'rebels' from BDO tournaments, and has been resistant to any kind of rapprochement.

You can view the split in two ways; either that the 'rebels' sold their soul to Sky TV, or that they took a heroic risk, organising, taking matters into their own hands, and getting themselves on TV (It was a risk, says Chaplin. In 1994, the first rebel tournament, there wasn't enough in the kitty for winner Dennis Priestley's prize money).

The standard of play in the PDC tends to be a touch higher than at the BDO, and the atmosphere in Ally Pally is certainly more exuberant than at the Lakeside Country Club, Frimley Green.

'The PDC has done for darts what the FA did for football in the 1920s and 1930s, turned it into a massive spectator sport, more than a participation sport,' says Chaplin. 'Barry Hearn has made the championships an event.' (Sports promoter Hearn, who has done similar work with snooker, became chairman of the PDC in 2000). 'You don't even have to be a darts fan. Bunches of guys – and girls these days – go purely for a good night out.'

It's true. I watched a YouTube clip of the 1980 final between Bristow and Bobby George, and there was not a female face to be seen. That's not the case now. Not that darts is in immediate danger of winning any diversity awards; not while the players are accompanied to the oche by what I suppose we have to call 'glamour girls', and the participants remain predominantly, if not exclusively, white men.

Working class heroes, Sid Waddell called them. It was Sid, long before he became the unparalleled voice of the TV coverage, who first brought darts to our screens in a programme called *Indoor League* he produced for Yorkshire Television in 1972, featuring skittles, a darts tournament, and compere Fred Trueman smoking a pipe and swigging a pint of bitter.

'It was a magnificent sub-culture,' Sid recalled on Sky TV in 2011. 'Big guys with tattoos, who liked a pint and a bet. Leighton Rees from the Valleys, who lived with his mam, Alan Evans, whose dad had a pub, and used to stand him on a box to play at the age of eight. Later there was Keith Deller whose mum used to fry chips with one hand, and throw darts with the other, and Jocky Wilson, who would bring his own optic to tournaments and a bottle of vodka with his name on it. He'd win darts matches when other people would have been in intensive care.'

A BBC producer, Nick Hunter, to whom the Corporation assigned much of its working class sports output – rugby league and snooker, as well as darts – was responsible for the next big breakthrough in televised darts, introducing the split screen in 1978. 'It was all there at last,' said Sid. 'The agony and the ecstasy. On one side, a close-up of the player's face, on the other the board. It was made for TV.'

The popularity of darts even spawned a quiz show, *Bullseye,* which ran from 1981 to 1995, in which darts champs partnered amateurs, hosted by comedian Jim Bowen, who always seemed to be showing sheet metal workers or glass blowers how close they had come to winning a new car, or a speedboat. 'Look at what you could have won,' was his catch phrase, alongside 'super, smashing, lovely.' It attracted 17 million viewers, and a host of jokes about council houses with two speedboats in the drive.

Even then, it seems, the undervaluing of darts had more to do with class prejudice than anything in the sport itself. It's a very difficult skill, and arguably demands as much dedication as sports such as golf if you're to reach the top. As darts fan Stephen Fry says, 'The ability to send tungsten into a small area reliably and consistently is breathtaking.'

It really ought to be an Olympic sport, and the only reason I can think of for the demands not being more urgent is because of a reluctance to see the nation represented on the world stage by a chap with a Mohican hairstyle, wearing a Hawaiian shirt.

In the meantime, though, Sid's working class heroes seem to be having the last laugh. The PDC championship has a record prize fund this year of just over a million pounds, and tomorrow's winner will be rewarded for his steady hand and eye, hours of practice, and nervelessness unseen outside the field of bomb disposal, with a lot more than a speedboat.

All Our Yesterdays

No 52: **The Galloping Gourmet** (1968-1971),
The Independent

● Before Keith Floyd, before Nigella Lawson, there was Graham Kerr, who came from New Zealand with a family size bottle of wine, and enough double cream to administer a heart attack to the whole of Britain.

The devilishly handsome Kerr - who twinkled in a sort of Robert Vaughan way - was constantly taking 'a short slurp' of wine, while cooking outlandishly rich dishes, and delivering double entendres of which Ainsley Harriott would be proud. A typical Kerr sequence would see him slinging industrial quantities of cream and clarified butter into a frying pan, before turning to the camera with a sly grin and saying, 'That's not sweat on my forehead, that's fat oozing from my pores.'

Not that he wasn't a damned good cook. Before emigrating from the UK to New Zealand at the age of 24, he had already managed the Royal Ascot Hotel, and served as a catering consultant for the army, a job he returned to with the New Zealand air force, where he got his first TV exposure. In 1971, though, his TV career was cut short by an horrific car accident. When he returned to TV some years later, he had found religion and low-fat cookery. Maybe he was cookery's Martin Peters - fifteen years ahead of his time.

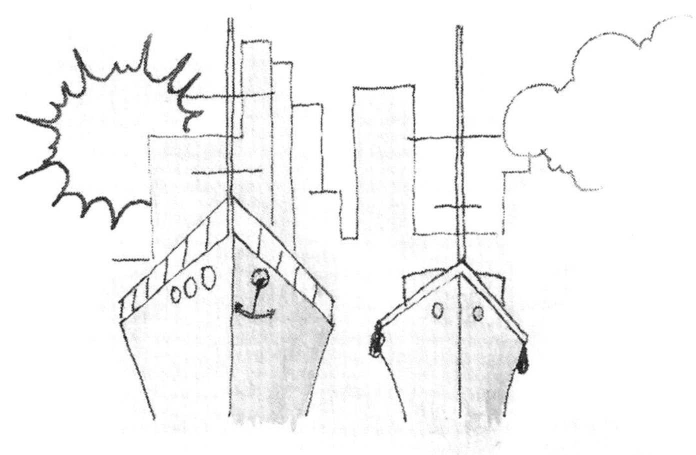

12. Footballers: What Are They Like?

'The new manager was able to reveal the previously well-kept secret that Ken Bates's heart "is in the right place," by which I assume he meant Monte Carlo...'

It will not startle you to learn that this piece pre-dates my employment on Ken Bates's radio station.

While Manchester United tucked into salt and pepper spiciness, gruel remained thin at Elland Road

Screen Break, The Guardian, *5 March 2012*

Despatches from the front line: Ryan Giggs's favourite Chinese meal is chilli lamb. There is a plate on the wall of Wing's restaurant in Manchester signed by Giggs, endorsing the dish. According to the owner Wing-Shing Chu, the Manchester United veteran, despite his well-advertised preference for variety in the boudoir, orders the same thing on every visit. I am able to bring you this latest intelligence thanks to my subscription to MUTV.

The many millions of you not similarly endowed may also wish to know that after Sir Alex Ferguson removes his chewing gum of an evening, he likes to get his laughing tackle around some soft noodles – you would have thought the word 'soft' might deter him, but until they start serving 'well hard noodles', that's what he gets – and Wayne Rooney's favoured starter is salt-and-pepper spare ribs.

These latest revelations were in a programme called *Red Dragons' Kitchen*, one of countless shows on MUTV featuring United players in smart restaurants, the channel's favoured ballast, in between the lame-brained phone-ins and coverage of reserve matches.

As it happens, I have eaten in Wing's and found it perfectly fine, if a little pretentious and overpriced for food not vastly different from the cheap and cheerful places elsewhere in Manchester's Chinatown. Not that that would be a consideration for those earning bulging weekly envelopes in the bright, shiny world of Premier League football.

Lower down the league ladder, things are different. If you were looking for a handy metaphor for the state of football below the Premier League, Blackpool v Hull City on Sky on Friday night would do. Blackpool took to the field in shirts carrying the name of their sponsor, Wonga.com, while Hull's bore that of Cash Converters; a loan shark versus a pawnbroker, more or less. Hard times. The fans' chants, echoing round a half-empty stadium (or half-full, if you are one of those people), Sky's Friday night second team, and a deal of banal football completed the picture.

It was not much more festive at Leeds United on

Saturday. The appointment of Neil Warnock means Leeds now have a charmless manager to go with their charmless chairman – which was obviously not the line being sold by Sky, who spoke to Warnock before the match. The new manager was able to reveal the previously well-kept secret that Ken Bates's heart 'is in the right place,' by which I assume he meant Monte Carlo.

He also declared himself pleased with the way Leeds fans had taken to the Warnock-Bates axis, which is clearly not the whole picture. As someone living rather closer to Elland Road than the Principality of Monaco, I should say the fans' resistance has been so lowered by administration, points deductions, the sale of their best players, and various other indignities, that you could install a regime of Pol Pot and Piers Morgan and they would just shrug, and turn up as usual.

Some of them would anyway. Sky pundit Gary McAllister's pre-match prediction of a full house, attracted by a match against the league leaders, and the 'two big egos' now guiding Leeds, was way out. A crowd of 20,000 of the most tribal fans in the country tells me that in these difficult times, several thousand others are taking the line that, like Wing's, Bates might be charging rather too much for moderate fare.

Still, if you have missed the cutaways of Warnock snarling in his technical area, berating the fourth official, and his post-match whinging, you will welcome his return. 'I expect a referee and a linesman to spot a blatant handball,' was his typical whinge after Leeds's defeat in a match they dominated. Others might say that Southampton had benefited from the eternal Championship truth that with a decent goalie, a well-drilled defence, and a reliable goal scorer, it is a league in which you will often get away with it.

If Southampton keeper Kelvin Davis was instrumental to the win at Leeds, his performance was eclipsed by the goalkeeping display of the season so far in the thrilling Liverpool–Arsenal match on Saturday. But for Wojciech Szczęsny in Arsenal's goal, Liverpool would undoubtedly have been out of sight by half time, gratefully acknowledged in post-match interviews by manager Arsène Wenger, and goalscorer Robin van Persie. The cheerful Dutchman demonstrated his command of idiomatic English by graciously admitting 'we nicked it,' without losing sight of the footballer's sacred duty when faced with a post-match mike, to preface every observation with 'To be fair.'

The three Championship matches over the weekend – the BBC televised Cardiff v West Ham yesterday – were always going to look a little drab measured against another exciting and unlikely Arsenal comeback. BBC commentator Jonathan Pearce did try his hardest, though, to sell us yesterday's game, with some nonsense about the 'haunted eyes' of the Cardiff players after defeat in the Carling Cup final, and the indispensable information that the last time West Ham won in Cardiff 'the nation was dancing to the number one in the charts, "Working My Way Back To You" by the Detroit Spinners.' I'd drop the scripted intro if I were you, Jonathan.

Finally, thanks to ITV sports journo Luke McLaughlin, who noted a rare appearance by Matt Le Tissier as Sky co-commentator for the Liverpool match. 'Le Tissier said "he'll be disappointed with that" an awful lot,' Luke tweeted me. 'He'll be disappointed with that.'

Political Correctness gets a bad press. I'm in favour of it mostly. In many ways, it's just being polite. It only becomes a problem when free speech is under attack and sincerely held views, like those of JK Rowling or Salman Rushdie are threatened by religious or liberal zealots. But it should be possible to be funny without being deliberately unkind or insulting. Sadly as a tearaway young journalist in my fifties, I was more cavalier, and I'm mildly ashamed of this piece about Stan Collymore, whose issues, including some car park based romantic adventures, had been exposed in the national press. But there are a couple of decent jokes in it, so I thought it merited a re-print. If only to demonstrate how more mature we have all become.

The Stan Collymore dilemma

Screen Break, The Guardian, *6 March 2006*

What next for Stan Collymore? The question was forming in my mind towards the end of a programme called *My Childhood* on BBC Three, when suddenly the answer popped up on screen.

Next: *Two Pints of Lager and a Packet of Crisps*.

A little modest, I thought, for a millionaire ex-footballer whose normal routine when bearded by the black dog of despair is to shove off to Australia for a couple of months of light scuba diving; but naturally the slogan referred not to the troubled former international striker, but to the following programme, the monumentally witless 'comedy' show (four series, one joke), intended one suspects to lighten the mood in some mysterious way after an hour of Stan in the psychiatrist's chair.

Mental illness, of course, is no laughing matter – something it has in common with *Two Pints of Lager and a Packet of Crisps* – but sometimes it is difficult to take Stan entirely seriously, or at least as seriously as he takes himself. Maybe we are just a little too familiar with Stan's inner demons. I don't know who is handling the PR for those IDs, but in recent years they seem to have had more airtime than Carol Vorderman, as a result of which we know all about Stan's depression, the weeks he was unable to get out of bed, and the lack of sympathy and understanding he encountered in the macho world of professional football.

In *My Childhood*, Stan was encouraged to trace his problems back to his early years by psychiatrist Dr Linda Treliving. The sweetly sympathetic Dr Treliving, whom one imagines Stan found more *gemütlich* than some of the central defenders he came across on a Saturday afternoon in the Premiership, is an expert in early trauma, of which Stan could claim barrow loads.

His largely absent Barbadian father, a journalist from whom Stan possibly inherited the plausibility the late Nicholas Tomalin reckoned was one of the essential tools of our trade, was in the habit of turning up out of the blue to give Doreen, Stan's mum, a good hiding, leaving her understandably a bundle of anxieties, many of which little Stan took on his own shoulders. Once Collymore Senior flew off to Barbados with his latest girlfriend and five-year-old Stan in tow, after telling Doreen he was just taking the boy to London for the weekend.

The programme combined Stan's sessions with the Doc with a *This Is Your Life* element in which the patient wandered the not particularly mean but rather uninspiring streets of his native Cannock, meeting childhood friends, chatting to former teachers and so on.

Alongside Stan's early trauma, the more recent nightmares – signing for Leicester City, going out with Davina McCall – were rehearsed, and I do not intend to give them more currency here, except to endorse the popular view that nothing he has been through excuses his despicable behaviour towards Ulrika Jonsson in 1998, and also to observe in passing that if it weren't for dogging and piking many of the car parks in our areas of outstanding natural beauty would remain sadly neglected.

Stan, Dr Treliving and her colleagues concluded, has Borderline Personality Disorder, requiring anti-depressants and daily psychotherapy for up to two years. Therapy is a long-term commitment – as Woody Allen says in *Annie Hall*, 'the therapy is going really well, they reckon in six months time I should be able to take the lobster bib off' – which is clearly as alien to Stan as a quiet night in with a plate of chocolate hob nobs and *Holby City* on the telly. Sure enough, by the end of the show Stan had set off round the world again 'hoping that will bring him some happiness.'

As previously indicated, one does not wish to make light of mental illness, not in real life anyway, so thank goodness for *Footballers' Wives*, in which, I feel absolutely safe in saying, all the characters are as barmy as badgers.

It was actually possible to flip straight from Stan's analysis to that of Amber Gates, whose husband Conrad was murdered in the last series by Earls Park team-mate and captain Bruno Milligan. Amber is even more reluctant than Stan to embrace the world of psychotherapy, flouncing out on her shrink, saying, 'Jesus, I thought I was the one with the mental problems,' one of many rich insults adorning episode one of the new series.

Earls Park's exciting new midfield signing Tremaine Gidigbi, played by Chucky Venice – the only actor in the show whose real name is possibly more outrageous than his character's – is said by Bruno to be 'so full of shit you could fertilise the pitch with it,' although my favourite line comes after the obligatory cat-fight between two of the wives, when one laments, 'She's ruined mi bleedin' Versace.'

By the way, feel free to disagree with any of the above. I got an entertaining email this week from one Kirsty Edwards taking me to task for my recent dismissal of her 'favourite reality TV programme,' *Dancing On Ice*. She says she is annoyed by the negative tone of my piece, accuses me of poverty of imagination, and one of the jokes I was quite pleased with she describes as 'somewhat pathetic and not amusing.' Mystifyingly, she signs off with a kiss.

One of her comments struck home, though. Kirsty asks if I have nothing better to do than 'sit around eating pizza on your own, watching programmes you don't like.'

Bloody hell, bang to rights.

Manchester United defender Patrice Evra had been involved in an 'incident' with famously hot-headed Uruguayan Luis Suárez which may very well have had a racist element – I forget – but there was outrage when the Liverpool player spurned the Frenchman's proffered hand.

Dining out with Manchester United's own TV Channel

Screen Break, The Guardian, *13 February 2012*

Did you know Manchester United has its own official Cabernet Sauvignon? It's a Chilean number called Casillero del Diablo. They advertise it between the programmes on MUTV, the club's TV channel. Ryan Giggs, Patrice Evra, and Wayne Rooney sit around exchanging anxious looks as they discuss the new 'devil' the boss is bringing to Old Trafford, which turns out to be the wine.

I doubt Sir Alex drinks it himself, as it is sold in supermarkets for £5.99, and legend has it the gaffer's taste runs to something a little ritzier. 'Let them drink Chilean plonk,' I imagine him cackling, as he pours himself another glass of the Château Margaux '95, not I expect the kind of image they were hoping for when they set up MUTV.

They probably thought the station might help fans feel part of the club, but actually it emphasises the divide between the players and the poor bloody infantry who pay to watch them. A lot of time is spent in smart restaurants – certainly more than the man on the Collyhurst omnibus would expect to spend – as the stars share their thoughts over green salads and soft drinks.

A programme called *Dining With Rio and Ryan*, for instance, begins with a lingering shot of the exterior of Rosso Restaurant & Bar, while inside Giggs and Ferdinand are answering searching questions like, 'What's some of the funny stories you do on people in dressing rooms?' It's not *Newsnight*.

Rio reveals that much dressing room hilarity centres on the always reliable comedy topic of 'dodgy gear', and takes us back to the time 'two of the lads had dodgy trousers on.' And, guess what? 'They cut all his trousers up, cut up all his gear and that. He was devastated.'

'They cut up his T-shirts as well,' added Giggsy.

Another programme, interviewing the da Silva twins, is shot in a Brazilian restaurant, Bem Brasil. What makes all this restaurant action particularly bogus is that it is well known – confirmed by Danny Welbeck in a *Guardian* interview on Saturday – that when footballers dine out, they mostly go route one, and eat in Nando's.

Granted, I am not the target market for MUTV – I am going out on a limb here, and guessing that would be

Manchester United fans – but I took out a subscription last week to keep up to date with the official line on handshakegate. Those are the kind of lengths to which we diligent correspondents on the front line are prepared to go, to keep on top of a breaking story like this.

Disappointingly, the line was that Luis Suárez had let his team down, his manager down, and well, you know the rest, by refusing Evra's proffered hand, which is more or less what the glorious leader had said in his post match interview. MUTV didn't even bother taking us to a fine Manchester tapas bar to reveal it.

You could tell how important the handshake story was by the fact that *Match Of The Day*, to whom Liverpool manager Kenny Dalglish declined to share his thoughts on the topic, borrowed an interview from Sky's Geoff Shreeves, who had bearded the Liverpool boss after Saturday's final whistle.

Even for Shreeves, a man who has seen more hair-raising action in the tunnel than Tim Robbins in *The Shawshank Redemption*, quizzing King Kenny shortly after a defeat against United, on a matter of pre-match etiquette, must qualify for one of those hazard payments war correspondents get.

Predictably, Kenny told Geoff he was 'bang out of order', and left him standing, rather as Suárez did to Evra, a not entirely unheard-of denoument to one of Shreeves's difficult encounters.

My view is that humour could have been used to take the heat out of the Suárez-Evra meeting. The problem with Kenny and Sir Alex is they are too fixated on football matters to have built up a decent knowledge of Marx Brothers' films. I would like to have referred them to the one where each time one of the brothers holds out his hand for a handshake, another puts his leg in it. Trust me, done quickly in a vaudeville style, it's very funny.

Imagine if, instead of his peevish refusal, Luis had put his leg in Patrice's hand, and then Rio had turned the tables and put his leg in Luis's hand, and they had repeated the routine to fill five of those tense pre-match minutes. Laughter would ensue, all enmity would be forgotten, and in no time at the boys would be breaking bread together in swish restaurants, exchanging hilarious 'dodgy gear' anecdotes, and, who knows, maybe ending the evening by amusingly cutting up each others clothes.

All Our Yesterdays

No 13: **The Incredible Hulk** (1978–1982),
The Independent

For those of us scratching a living as journalists at the time, the most intriguing character in this show was tabloid reporter Jack McGee (Jack Colvin), relentless in his search for the secret of the Hulk. Through five series, he harried Bill Bixby's Dr David Banner, trying to stand up his very reasonable theory that a raging creature was out and about, causing havoc. By breaking this story, McGee hoped to revive his stagnating career.

Who, we asked ourselves, was bankrolling this four-year investigation? Was there no news editor telling McGee to leave it be, and go after some other stories, do some police calls or something? And how likely was it that anyone's career would be saved by just one story? It'll be fish and chip wrapping tomorrow, lad.

The McGee character was just one of many implausibilites on display. For instance, how come Banner's clothes were ripped open when he became the Hulk, but mysteriously reverted to their original state when he became Banner again?

And – a favourite of comedians of the time – how come nothing burst open below the waist? The answer to all these questions, of course, was that the Hulk's origins were in a comic, and so the series quite properly used the logic – or lack of it – of comic books.

13. Football: The National Pastime

'Pablo Escobar was a philanthropist and a murderer, loved in the Colombian slums for building football grounds, and houses... but not averse to having those who crossed him slaughtered or dismembered...'

Little did I realise that ten short years later I'd be working for Ken Bates's radio station. Also, I was wrong about Love Actually *and Martin Freeman.*

Football, a matter of life and death

Screen Break, The Guardian, *17 April 2006*

How important is football? Very, according to Melvyn Bragg, who chose The First Rule Book of the Football Association alongside Darwin, Shakespeare, and the King

James Bible as one of the *12 Books That Changed The World* for his new TV series last night. Bragg was on *Parkinson* on Saturday plugging the show, justifying footy's inclusion in his list, at the expense of Dickens and Dostoevsky.

Actually, forget Dostoevsky, it being Parky, Bragg mostly found himself arguing for the primacy of football over cricket. One of his arguments was that football has been a force for combating racism, on which point Parky begged to differ slightly. He thought the word 'combating' should be omitted. It made for an entertaining dust-up between two of the old buggers of British broadcasting, whose careers and hairstyles have diverged so spectacularly over the years.

Back in the Seventies, both went for the collar-length, post-Beatle comb forward, and generous sideburns; sort of Los Angeles Aztecs-era George Best, and while Parky's career in the intervening years has been, in the rather indelicate words of an Australian broadcasting executive I once knew, 'all over the place like a mad woman's shit' – remember *Give Us A Clue* and an old LBC show he used to do where he would babble interminably about Sarah Vaughan and Denis Compton – his hair has experienced minimal meddling. The sideburns have gone, the hair stops before the collar now, but it has been left to turn silvery in the style of a man who spits in the face of Grecian 2000.

Bragg, on the other hand, boasts a more linear CV, encompassing a succession of novels I am told could be categorised as steamy (I am afraid I have never read one; like snowboarding and learning the bassoon, it is one of those things I have just never managed to find the time to do) and various TV arts programmes. Bragg's programmes have become a little more cerebral recently, as his latest project demonstrates, and one is almost tempted to call him an egghead, except his lightly hennaed bouffant could only be compared to an egg whose whites had been separated and beaten into a stiff peak for a soufflé of some sort.

In truth, I was only watching *Parkinson* because an appearance by José Mourinho was promised, but it turned out the Special One was too special even for Parky, and instead we had Kathleen Turner promoting her new play, actor Martin Freeman plugging a forthcoming film, and Bragg beating the drum for his TV show.

I have to say the programme engendered in me some sympathy for Davina McCall, whose recent talk show flop has made her the most reviled broadcaster since Lord Haw Haw. There seemed little qualitative difference between McCall interviewing Eamonn Holmes, and Parky talking to a young actor, about whom the most interesting thing was that his naked bottom had been on display briefly in the worst film of the past fifty years (*Love Actually* – this is not opinion, it is provable fact). But then the Parky – Bragg spat pulled the show back.

The Yorkshire curmudgeon's view was that football had done little to foster any sort of understanding. What is more, when the young Parky used to go to Barnsley, he 'didn't need 2,000 policemen to control me.' And, as for black players, 'Charlie Williams used to play for Doncaster Rovers.' I should have been interested to hear Kathleen Turner's view on Doncaster Rovers's recruitment policy in the 1950s, but she wore the smile of the Sphinx. What a professional.

If Bragg were looking for historical reinforcement for football's presence in his list of world-shattering books, it was there in spades in a terrific documentary on BBC Four called *Communism and Football*, a vivid picture of a time when Bill Shankly's oft-quoted dictum about the importance of football could be taken literally.

Among the stories the programme told was that of

Spartak Moscow, founded in the 1930s and a lifeline for thousands of oppressed Russians, as it owed no allegiance to the army or secret police. Supporting Spartak became an act of resistance against Stalin's tyranny, infuriating the fearsome Lavrentiy Beria, one of Stalin's henchmen and president of Moscow Dynamo, the KGB's team. He ordered the execution of Spartak's main political supporter, and sent the club's founder and best player to a Siberian gulag for ten years. I mean, even Ken Bates...

What were the secret police doing with their own football team anyway? How did anyone know when a match was on? Did potential spectators have to find some shadowy figure in a dark overcoat, collar turned up against the icy wind, and wait for him to whisper, 'The sparrows fly south in the winter,' which meant Lokomotiv at home next Saturday? The players presumably would then be rounded up for the game by a knock on the door in the middle of the night and a torch shining in their face? And did the fans taunt rival supporters with chants of 'You're shit, and we know where you live'?

Well, no. In Russia, as in Hungary and East Germany, football was a deadly serious matter, its joys to be savoured surreptitiously. In those dark times, it was unarguably more significant than poetry or politics, in the conventional sense.

And to think it all started with some public schoolboys in England in 1863. Bragg is right, and Parky wrong, although on the hairstyle issue, the jury is still out.

Until BT and the streaming giants, with their famously deep pockets, joined the fray, Sky Sports won the Premier League every season. Plucky Irish challenger Setanta's UK operation lasted little more than a season. The seemingly indestructible Apprentice, *meanwhile, was only up to series three by 2007-2008 so the nation had not yet tired of delusional numb nuts playing market traders, and the programme was still creating water cooler moments (teenagers, ask a grown-up to explain water cooler moments, and indeed water coolers, to you).*

But what of The Apprentice*'s Jennifer Maguire? Turns out I was right about her, except her broadcasting career has been mostly in Ireland rather than the UK. She now trades under her married name of Jennifer Zamparelli, and has presented or co-presented several radio and TV shows in the Republic. If Google Images are to be believed, her lipstick is still very bright red.*

Climax of the 2007-08 Premier League Season

Screen Break, The Guardian, *12 May 2008*

It is difficult to diverge from the received wisdom – and the Sky Sports mantra – that yesterday was the most unprecedentedly, knicker-wettingly, orgasmically thrilling end to a Premier League season, as, for the first time, we arrived at the final day with two teams still in contention; Sky and Setanta.

With Sky having long ago gathered in most of football's glittering prizes, the plucky newcomers were left with a relegation tussle at Portsmouth to cover, but as it happened they got the best story. Fulham, at one time 1/50 for relegation, escaped thanks to three successive away victories, a feat they last achieved when Queen Victoria was a lad (I might not have that absolutely right; Setanta's commentator Jon Champion tends to throw more facts at you than it is possible for even a moderate drinker like me to absorb.)

Danny Murphy's late goal gave Setanta the opportunity for some fine shots of Roy Hodgson not getting excited. For the players, meanwhile, as the final whistle confirmed their survival, joy was unconfined. I am no expert, having a pretty well unblemished record of staunch heterosexuality going back more than thirty-five years, but the celebrations seemed something of a homo-erotic delight, with the players all stripped to the waist, hugging each other, watched by Fulham fan Hugh Grant in the stand, giving one of his winning smiles, and looking way more convincingly ecstatic than he ever did with Martine McCutcheon in *Love Actually*.

Hodgson had already suggested his joy would be more confined, saying he planned to celebrate a satisfactory outcome by going to bed with a glass of water and one of JP Donleavy's lesser works, *Schultz*. I did not hang around to find out if Hodgson was quizzed on the Donleavy issue by one of Setanta's young blonde pitchside reporters ('Why *Schultz*, Roy? Surely you would find *The Ginger Man* or *The Beastly Beatitudes of Balthazar B* more palatable after a long hard season?').

The money shot, I reckon, on the final day is at the home of one of the relegated clubs, where a dad will be giving a consoling hug to his heartbroken young lad, or a young man in a nearly empty stand lends a shoulder for his girlfriend to weep on, so I flipped to Sky interactive for the dénouement of the Birmingham – Blackburn match.

Maybe Brummies are made of sterner stuff than most football fans – or inured to disappointment – but there did not seem to be too much weeping going on at St Andrews. Fans looked crestfallen all right, and the cameras dutifully scanned the stands for fallen crests. 'You almost feel like you are intruding on private grief,' said commentator Alan Parry. Like that has ever stopped Sky.

Regular readers will know I am an inveterate flipper,

but yesterday I felt the nation was with me. As it became apparent the way the wind was blowing at Wigan and Stamford Bridge, those of us for whom the sight of Sir Alex Ferguson celebrating once again is about as welcome as another re-run of *Last Of The Summer Wine*, looked elsewhere. Excellent team, Manchester United, of course, but seeing Ferguson haranguing the fourth official in the first half when almost every decision had gone his way, made me yearn for the quiet dignity of Roy Hodgson.

I felt I had something of a personal stake in Fulham's survival as well, having appeared on Simon Mayo's sports panel on BBC Five Live on Friday, and alone in a line-up way more expert than me, having picked Hodgson's team as the likely survivors. It is so rare I get anything right, as Messrs William Hill, and my wife, will confirm, that here was more cause for celebration than another title for Manchester United.

Setanta has some way to go before catching up with the slickness and professionalism of Sky. As Dean Windass and Nicky Barmby demonstrated for Hull City in the Championship play-off, there is no substitute for experience, and Sky's presenter Richard Keys left an unsteady Angus Scott, his opposite number on Setanta, trailing in his wake. Scott promised us Setanta's cameras would be at Reading, which would have made for a quiet afternoon with the team away at Derby. Nonetheless, they lucked out, going to Fratton Park.

The relegation showdown is often more interesting than the title. There is, after all, something of *The Apprentice* – the nation's number one topic of conversation – about it, as teams are fired from the Premier League. On which topic, here is a prediction, while I am on a winning streak. If Jennifer Maguire, the Irishwoman with the rather too vivid a shade of lipstick (I believe it is marketed under the name Mad As A Mongoose), who was fired last week, is not presenting her own television show within a year, I will eat my socks.

No, I will eat Alex Ferguson's socks.

After the disaster of the 2010 World Cup in South Africa, a new Premier League season arrives to assuage the pain. But at least, unlike in Colombia, failure on the football field is not a matter of life and death.

Opening day, 2010-11 Premier League Season

Screen Break, The Guardian, *16 August 2010*

I always feel a new Premier League football season has not really started until Alan Shearer says, 'You can only beat what's put in front of you,' and we were less than fifteen minutes into *Match Of The Day* when he inaugurated the season thus, saluting Blackpool's victory over a Wigan side still more or less on their summer holidays. And lest you did not feel entirely at home, there was Steve Bruce's post-match interview, beginning, 'The last thing I want to do is come on here and criticise referees...', before – guess what – proceeding to not so much criticise Anthony Taylor, as suggest he should not be in the job.

The post-match roasting of referees, as keen-eyed habitues will know, is a role traditionally shared on *MOTD* between Bruce and Sam Allardyce, but with Alex Ferguson reportedly on the brink of renouncing his vow of BBC silence, there may be a new player in the mix, so it was as well Steve got in early doors, as we nostalgists like to say.

Harry Redknapp completed the first day feeling of *plus*

ça change by confirming that his adverbophobia – a condition involving the avoidance of adverbs in all circumstances – has still not cleared up. 'We moved the ball fantastic,' said Harry.

Actually, that sums it up good. I watched the Spurs match live on Sky, and in the first half at least their football was the most pleasing of the day, played in front of Sky's new host, close-season signing from *GMTV* Ben Shephard. The new anchor did not seem overawed to find himself occupying Richard Keys's hallowed seat, coping rather well considering he had been lumbered with Sven-Göran Eriksson as a pundit. Sven's track record in football speaks of solid managerial qualities, but on TV he always brings to mind the title of that fine Coen brothers movie, *The Man Who Wasn't There*.

'What would you be saying to Manchester City at half time if you were their manager?' asked Shephard, to which the Swede responded with his trademark extended 'We-e-ll,' an enigmatic smile, and the following wisdom: 'They'll have to play better, that's for sure.' Gee thanks, Sven.

In all, though, it was fun not to be taking football too seriously, after the World Cup, when everything seemed so important. As my colleague Simon Burnton pointed out in Saturday's paper, nothing seems to matter terribly on opening day. The sight of English goalkeepers – Green, Carson, Kirkland – flapping comically, West Ham's masterclass in supine defending, all can be smiled upon indulgently in the knowledge there is plenty of time to put things right.

The Colombian national team had no such luxury, after World Cup failure in 1994, as a gripping documentary, *The Two Escobars*, on ESPN, made clear. I would urge you to seek out a repeat of Jeff and Michael Zimbalist's stunning film chronicling the rise to Latin American pre-eminence of football in Colombia, fuelled by drug money, notably from notorious gangster Pablo Escobar.

Wrestling in Honey

There is an old Marty Feldman sketch in which he describes some long-gone East End hoodlum as 'a gentleman'. 'He was a gentleman, and a murderer,' said Feldman admiringly. In similar vein, Escobar was a philanthropist and a murderer, loved in the Colombian slums for building football grounds, and houses for people living on rubbish dumps, but not averse to having those who crossed him slaughtered or dismembered.

'He managed the underworld,' said an associate. 'If you messed with Pablo's people he'd find you and make you pay. With my own hands I've killed around 250 people. But only a psycopath keeps count.'

The film was full of sly, darkly comic moments like this, and was admirable for the depth of research, boasting interviews with every key figure from one of the most turbulent periods in Colombia's recent history, and for turning up remarkable contemporary footage.

Football, the film explained, was a handy channel for laundering drug money, with ticket sales being in cash, and figures easily doctored. What particularly resonated for a British audience was the way fans were prepared to look the other way, when the football was as exhilarating as that played by Atlético Nacional of Medellin in the Copa Libertadores, and the Colombian national team in their run to the 1994 World Cup finals.

But the finals took place in the US with bloodshed rife back home in Colombia, following the murder of Pablo Escobar, as drug cartels fought to fill the vacuum, and the US continued to wage its unwinnable War On Drugs. With the team riven by worries about loved ones back home, the exemplary Colombian full back Andrés Escobar (no relation to Pablo, and nothing in common bar surname) had the misfortune to score the own goal that all but eliminated

Colombia, and ten days later was shot dead back home. The film suggests that the shocking murder was little more than a consequence of the lawlessness at the time, but did tend to confirm that Bill Shankly's much-quoted maxim about life, death, and football could not be more wrong.

Premier League v FA Cup; Sky v BBC, and the joy of Lineker

Blog post, 18 April 2015

I yield to no-one in my love of the old days – warm beer, cricket on the village green, bobbies on bicycles two by two, all that – but it's rare a chance arises to compare the rose-tinted past with the brave new world, as it did yesterday evening when Sky's high-octane Premier League coverage went head-to-head with Arsenal-Reading in the FA Cup semi-final on the BBC.

As we know, the Premier League may have the money, the prestige, the global renown, but what the FA Cup has is history, and boy does the BBC love a bit of history.

Lest you were in any doubt, its coverage of the semi-final kicked off with footage of the late Sir Laurence Olivier doing the St Crispin's Day speech from the film of *Henry V* ('We happy few, We band of brothers,' and so on).

The excuse, I guess, was that Reading's nickname is The Royals, but as the Championship team are also known as The Biscuitmen (a reference to the town's major industry in the halcyon days) I assume the only reason Sir Larry got the nod is because no footage exists of Dame Edith Evans dunking a cream puff.

The BBC even gave us a moment of history at half-time

with a breakdown, something that used to be a regular feature of TV outside broadcasts, when a feature on Crystal Palace's shock semi-final victory over Liverpool 25 years ago came to a shuddering halt halfway through.

In those circumstances the BBC is fortunate to retain the services of Gary Lineker, by some distance the best presenter of live football on TV. Sky have never really replaced the disgraced Richard Keys, who wasn't universally loved, or even liked much, but had the benefit of longevity in the post, something often undervalued. The BBC, if it remains serious about sport, needs to fight hard to avoid Lineker falling into the hands of rivals.

Not that Sky's presenters are less than perfectly competent – David Jones did the job yesterday – but it's never a good sign when you have to go to Google Images to check on which one it is.

Clearly, the price of live Premier League football has now soared way beyond the reach of the BBC, which may be the clincher in Lineker's future. While the BBC's match had the lion's share of the goalmouth action, even a channel flipper like me, who considers himself more or less immune to Sky's hype, and has a real interest in who reaches the FA Cup final (I backed Liverpool to win it several rounds ago at 9/2), found it difficult to resist turning over to Sky from time to time.

Having invested its eye-watering billions in the Premier League, Sky doesn't skimp on the peripheries (although it might have to when the new, tooth-achingly, eye-watering deal kicks in).

The sound always seems a little crisper, and in punditry, where Sky offers us the Rolls Royce of analysts, Gary Neville, the BBC counters with the comfortable, but mid-range Danny Murphy. In the commentary box, Sky fields

Martin Tyler for its big matches in the certain knowledge he'll rarely make a bad call, while the BBC never seems sure who its best commentator is.

My view is that the top man was on the job yesterday. Steve Wilson is commendably unfussy, and made the most of what was undoubtedly the evening's bigger story. The outcome on Sky was depressingly predictable.

The BBC may miss out on the Premier League's pricey weekly thrills, but took the biscuit last night.

All Our Yesterdays

No 58: **The Benny Hill Show** (1955–1989),
The Independent, 24 June 2002

If a skilled farceur like Benny Hill had been French, he would have been garlanded with every honour the arts world has to offer, and would not have been allowed to slip away virtually uncelebrated in 1992, at the age of 68.

● Forget the sexism, forget the scantily clad Hill's Angels (of whom Jane Leeves, Daphne in *Frasier*, was one; her last credible performance). Hill was simply Britain's first and greatest television comedian. That is, although he had appeared on radio and in the halls, he was the first comedian to make his name on the TV, the first to develop a style exclusively suited to the tube. He appeared on BBC television in 1949, when many performers still thought it a fad that would never replace the wireless, and from 1955 until 1969, when he defected to Thames, there were regular series and eagerly awaited Christmas specials. Hill was best known in those days for surprisingly sharp parodies of other TV shows, like Fanny Craddock's cookery programmes and *Watch With Mother*, and for his saucy comic songs, like 'Harvest of Love' which made the charts.

The Thames shows became a little broader, although it is often forgotten that the 1970s were that kind of decade – compare the *Carry On* films of that era with the earlier ones – and in 1989, Hill became a hapless victim of the new prudery and his show was cancelled. It did not stop the Americans lapping up Hill's old shows and hailing him a comic genius. The Americans were right.

14. Euros, World Cups and Olympics

'Nobody, it seems, yngles quite like we yngle...'

England, Fabio Capello and Adrian Chiles, what fun!

Screen Break, The Guardian, *6 September 2010*

Who, I should like to know, is spending £2.99 a week on the part work, offering 'three full episodes of the TV show *Bonanza* on DVD, and a companion guide'? And why would you need a 'companion guide'? I seem to remember the show, which ran from 1959 to 1973, as fairly routine soap opera, which could easily be followed without guidance, even if viewed through the wrong side of a balaclava while humming Rosemary Clooney's latest toe-tapper.

Bonanza was chiefly famous for its theme tune, which went dum da da dum dad a dum dum *Bonanza*, and for the fact that for unspecified reasons, they used to set fire to a map at the start of the show. It starred Lorne Greene, an actor with a dark brown voice and a silvery grey toupée, as the patriarch of the Ponderosa ranch, a widower living with his three sons; one obese, a handsome one always dressed in black, and another I have forgotten. Each week one or other would get into some sort of scrape, but the family would rally round proving that a good, wholesome American family could defeat any kind of evil (code for Communism, I suspect, although I missed that at the time).

My parents enjoyed the show, ignoring my innuendoes about the boys, who were often to be found in the proximity of pretty girls with pinched waists and neat bosoms, but, like Liberace and Edward Heath, could 'never find the right woman to settle down with.'

I perhaps paid more attention to the *Bonanza* ads than I should have, as they were running in the build-up to the England match on ITV on Friday, and were more interesting than the uncomfortably stilted badinage between host Adrian Chiles and his pundits. I found myself looking out for that little black and white spinning wheel in the top right hand corner of the screen, signalling an imminent commercial break, and relief from the tedious pre-match Capello-centric chitty chat.

It does not help that Chiles currently has all the relaxed charm of a hostage being forced at gunpoint to make a video asking his relatives to leave a large sum of money in a hollow tree, before they start receiving body parts by registered post. I do not know what has happened to Chiles. Without being funny himself, at his best, on programmes like *The Apprentice – You're Fired*, he engendered an atmosphere of good humour through his ease with live television – not a skill to be undervalued – and a certain bluff geniality.

On Friday, though – maybe under the pressure of being chosen to satisfy the overwhelming national desire for a new breakfast TV show – all that seemed to have disappeared. He was laboured, and actually appeared nervous. While his panel bludgeoned home the familiar complaints about Capello's tactical intransigence, and inability to connect with some of his players, actually talking at one point about 'losing the dressing room', the host ploughed his usual West Brom furrow: 'We're rubbish, us, but we'll support us till we die, because that's the kind of wacky folk we are. Back with more after the break.'

Danny Murphy was an addition to the regular punditry duo of Andy Townsend and Gareth Southgate, presumably in a bid to recreate the rapport Chiles used to have with Lee Dixon on *MOTD2*, but on Friday's evidence that may be some distance away.

One further complaint; whoever told ITV that shooting the England manager at a 45 degree angle as if he was *Citizen Kane* would make his pre-match interview with Gabriel Clarke more interesting, was wrong. Oh, and I am fed up with The Verve, and the 'England band' endlessly playing 'Tom Hark' and *The Great Escape* is only marginally less annoying than the vuvuzela.

I am conscious of having been something of a cross patch this week, so allow me to finish by applauding BBC Four for its North of England stuff. Last week the channel, which has lifted television archaeology to new heights, had some magnificent archive programmes about Blackpool; and tomorrow night (Tuesday) it does a similar job for another distinctly northern phenomenon, rugby league.

There is an exceptional new documentary about Eddie

Waring, of which I have seen a preview, which while largely sympathetic explains why Eddie's efforts on behalf of the self-styled Greatest Game were sometimes viewed sceptically on his home turf, a classic Cup final from 1978, and a screening of Lindsay Anderson's epoch-making film, *This Sporting Life*. It is no *Bonanza*, but it remains the best film about sport you will ever see.

❧

I leave the sofa for the 2010 World Cup – not a wise move

Screen Break, The Guardian, *28 June 2010*

If your Sunday afternoon was ruined, at least you did not suffer in front of an angry mob.

I have been doing a little work for Leeds City Council during the World Cup, hosting England's matches on the big screen in Leeds's Millennium Square – while local councils are still able to afford things like hosts (and indeed Squares) – so I am more or less the public face of the England team in the city, and possibly for visitors from as far away as Ossett and Cleckheaton. Round this manor I am the public face of what I believe we are now contractually obliged to call England's World Cup debacle.

As many as 8,000 people have been packing into Leeds's grand piazza for big matches according to the council, although attendances have looked to me to be more in the order of five or six thousand. It is possible I was hired to keep the numbers down to manageable levels. The point is, whatever the exact tally, it is a bigger crowd than I am accustomed to entertaining while preparing this piece, and has given me a different perspective on the TV coverage.

My normal routine would be to watch both channels

carefully through the week in the comfort and (occasional) quiet of my own home, consider their relative performances, and deliver some sort of fair and balanced assessment.

The verdict of the common people tends to be more instant, and frankly more unforgiving, as I discovered during the England – USA match when I was met with a hail of (thankfully) plastic bottles (*Telegraph* readers, I guess), as I first took the stage to draw the mob's attention to the fine temporary toilet facilities provided by their caring council and recommend them over any ad hoc arrangements they might have been considering. I realised then I had been engaged less as a presenter, more as a target.

Equally muscular responses were prompted by the sudden appearance of the giant heads of presenters, pundits, and commentary teams when we switched on TV coverage of the matches. There was not so much in the way of missiles – even a well-refreshed rabble is smart enough not to waste its ammo on targets several thousand miles away – but plenty of what PG Wodehouse used to call chi-iking.

Giant Adrian Chiles, I have noticed over the tournament, has been greeted with particular, not venom exactly, but definitely disrespect, as a knot of the more forthright critics began a chant relating to a solitary sexual pursuit. I am assuming this kind of abuse is an inevitable consequence of recent publicity, reports of his salary, and the fact that he gets to share a sofa with Christine Bleakley. Giant Gary Lineker, interestingly, provoked a more muted reaction, despite the crisp commercials, the young girlfriend, and probably being far better rewarded than Chiles, which shows what a fickle beast *La Foule*, as Edith Piaf called it, can be.

Before switching to TV coverage, I have been leading the crowd in football karaoke, lusty renditions by the assembly of the better-known football anthems – a job I have dreamt of doing since I saw Ed 'Stewpot' Stewart do something similar at a rugby league cup final at Wembley in the 'Eighties, and which yesterday turned out to be the highlight of the afternoon – and showing footage of great World Cup moments presented by John Motson. Motty is always warmly received, pointing up the Motson-shaped hole at the heart of BBC's commentary team, currently being occupied by Guy Mowbray.

Mowbray, neither a compulsive phrase maker like Peter Drury nor a screamer (not in the slang sense, not that there is anything wrong with that) like Jonathan Pearce, strikes me as a good choice. In as much as you can make much of an impression in an atmosphere swinging from febrile to funereal, Mowbray seems sure-footed and his unfussy style does not invite nostalgic comparison with Motty's schoolboy enthusiasm nor with Barry Davies's occasionally schoolmasterly pedantry.

The mob was not too happy with him yesterday, of course, nor with anyone else, including obviously the local face of England's World Cup. 'Night begins to fall,' said Mowbray as England's challenge dribbled out. Mine fell not under the expected hail of plastic bottles, but before a departing crowd too stunned to throw.

'Who's On First?' is a 1930s comedy routine popularised by American vaudevillians Bud Abbott and Lou Costello. It revolves round a baseball line-up of players with names that could serve as questions. The first baseman, for instance, is called 'Who.' The hilarity starts from that. Jon Champion is the only commentator I've heard reference the gag, for which in my view he deserves a BAFTA of some sort.

Maradona's Arse – star of World Cup 2010, South Africa

Screen Break, The Guardian, *14 June 2010*

If we remember the 1990 World Cup for Gazza's tears, or Roger Milla's dance, there is a fair chance the enduring image of this competition will be Diego Maradona's backside. Boy, that is some tuchus. And when you are the proud possessor of a heiny the size of a small South American republic, what shows it off better than a lightweight grey suit?

Clearly, there is pride involved, because the little magician is turning his mighty caboose to the camera at every opportunity. First there was the training/bonding exercise where the winning team was invited to fire shots at the manager's behind, footage that seemed to be on some sort of a continuous loop so often was it shown in the first couple of days of World Cup coverage. Then there was Diego's celebration of Heinze's goal against Nigeria, a joyous rear-view shot of the great man cuddling one of his subs, and shaking his booty like a five-bob stripper. I swear it was still moving when Nigeria kicked off again.

Instead of yet another otiose South African travelogue (memo to BBC and ITV: we do not need to see one more reporter in a township 'bantering' with the locals – we get it) why not take us on a Cook's tour round Diego's gluteus maximus, possibly looking at the place of the rump in football iconography (keen students of the low centre of gravity in our national game will know that Leeds United's well-upholstered forward Tony Yeboah is the only player to have won *Match Of The Day*'s Goal of the Month contest two months in succession)?

I am hoping Argentina go all the way, because I believe

Diego has so much more to give. This is a man, remember, who, while recovering from addictions and weighing in at around 20 stones, allowed a TV crew to film him being hosed down in Cuba as part of his 'treatment', a man who chose to host a chaotic, off-the-wall TV chat show as part of his recovery. In many ways he is the bastard love child of Bobby Charlton and Russell Harty (kids, ask your dad). Gabby and Gabriel, you must leave the England camp now. Nobody in there has anything interesting to say. On behalf of the audience back home, we need you both on 24-hour Diego-watch.

Another highlight of the Argentina-Nigeria match was Mick McCarthy, BBC co-commentator, not only for his no-nonsense approach to the game ('Gerr 'old o' someone an' mark 'im' was his sound advice to the Nigerians at corners, that fancy zonal marking being summat they have no truck wi' round Barnsley way), but also for his adherence to the aberrant Yorkshire 't,' indicting Nigeria for their 'drettful' marking.

I believe banks often site their telephone services in Yorkshire because surveys show we associate the accent with common sense and financial probity (How is that going, by the way, banks?), so when McCarthy calls a spade a bloody shovel, one is similarly inclined to believe he knows of what he speaks. He may turn out to be as wrong-headed as the banks, but for the time being he seems a good signing for the BBC.

The only problem was my ears had become nicely attuned to Mick's flat vowels and deliberate delivery, when I was confronted by studio guest Emmanuel Adebayor's 200 mile-an-hour punditry. I received a tweet suggesting IwritethewholescreenbreakcolumninthestyleofManu, who is the vocal equivalent of a typewriter (kids, ask your dad again) without a space bar. I got about one word in every three.

Finally, hosannas to ITV commentator Jon Champion for the most enjoyable commentary of the World Cup so far, on the Greece-South Korea match. 'Who is the South Korean coach?' Jon asked summariser Craig Burley, a jokey reference to Huh (Jung-Moo), who is indeed the South Korean coach, not, as the commentary made clear, casual racism, but an Abbott and Costello reference (kids, I promise you, you will not have to trouble your dad again), something in which modern football coverage is sadly deficient.

The other chucklesome moment enlivening a dull match was Jon's description of Greece coach Otto Rehhagel's hair as 'unfeasibly dark for a man his age.' 'How appropriate,' said Champers, 'that a Grecian should stand accused of colouring his hair.' All right, Otto is actually German, but anyone unwilling to let the facts get in the way of a good joke has my support for the rest of the competition.

Summer 2007, Britain was preparing for the 2012 Olympics, and it seemed it was just me and comedian Frankie Boyle holding out against it.

Yngling confusion eased by reverse Shankly

Screen Break, The Guardian, *16 July 2007*

It is difficult to get fully involved in a sport you cannot pronounce, which may be just one of the reasons yngling has never really caught on with me. I mean, are you supposed to say yingling, ingling, or ngling? Or is it one of those words like Cholmondeley, which sound nothing like they are spelt, created purely to confuse foreigners? The commentators on the BBC on Saturday were going with ingling as far as I could hear, although mostly they copped out and covered it in a caption.

For the uninitiated, it is a form of yacht racing, restricted, I think, to hearty blonde types called Sarah mostly, with the odd Pippa thrown in for comic relief. Britain is rather good at it, and can usually be relied upon to pick up an Olympic medal or two in the discipline. Nobody, it seems, yngles quite like we yngle.

There are, of course, scandalously, for a variety of historical class-based reasons, far too many Olympic medals doled out to people in boats, and too few to darts and snooker players, but that is a separate issue. I would not, for one moment, suggest yngling medals are easy to come by. Though I have never actually yngled myself, not as such, I imagine propelling a sailing boat through the water at speed takes some strength and skill; not as much as a seven-dart finish, but skill none the less.

The problem with it as a television sport is that, unlike, say, darts, to take a sport at random, it is not always easy to make out what is going on. Apart from the overhead shot of the yachts in a line shortly after the start, and the odd zoom in on one of the Sarahs or Pippas having trouble hoisting the whatsit up the thingy and maybe getting a slight dunking for her pains, there is not a great deal in it for us landlubbers, born, in the immortal words of Pete Townshend, with a plastic spoon in our mouth.

The BBC coverage of the World Sailing Championships from Cascais in Portugal homed in, therefore, on the apparent animosity between yngling skipper Shirley Robertson, and Sarah Ayton, who was in another of the British boats. As it turned out Ayton and Sarah Webb won yngling gold, and

Robertson a mere bronze. 'This, I guess, is about as hard as it gets,' presenter Richard Simmonds said to Shirley. 'It's only sport. It's not real life,' she replied, in what, in yngling terms, you might call a reverse Shankly.

I notice, by the way, that the BBC is now billing itself before events such as this as 'The Olympic Broadcaster', hoping, one presumes, to snaffle a little bit of the kudos of the games, in much the same way as 'Mayor of London' was plastered over all the Tour de France signs last weekend, creating the impression that the Tour was in fact the personal invention of Ken Livingstone.

The BBC should be careful, though. Not everyone is cheerleading for the games quite as enthusiastically as the Corporation. As comedian Frankie Boyle said on *Mock The Week*, the best of the extraordinary proliferation of topical quiz shows currently being broadcast: 'The Olympics are supposed to restore our sense of national pride and self-worth. For 9.2 billion pounds, we could have written "Fuck off Germany" on the moon.' That was one of a number of solid gags the brilliantly abrasive Glasgow comedian delivered, assuring the programme a good showing in this year's very narrow BAFTA category of 'Best Topical Quiz Show Without Marcus Brigstocke In It.'

Frankie, I suspect may have missed out on the polo, broadcast by Sky yesterday, which I watched as part of this week's round-up of posh sports, or at least sports you were unlikely to conceive an undying passion for growing up in Salford 6. The England Ladies strolled to victory over the Rest Of The World, 9- 3, which may not go quite as far in restoring our sense of national self-worth as Frankie's suggested lunar manifesto, but was an impressive performance nonetheless. There cannot be many sports in which we can take on a Rest Of The World team and give them such a sound thrashing.

Like the yngling ladies, the England polo players – Emma Tomlinson and Nina Clarkin were the ones interviewed – glowed with good health, good sense, and team spirit, and brought to mind irresistible echoes of John Betjeman's Miss Joan Hunter Dunn, 'Furnished and burnished by Aldershot sun.'

I always feel the horses get a rough deal in polo, though. They get balked an awful lot, and just as it must be difficult for the riders to keep changing pace and direction in order to whack the ball, it must put a tremendous strain on the horses' joints as well, and nobody talks much about them.

Finally, thank you to not one but two distinguished academics who wrote to comment on last week's column. In a three-page email, Karl Baker of the University of the Arts, London, quotes Kierkegaard and Paul de Man to draw parallels between tennis commentator David Mercer's use of the word 'ironic' and Laurence Sterne's continual use of parabasis in *Tristram Shandy*.

On the same topic, Mark J Jones, Research Fellow in the Department of Linguistics at Cambridge University, points out that language change is constant and unforgiving, and my railing against it is like Cnut trying to stop the tide.

At least, I think he said Cnut.

We have already agreed that I was wrong about almost everything, so it was no surprise to find me doubting the wisdom of the escalating costs of the London Olympics, back in 2011. In fairness, my cynicism was in support of the excellent BBC satire, Twenty Twelve. *Also I appear to have been spot on about Gary Neville.*

Sex, the Olympics, and, er, Ken Bates

Screen Break, The Guardian, *22 August 2011*

There has been much amusement round my manor of late following Leeds United chairman Ken Bates's latest programme notes in which, after his customary rant about chucking out asylum seekers, and bringing back capital punishment, he likens his stewardship of the club to the sex act.

'In an age of instant gratification,' wrote Bates, 'Leeds United is like having a long, drawn out affair with plenty of foreplay and slow arousal.' Cue widespread spluttering over half-time Bovril, especially by those taking the view that there are no circumstances in which the concepts of foreplay, slow arousal, and Ken Bates should ever be allowed to appear so closely together in any one sentence.

It was certainly a tough image to shake off, and I fear I found myself returning to it when watching the brilliant satire on our preparations for the Olympics, *Twenty Twelve* on BBC Two. If supporting Leeds United, I thought, is akin to being slowly pleasured by a bearded bigot, then hosting the Olympics is like being locked in a loveless marriage.

Oh, it started well enough, as is often the case, amid what the great philosopher Mama Cass, in an entirely different context, called 'rockets, bells, and poetry.' That is when somebody should have had the sense to plead just cause and impediment, but instead we are left looking in the mirror each morning and realising we are stuck together, us and the Olympics.

Fortunately, this is exactly the kind of sad condition in which the British situation comedy specialises; from Steptoe trapped with his dad, through Basil and Sybil Fawlty, to Tim in *The Office* destined never to escape Wernham Hogg.

Twenty Twelve continues that downbeat tradition. It is set in the offices of the Olympic Deliverance Commission (deliverance, geddit?) around two years away from the start of the games, with Mama Cass's rockets and bells having long since faded.

Instead, a quote from the fourth Earl of Chesterfield seems more pertinent: 'The pleasure is momentary, the position ridiculous, and the expense damnable,' he said, speaking neither of Leeds United nor of Olympic bids as it happens, but getting it about right.

Like much of writer and director John Morton's work, *Twenty Twelve* is full of sly humour that creeps up on you and takes you by surprise, like a lubricious partner in an early morning shower (anyone can do this stuff, Ken).

For instance, when Sebastian Coe's representative on earth, the permanently harassed Head of Deliverance, played to the hilt by Hugh Bonneville, reports, 'Seb has come up with an idea we take part in the London Marathon,' his Head of Sustainability's deadpan, almost throwaway, response is: 'When you say enter it, you mean what? Run it?'

The Commission's task in last week's episode was to find a new head of the Cultural Olympiad after the 'departure of the previous incumbent because of uncreative differences of vision.' The candidates are a voluble woman, fresh from her triumph in charge of Belfast, European City of Dance, who promises 'a real commonality of creative purpose through a shared awareness of diversity,' a laid-back hip-hop performer, and an attractive young woman with nothing much to say, but who boasted 'a brief spell as younger sister of one of Boris Johnson's girlfriends at Oxford.'

Sure, *Twenty Twelve* arrives rather at the fag-end of the spoof reality / mockumentary craze, whose apotheosis was *The Office*, but some of the detail does not suffer greatly from comparison with Ricky Gervais (the name of the PR company, Perfect Curve, for instance, is spot on, as is the way the candidates for the culture job, however artsy and away with the fairies they may appear, make sure they get a receipt from the taxi driver who drops them off).

Olympo-scepticism may not be the main point of the show – the familiar targets of meeting-speak and office politics take more of a pounding – but even a tiny dissenting voice is welcome in an atmosphere where we are all being encouraged to paint on our brightest smiles, forget the damnable cost, up from an estimate of around £2.4 billion to £10 billion, and fondly imagine that, even with the battalions of Pringles Crisps and Coca Cola firmly in cahoots, the event might lead to one less obese kid in Britain.

Finally, I do not often do requests, but I received an email this week from J Spencer of Warrington, asking me to comment – unfavourably, I got the impression – on Gary Neville's debut as a football pundit on Sky. Sorry Mr Spencer but I think punditry may be the job the former Manchester United man was born to do.

Though he looked a little edgy, shifting uneasily from foot to foot when Sky made him do the standing-up-playing-video-games thing, he seemed sensible, knowledgeable, and delivered his wisdom without frills, and at a time when others are opting for amiable novelty acts like Robbie Savage in the pundit's chair, that is as cheering – this one's for you, Ken – as a long snog in a shop doorway on a winter's night.

The great joy of big international soccer tournaments is that you get to whore yourself out to a whole lot of new people.

2016 European soccer championships, England drawn in group with Wales

FourFourTwo *website, 16 June 2016*

Don't you love these two o'clock in the afternoon kick-offs? Watching a football match during office hours always feels delightfully sinful, even if like me you had nothing else to do anyway, and would probably have been watching *Duel at Silver Creek* (PG, 1952) on Film 4 if the match weren't on.

On the BBC, though, the early kick-offs – or kicks-off for my pedant audience – put the presenter under added pressure, given precedent on the channel, notably the sainted Desmond Lynam's performance in similar circumstances.

'Good afternoon, shouldn't you be at work?' (with suggestively raised eyebrow) was Sir Des's famous welcome to the England-Tunisia group game at France '98. He didn't quite twirl his moustache, but the thought was there.

As early as Euro '96 Des had set the benchmark for ironically low-key intros: 'Good evening, you've obviously heard there's a football match on tonight,' he said, in advance of the keenly anticipated semi-final between England and Germany. It made Gary Lineker's 'Thought you'd find a way. Glad you could make it,' yesterday seem a little under-powered. Perhaps he needs to grow a moustache.

Actually, Gary was more hesitant than usual all afternoon, and I'm wondering if there were technical problems, because during the post-match chat his talkback was clearly audible on my sofa.

He also had an extra pundit to cope with. The BBC likes

to arrive mob-handed at moments of great national significance and fielded a four on the 'experts' bench, where the industry standard is a three. With Wales's John Hartson and Dean Saunders joining regulars Alan Shearer and Rio Ferdinand – 270 caps between them, Gary reminded us – it meant an extra voice to tell us what 'a massive, massive match' it was (I counted five reminders before kick-off of the inescapable massiveness of it all).

Not that there was any need to keep telling us. The extra seat was reminder enough, and it even seemed to get to Roy Hodgson, who, in his pre-match interview with Gabby Logan, seemed, in the words of one of my Twitter friends 'as nervous as a kitten in a tumble dryer.'

He got away with it though – no more than that – and was commendably humble post-match, which can't be easy with Gabby screaming at you about how much of a genius you are with your substitutions. He smiled winningly, and gave thanks to circumstances: 'Er, I wasn't counting on being 1-0 down,' was his explanation of his tactical acumen.

As much as I join the rest of the nation in cursing Hodgson when it seems appropriate, there are times when you can't help liking him.

Unless she had been overdosing on Haribo or had taken too much caffeine on board, problems with the microphones were probably to blame for Gabby sounding so shouty and over-excited in her post-match interviews, which makes it all the more ironic that the mic in the tunnel pre-match caught perfectly Joe Hart's battle-cry to his team-mates to 'keep the fucking ball.'

Commentator Guy Mowbray apologised – because obviously you would never expect to hear swearing at a football match – but how doubly ironic that it was Hart himself who failed to keep the fucking ball from Bale's free-kick.

Potty mouth Hart was given a wide berth post-match. The deeply religious Daniel Sturridge was unlikely to test the BBC's profanity filter, and predictably perhaps, he ascribed his winner to divine intervention. Twice in his post-match interview he pronounced himself 'grateful to God for allowing me to score.' As someone without religion, it's an attitude that always puzzles me – equally when you see players cross themselves after scoring. If God is with you when you score a vital goal, where is he when you miss that sitter?

And now for England's final match it's over to ITV, who have been a smidgin more continental in their selections for the punditry seats. I shall be disappointed if they don't stick with the impressive Slaven Bilić in the middle of a mobile three.

By 2018 and the World Cup in Russia, nobody was looking for colourful essays – not from me anyway – to adorn the newspaper two days after the match, so instant reaction for the website became the norm.

England 2 Sweden 0

Instant reaction for the Guardian *website, 7 July 2018*

Say what you like about the BBC, they're invariably by our side at moments of great national celebration; the Coronation, the wedding of Prince Harry and Meghan Markle, the end of another season of *Question Time*.

And we were happy they were in charge yesterday (and not only because a majority of recent England disasters have been hosted by the commercial channel) despite a start that could have gone badly wrong, with Gary Lineker's unnecessarily downbeat: 'Where's Des Lynam when you need him?' Relax Gary, you're playing a blinder.

The nervy start wasn't helped by a montage of our last successful quarter-final, against Cameroon at Italia '90, inviting those of us who are veterans of tournament football, to rue the absence of such outspoken Ron Managers of yesteryear as Terry Venables and Jimmy Hill. No need; pundits Shearer, Ferdinand, and especially Klinsmann, were spot on in their judgement.

Klinsmann, for instance, warned us that the first twenty minutes would be slow, so when it turned out to be not so much slow as narcoleptic – a couple of bookie ads would actually have been blessed relief – we were prepared.

One of the major differences between yesterday and Italia '90 was the knowledge that big matches like this are now social media occasions as much as TV showpieces. It means a new awareness that the audience at home – with our 'trotters up', as recommended by Danny Dyer in the build-up – or in town squares throughout Britain are part of the occasion, as much as those at the centre of it.

Shearer urged us to shout and scream and go crazy, suggesting the players can hear it. For a man who reportedly used to spend summer Saturdays creosoting his fence, this was quite a conversion. But Lineker does that. He relaxes his team. It's a chat in the snug of a favourite pub, where Mark Pougatch on the other side, albeit perfectly professional, hosts a rather stiff dinner party.

Scenes of celebration in Newcastle, Croydon, and Leeds punctuated the action yesterday, and England's Fabian Delph, recently returned from Leeds where he attended the birth of his third child, assured he had passed on West Yorkshire's good wishes to his colleagues. Invited by Gabby

Logan to comment on his happy event, he described his wife as an 'absolute machine', which I can assure you passes for praise in Leeds. Picked up by Lineker, it was soon all over Twitter.

Also on Twitter, and reported to me by my daughter who was in Millennium Square, Leeds, was a boisterous chant disparaging the Swedish team, while praising the looks of their female fans. In some venues, social media tells us, Swedish fans responded with 'Go home to your ugly wives,' to the tune of 'Go West', the one battle of the afternoon the Swedes convincingly won.

In fairness to the fans, even in the age of #metoo, it does seem to be the main task of TV at a big match to find a lingering shot of an attractive female fan or two, which is undeniably easier when Sweden or Brazil are playing.

'It was never going to be a blockbuster,' was Gary's honest verdict on the match, but these days whatever the quality, the fans miles away from the action can make it one.

15. Cricket Lovely Cricket

'The thwack of leather against willow, the village green, Joan Sims as the district nurse on a bicycle, and is there honey still for tea?'

Five years before the triumph of the 2012 Olympics it was still OK to make jokes about the cost, and Lord David Gower with 'a cigar on', becoming a regular theme of these columns. The attenuated Liz Hurley wedding I can't remember. Nor probably can she.

Cricket World Cup in the Caribbean, Lord Gower presiding

Screen Break, The Guardian, *19 March 2007*

The cricket World Cup is going to be with us for some time so we may as well get used to it; 54 matches stretching out over eight whole weeks. That is an awful long time for one sporting tournament, a cricketing eternity. By the time it is finished, we will be inhabiting a different world. The cost of the London Olympics will have risen to a figure so immense that the only way to pay for it will be to persuade Philip Green it is his birthday party, I will have had to renew my car insurance, Liz Hurley's wedding may even be over. In the meantime, I am not sure I can stomach another presenter in the West Indies telling me: 'It doesn't get any better than this.'

David Gower was first off the mark on Sky's preview show: 'Welcome to Barbados,' said Lord Gower, addressing the huddled masses at home, adjusting our mufflers and trying to warm our hands on mugs of Cup a Soup, 'The bananas, the coconuts, the sun, the sand, and the sea...' Guess what? 'It doesn't get any better than this.'

In case we did not entirely get the message, Sky's set was a wooden platform on a Caribbean beach at twilight, providing an appropriately colonial feel to Gower's cocktail hour chat-ins. Just out of shot, I expect, was a boy with a tray of expertly mixed large gin and tonics, while in a nearby bar a stubbly Graham Greene anti-hero downed neat whisky while suffocating in *weltschmerz*, or one of those other German things.

None of that for Lord Snooty, though, whom one hopes is well supplied with sun block, because as the week wore on, he grew steadily more burnished. Eventually I assume he will turn an attractive nut-brown colour, but at the moment he appears a little red and shiny, and with the grey/white hair spikier than previously, he looks like you imagine Sting might after a particularly strenuous demonstration of tantric sex.

And if Gower was rather sticking it to those of us condemned to follow the action from, say, a sofa in Wakefield, Manish Bhasin, presenting the BBC's highlights show on Saturday night, was simply – forgive my directness – taking the piss. I did not hear what he was saying because I was busy presenting my award-winning radio show and had the sound turned down – some of us have to work for a living – but I could see him walking along a beach, with the crystal clear waters of the Caribbean actually lapping around his bare feet. He was wearing Bermuda shorts, for goodness sake. I am sure there is something in the BBC charter forbidding that kind of thing outside the confines of the *Radio 1 Roadshow*.

I mean, these chaps are probably working very hard out there, and it is no fun living out of a suitcase; just ask Tich and Quackers (old variety reference – younger readers, ask your parents). They must be missing the comforts of home (the broadcasters, that is, not Tich and Quackers); family, friends, full-size soap, and so on, but I really could do with a few more shots of presenters indoors in shirt, tie and jacket to reassure me that my licence fee and Sky subscriptions are not going to finance two months of rum, reggae, and rumpy pumpy.

Interestingly, Gower's statement on the transcendence of the West Indian experience did not meet with universal agreement. The start of the cricket World Cup coincided with the Cheltenham Festival, better than which, according to Derek Thompson in his very opening link on Channel 4, it does not get, a theme the racing types returned to throughout the week.

'It's a glorious morning, the sun is shining, God is in heaven, and we're in Cheltenham on Gold Cup day,' announced Lesley Graham, while on BBC Radio 5 Live Clare Balding declared there was nowhere else in the world she would rather be. Reporter Rob Nothman weighed this up, and decided that on balance he would rather be at the cricket.

Either, I reckon, is preferable to watching TV at home in the service of a semi-humorous newspaper column, although Andy Murray's quarter-final at Indian Wells against Tommy Haas on Sky Sports Extra did provide two-and-three-quarter hours of truly gripping sporting drama. As studio pundit Peter Fleming said: 'Anything you could hope for in a tennis match happened.' Despite Murray's semi-final defeat, he emerges from Indian Wells worthy of his place among a golden generation of young tennis players.

Murray is even beginning to sound like one of the new young guns, having more or less replaced his Scottish accent with the standard ATP mid-Atlantic drone, like a young Croatian after a year or two in a Florida training camp.

Unfortunately, my late night flipping also brought me into contact with an excrescence called *Benidorm* on ITV, centring on the activities of a bunch of people from the North of England on holiday in Spain. 'I've gorra gob like Ghandi's flip-flop,' announced one character in the course of this ineffable garbage. The remarkable thing is, somebody actually wrote down that pathetic careworn old simile, it went through some sort of script editing process one presumes, and finally an actor said it, and it went out on television. No wonder I get fed up. David Gower and all you lotus eaters at the World Cup, you are well out of it.

Here's a piece about England having one of their occasional disasters on overseas tours.

England's grouchy captains

Screen Break, The Guardian, *18 November 2012*

It's a shame, someone once said, that all the people with the solution to the world's problems are busy cutting hair and driving cabs. Similarly, the chaps who might have been able to do something about the England cricket team's disappointing start in Ahmedabad are mostly sitting in a television studio just off the M4, impotently watching it on the TV, just like the rest of us.

Sky's impressive collection of former England captains is grounded in Isleworth after the Indian cricket board demanded half a million to let them into the ground, and Sky demurred.

I assume the experts are holed up in one of those hotels round there where all the airline pilots stay, and so they could have been getting testy on air for any number of reasons; the airless, overheated rooms, a melted after-dinner mint on the pillow, or airline staff cavorting noisily into the night before taking their plane across the Atlantic. (I'm joking of course, there being no evidence, our lawyers tell me, that airline personnel would conduct themselves in anything other than a responsible, highly professional manner).

Whatever the reason, Nasser Hussain was getting awfully grouchy with Nick Knight on Friday morning, as Cheteshwar Pujara and Yuvraj Singh contemptuously swatted away the predictable deliveries of the England bowlers, like somebody contemptuously swatting something away (I jotted that one down at 5.30 in the morning as a work in progress but it turned out to be one of those works in progress that failed to progress, a phenomenon you will be familiar with if you have ever watched a television sitcom).

'What about some Pietersen at him?' Nasser said with a note of some impatience. 'Everyone's talking about Yuvraj to Pietersen, what about the other way round? KP coming on and tossing a few up, why not?'

Knight, the token non-captain in whatever passes for a commentary box at Isleworth, swatted this suggestion away, not just contemptuously but sarcastically: 'So that's your suggestion as a former England captain to the present captain,' he snorted. 'Absolutely,' said Nasser. 'We've tried everything else. A bit of Pietersen, that's my cunning plan. In situations like this you've got to think out of the box.'

'It's very easy for us guys up here to think out of the box,' Nick responded, rather missing the point that that was precisely the reason for the three o'clock alarm call, the cold breakfast with the stale croissant and the tired slices of fruit, and the cab to the studio. 'OK, so we carry on bowling all the normal bowlers, and it's 394 for four,' spat back Nasser. Boys, boys.

As well as coping with hotel living – I like hotels myself, having things like shower caps and sewing kits that barely exist in ordinary life makes me feel thrillingly stateless – the team had to cope with the idiosyncrasies of Star Television, the host broadcaster, whose modus operandi seemed to include finding an attractive woman in the crowd, fixing the camera on her, and then all going off for a cup of tea. Where an attractive woman was not immediately accessible, other lingering crowd shots could be guaranteed to last just a second or two too long.

We also got shots of Star's team in their commentary box, just to stick it to the Sky boys back home, and regular plugs for the local phone-ins, *Ask Sunny*, a chance to put match-related queries to Sunil Gavaskar, and *Ask Ravi* – 'What was it like when you met the Beatles?' muttered David 'Bumble' Lloyd mischievously. 'Ooh, wrong Ravi' – with Sourav Ganguly responding.

The sound was a little disorienting too, the constant low-level crowd noise reminiscent of the early days of multi-screen cinemas when soundtrack would leak in from the screen next door.

The one man guaranteed to keep his head in the midst of the madness was of course David Gower, who to borrow the memorable phrase of Ron Atkinson 'had a cigar on' through it all.

Not literally, of course, cigars having strangely fallen out of fashion among broadcasters, but in keeping a sense of proportion over England's bowlers' – Swann excepted – inability to make an impact on India's batsmen, and then our batsmen's initial problems in playing Indian spin.

He contented himself with introducing Mike Atherton, Sky's only man in Ahmedabad, reporting from a car park outside the ground: 'Now let's go over to our man at the scene of the crime...'

On the argument over Monty Panesar not being in the side – 'If Monty doesn't play on this pitch, when will he be picked?' someone said – Gower offered wisdom that could apply to all sports, all the time: 'It's interesting,' he said, 'how the moment you're out of the side you become a better player,' casting Monty briefly, for those who remember international football in the 1990s, as the Matt Le Tissier of cricket.

It was all so different then, now time has rewritten every line. Russell Brand writing a column for The Guardian, *biscuit barons (that's barons, not barrels) taking over West Ham, but one thing had never changed. Overseas disappointment for England.*

Joan Sims, Russell Brand, and Steve Harmison's Head

Screen Break, The Guardian, *27 November 2006*

Some of you may be aware of an old hit by Peter Sarstedt, 'Where Do You Go To My Lovely?' It is not played much on the radio these days, but a line from the song grabbed me by the lapels the other night, and shook me into wakefulness as I half-dozed through the coverage of the first Ashes Test.

Wrestling in Honey

'Tell me the thoughts that surround you, I want to look inside your head, yes I do, na, na, na, na,' Sarstedt bleated in his chart-topper; and this seemed to be more or less what the assembled cricket sages were asking of Steve Harmison.

Ian Botham compared Harmison's predicament with that of a Somerset bowler he played with some years ago who had great talent but suffered a sudden inexplicable lack of confidence and never fulfilled his potential. Co-commentator Michael Holding, meanwhile, felt Harmy's problem was not so much in the head as in the arm. 'He needs time in the nets,' said Holding. 'He doesn't have an action that repeats. Maybe he has not done enough work.'

I should not like to venture an opinion either way, my feeling about cricket bringing to mind Sir Thomas Beecham's famous gag about the English and classical music. Though we know absolutely nothing about it, Sir Tom quipped, we rather like the noise it makes.

That is me and cricket; the thwack of leather against willow, the whiff of linseed oil, the village green, the men in whites, LP Hartley, Joan Sims as the district nurse on a bicycle, and is there honey still for tea? Love all that stuff, and got as caught up as anyone in the hype before this Ashes series, but when it comes to analysis I am very much at the mercy of the experts. Fortunately, both Sky and the BBC – who have brief highlights – have rounded up some top talent to interpret the noise for those of us ignorant of the nuances.

How is it that football suffers such a paucity of plausible pundits that Graeme Le Saux passed for an analyst for a time, mainly on the basis that he spoke nicely and was rumoured to read this newspaper (hopefully, not this morning); yet when an old cricketer leaves the crease he finds it possible to step in front of a camera and give us honest, worthwhile opinions about his sport – and also is able to broadcast for longer than five minutes without resorting to weak jokes about his own or his colleagues' careers?

I have come to regard the likes of Botham, Holding, Nasser Hussain, David Lloyd, and Michael Atherton as knowledgeable and trusted guides, while the ringmaster David Gower remains peerless. If you look up the word 'unflappable' in the dictionary, I believe you will find a photograph of him.

The cricket is actually on at quite a handy time for me, having reached that age when a gentleman can anticipate a wake-up call in the wee small hours from a demanding prostate (I think that is why they call them the wee small hours). I have been treating these nocturnal rest stops as opportunities to make a detour via the telly to check on England's lack of progress, before returning to the arms of Morpheus (insert own joke here, I am a little tired after all the late night cricket).

For younger enthusiasts, for whom the knitting of the ravelled sleeve of care continues more or less uninterrupted through the night, there are of course numerous other ways to keep up with the cricket; highlights, podcasts, internet scorecards and action replays, and text alerts sent directly to your mobile phone first thing in the morning, which I suspect many of you are now frantically trying to cancel in order to avoid starting each day with what we used to call a real downer, man?

The highlights on the BBC are anchored by boyish Manish Bhasin, understandably a little more flappable than Gower in the face of grizzled veterans Tony Greig and Geoff Boycott. When the presenter ventured a note of mild optimism, harking back to England's poor start and eventual triumph in 2005, he was summarily interrupted by Boycs: ''ang on. That's gone,' snapped the world's greatest

Yorkshireman. 'That's 'istory. Gerrit aht o' yer head.' I am not sure whether he called him 'lad' or not, but it was implied.

Finally, West Ham fans welcomed new owner, biscuit baron Eggert Magnússon, with a rousing chorus of 'If you made a lot of money selling biscuits, buy our club,' to the tune of the old Club biscuit TV advert, which information I pass on for the benefit of my colleague Russell Brand, who has been asking about original terrace songs.

Russell's new chat show started on Channel 4 on Friday night, so he may not have been able to make it on Saturday, when he was also incidentally the subject of another long profile in one of the papers, filling in any gaps that might remain in our Russell Brand knowledge. It was all there again; unhappy schooldays in Grays, the wicked stepfather, the sainted mother, the drugs, the day he went to work dressed as Osama Bin Laden, the relationship with Kate Moss he doesn't like to talk about; all fascinating. My only worry is that if I get knocked down by a bus, it will be his life that flashes in front of me rather than my own.

Almost unnoticed by me, Gary Neville became a star, of social media as well as TV, also Freddie Flintoff with his terrific 2022 series, Freddie Flintoff's Field Of Dreams. *Darren Gough became a colleague of mine at talkSPORT, so we can disregard anything written about him here.*

When an old cricketer leaves the crease

Screen Break, The Guardian, *7 February 2011*

The possibility – a distant one, I believe – of the newly retired Gary Neville taking over Andy Gray's role at Sky has prompted a fair amount of discussion/abuse on football fan forums, the more playful of which has focused firmly on Neville's upper lip. Even the great defender's staunchest admirers would admit their hero has always seemed more comfortable with a tricky opposition winger than with facial hair, and this view was reinforced last week by *Match Of The Day*'s very useful guide to the several ages of Neville's moustache.

Ostensibly it was a tribute to Neville's achievements, with shots of him lifting trophies at various stages in his Manchester United career, but the montage also acted like one of those speeded-up sequences of a flower blooming you used to see on nature programmes, giving one a snapshot of just what has been going on underneath the Neville nose through the Premier League era.

From the full-back's wispy my-first-razor days, through what a friend describes as the *Witchfinder General* period, to the time when Neville threatened to pre-empt comedian Richard Herring and revive the Hitler look, to more recent times when Alex Ferguson's representative on earth has mostly favoured the neatly trimmed Soho ad man style complete with little goatee, confusion has reigned in the region of Neville's shaving mirror.

Elsewhere, he seems a fairly self-assured character, and I would expect him to fill the unforgiving non-playing years stretching out ahead of him with something more fulfilling than standing in front of a touch screen screaming about how the referee's assistant got an offside decision wrong. It may be that TV punditry is best left to light entertainers like Steve McManaman and Robbie Savage, both on ESPN recently, adding nothing to the sum of human knowledge, but making a bit of noise, sporting wacky hair, and looking indecently pleased to be there.

The question of the post-retirement years, one of the stiffest facing the superannuated sportsman, was also raised by Freddie Flintoff in a programme on ITV4, *Freddie Flintoff Versus The World*, which I may have missed on its first run. Flintoff went with Darren Gough to Mexico, where the two former England cricketers competed in a series of challenges, after a spot of jokey travelogue action. 'Mexico is like really, really old, isn't it?' observed Gough, as the pair wandered round the capital's historic streets. 'It's not where I'd like to live but I'm sure lots of Mexicans enjoy living here.'

Gough – who seems in no immediate danger of stealing Bill Bryson's gig – has now taken his way with words and unique analytical skills to radio, as a presenter on talkSPORT, while Flintoff embraces his laddish image on TV shows like Sky's *League Of Their Own*, and crypto-reality exercises like this one, which saw him cliff diving in Acapulco, reviving for some of us memories of the golden days of Dickie Davies on *World Of Sport* (now there was an example of man and moustache in perfect harmony).

'The adrenaline rush was amazing,' he said after rather impressively hurling himself into the water. 'When you retire you wonder whether you are ever going to get it again,' which neatly encapsulated the problem facing sports stars after the pocket watch and the tribute on *Grandstand*. Some like Gazza – and Flintoff, I suspect – struggle to find a role away from the roar of the crowd, while others like Gary Lineker and Sue Barker, whose careers have maybe been less adrenaline fuelled, can more easily adapt to new arenas.

Where former England rugby union forward Brian Moore fits into this is difficult to say. Bachelor of law, writer of an award-winning autobiography, survivor of abuse, and *Daily Telegraph* columnist, he has clearly been through a good deal. I was on a radio discussion programme with him once, where he was sharp, witty, and almost forensic in exposing whatever specious argument it was that I was propounding.

So what happened to Moore on Friday night, in the commentary box for the England – Wales match on BBC? He was not so much analysing as chuntering, often starting arguments with himself. 'Well, that is debatable,' muttered Moore when Wales's Craig Mitchell was sent to the sin bin. 'Well, it's only debatable in the sense of theoretical, because you don't debate the referee's decision until he's made it,' he continued, uninterrupted. 'I'm not talking about the offence. It is an offence. I just wonder whether it's not in the red zone. Look, let's stop talking about it.'

You were the only one that was, Brian. Commentator Eddie Butler was stunned into silence, as he was when Moore referred to the Aussies as 'a race', talking about England's Ashes win.

Given Moore's chequered past, you expect and almost cherish the eccentricities, which you suspect will not be forthcoming from the single-track Neville, for whom, in the meantime, there is probably a role for the Manchester United hero as the new face of Gillette.

All Our Yesterdays

No 49: **The Magic Roundabout** (1965–1977),
The Independent, 12 June 2002

It was more than 20 years ago, but there's absolutely no trace of Mike Tough of Aberdeen on the Internet, which is odd because an embarrassing picture taken of me at a radio station in 1982 won't disappear however hard I try.

● This was a fairly decent five-minute filler for children, a fact sometimes lost sight of in the tiresome hippy nonsense that used to follow it round. Still does, in fact. A good measure of the cult status of a programme is the number of private websites devoted to it. *The Magic Roundabout* has many, including the one created by 39-year-old Mike Tough from Aberdeen, which begins thus: 'I don't have much time to update the web pages, as I have separated from my wife and we are now in the process of getting divorced. I'm young, free, and available again. Any takers out there?'

Maybe it was the laid-back rabbit called Dylan that persuaded Mike this was the show for people whose albums all had gatefold sleeves. Either that or Eric Thompson's beautifully whimsical narration. But now might be time to let go.

'Mike, I'm leaving you, I've had enough, I can't take it any more. Always on that computer. Mike! Mike!'

'Hang on a minute, darling. I've just got to download this brilliant jpeg of Ermintrude.'

'Mike, you're going to have to choose between the *Magic Roundabout* and me.'

'Be with you in a minute, darling. Right, click here. Start download. Great. Yes, darling, what was it? Darling...'

Time for bed, said Zebedee.

16. A Little Bit Political

'I am prepared to give evidence in the inevitable investigation into whether the FA is a bunch of what (Ashley) Cole says they are...'

This was written for half-decent rugby league magazine Forty20 *a week or so before the Wakefield by-election on two recurring themes: the parlous nature of the job I do in radio – and indeed more or less everybody's job these days – and the government's vain and hypocritical promises to level up.*

By-election looms

Any Other Business, Forty20 Magazine, *June 2022*

Some of you I expect are deep in the arms of Morpheus – or in some cases, your spouse – in the early hours of the morning and therefore will not have heard my occasionally mildly amusing radio show in the graveyard slot on talkSPORT, which I should say includes some red hot rugby league chat courtesy of this journal at 4.15am each Saturday. That's a.m., Saturday morning, sparrow's fart I think some people call it, although prime time in Ho Chi Minh City and parts of Adelaide.

We attract a small but enthusiastic audience, and are rarely short of people keen to take part in our phone-in quiz in the middle of the night, competing for a prize best described as nugatory.

The problem is one is quite vulnerable sitting out there in the weekend graveyard, and there is always the danger of falling off the edge of the schedule in one of those reorganisations that are an occupational hazard of pretty well every business these days. So I am constantly thinking how I might occupy my time should this happen.

I don't play golf, ski, bird spot, train spot, collect beer mats, sing in a choir, go to swingers parties, take part in triathlons, meditate, practice yoga, play five-a-side football, take on DIY projects, large or small, or stand in shopping centres advertising Jesus on sandwich boards, so there seems to be a distinct lack of absorbing and rewarding hobbies with which to fill those unforgiving jobless days before the graveyard slot becomes a little more literal.

Motivational speaker, there's something I could possibly take up. But I really can't be bothered.

It's a shame because it's not a million miles from what I'm doing now, and I could see myself as one of those guys on a cruise ship filling the forty-five minutes between the lunchtime buffet and afternoon tea with a few diverting anecdotes and an uplifting message that I'd have to borrow from Confucius or some other dead guy to get round any copyright issues.

'How To Turn Your Life Around' was the title of the lecture I thought I might deliver to the cruise ship crowd, but it occurred to me that if they were eating five course meals three times a day and drinking cocktails on the sun deck, they'd probably already turned their lives around. Maybe it would work on one of the cheaper Mediterranean trips: 'Listen people, follow these simple tips, and you could be stepping off the boat in Martinique instead of the docks twenty-five miles outside Rome.'

For the time being, though, I am still gainfully employed – the Kuala Lumpur massive and chaps with prostate issues breathe a sigh of relief – and was in London presenting my show on Cup final weekend.

It was an interesting time to be in the capital, Port Vale playing Mansfield at Wembley at the same time as the rugby league final, and then Huddersfield meeting Nottingham Forest the following day. What a unique opportunity for people from some of the most deprived communities in Britain to check on how the Government's much heralded (by the Government) levelling-up programme is going.

How charming it was to see people from North Nottinghamshire, the Potteries, and other areas in the North that are hanging on for dear life – Mansfield, I think, has been boarded up – wandering up Oxford Street wide-eyed at seeing shops still open, all lit up, not charity or betting shops either, shops actually selling consumer goods; clothes and gewgaws that people were actually buying. It's very rare you get the chance in real life to feel like Joe Gargery when he visits Pip in London, or a character in a depression-era American movie.

The inescapable conclusion of all this is that 'levelling up' (it fully merits the quotation marks) is going about as well as David Irving might at a Rosh HaShanah afternoon tea

(Google it), as will no doubt be reflected in the Wakefield by-election later this month.

Given the prevailing conditions, Tottenham Hotspur stadium's pricing policy was relatively benign for visitors from the benighted North. Ten quid odd for some chicken burger thing with a few chips seemed pretty standard, and the meat was apparently 'buttermilk chicken', so a step up I suppose from something you might eat late at night on the Burslem omnibus. Oh, hang on, we don't have late night buses up here, I'm thinking of London.

(The joke this month, by the way, is paragraph five)

It seems a lifetime ago, but there was a moment when Sky Sports' Sunday morning football chat programme, Sunday Supplement, *at one time the province of Jimmy Hill, later* Sun *journalists such as Neil Ashton and the late Brian Woolnough, was considered lively, agenda-setting, required viewing for anyone with an interest in sports journalism, which made this piece appropriate if nothing else for the Sports Journalists Association website. I presume I wrote it in return for a ticket for the annual SJA awards' dinner, under the kind of bartering system which occasionally has replaced actual employment for me.*

Loris Karius was a German goalkeeper who played for Liverpool from 2016-19, about whom I assume Gary Neville had said something disparaging. Neville's property developing, about which you can read elsewhere, included developing the Jackson's Row synagogue in Manchester about which, as a former habitué of its youth club dances, this writer was outraged.

Former Tory MP David Mellor used to host a football phone-in on BBC Radio 5 Live, often referring to its piss-poor contents as 'red-hot soccer chat'.

Gary Neville in the lions' den

Sports Journalists Association website, 20 December 2016

Bad news for those of us with an interest in newspaper sales, which I guess would be most vistors to this site; Sky pundit Gary Neville never picks up a newspaper. Never. He dropped the bombshell at the start of his much-discussed appearance on *Sunday Supplement*, Sky Sports' weekly sports discussion programme, whose very existence depends on a big bundle of physical newspapers, three sports journalists, and a large bowl of fruit.

The former England international had been invited on to the programme to face sportswriters Olly Holt and Martin Samuel, of the *Mail* group, and Henry Winter of *The Times*, after comments he had made – I never saw the original piece – about declining standards in modern-day sports journalism.

As host Neil Ashton put it, Neville was facing 'three titans of Fleet Street' so his early admission that he would never go to the trouble of actually going out and paying for their stuff was very much the TV equivalent of getting a tackle in early, letting the star player know you're there, putting a reducer on him as Ron Atkinson used to say.

Not that Olly, who was first to take on the much-admired pundit and property developer (much-admired for his punditry, the jury is still out on his property development), seemed overly daunted, naming some brilliant young journalists and the work they are doing to keep the titans' flame burning, an argument I found incontrovertible, and not just because one of the roll of honour will be spending her 26th Christmas dinner round our table.

The dispute between Neville and the Fourth Estate arose apparently from the way some of his comments on

Liverpool goalkeeper Loris Karius had been interpreted in the press, the reaction of coach Jürgen Klopp and the player himself, and the inevitable brouhaha on social media that followed. You might have thought Neville would be the last person to want to go back to a time when if you had a view on football you had to wait till Saturday to ring, god help us, David Mellor; but he explained that he felt journalists, especially those new to the game, without the heft of the titans, were under pressure to produce 'quantity rather than quality,' to get content, however flimsy its basis, online 'within 15 minutes' (that might be where his argument falls down, that's barely time to make an instant coffee and select a biscuit). As a result, he felt balanced, informed coverage of football was in peril. He didn't actually use the word 'clickbait', but the implication was there.

Neville, though, tended to destroy his own argument, admitting that his job as a pundit was to be opinionated and prompt debate, in which case he should have been delighted that by responding Liverpool had, in his words, 'added fuel to a fire that wasn't there,' a concept that merits closer analysis.

And as Henry Winter pointed out, serious discussion of football is far from dead, with eleven pages in Saturday's *Times* and *Telegraph*, and twelve in the *Mail* – though the concept of pages of print sadly might have been lost not just on Neville but much of his and succeeding generations. Holt pointed to the proliferation of sports journalism courses in colleges and universities. If you are on one, I would urge you to download this edition of *Sunday Supplement*, and not just for the presence of the titans. Aside from his argument about the Karius coverage, Neville, who is always brilliantly watchable on TV, had some fascinating insights on the relationship between players and the press, and his role under Roy Hodgson with the England team, amongst other issues.

I don't often watch *Sunday Supplement*, preferring to catch up on politics with Andrew Marr or Robert Peston, and guests who have gone to the trouble of having a shave and wearing a shirt and tie – exception made for the always elegant Henry Winter – but while not developing into the studs up row that might have been anticipated, this programme was riveting viewing.

Apart from anything else, I was fascinated by what appeared to be a *pain au chocolat* or a *pain au raisins* in front of Martin Samuel. It remained in front of him, as far as I could see, untouched for 90 minutes, so unless they were renewing it during the ad breaks, the *Mail*'s chief sports writer is to be applauded for admirable restraint.

In one of British media's more fanciful deals, Screen Break was sponsored for a while by the UK Concrete Show. This was thanks not to the content of the column, where any reference to concrete tends to be accidental, but to my work on radio and podcast, of which Steve Callaghan, CEO of the Concrete Show, was a big fan.

Bless him for it, I linked to the show's website where I could, and I am happy to declare here and now that the show is the Number One Concrete Show For The UK and Europe.

I am sure members of the concrete community everywhere will be thrilled to have paid for this piece about football pundit Gary Neville, and the Jewish youth club I attended as a teenager.

What Are You Playing At, Gary Neville?

Blog post, 28 August 2016

Who the hell does Gary Neville think he is, trampling all over my childhood?

You'll be familiar with Neville's excellent work on TV; as a commendably plain-speaking pundit on Sky, and in a cameo role in *Class of '92 – Still Out Of Their League,* the chucklesome BBC documentary about the non-league team bought by ex-Manchester United players with more money than sense.

In fact, so entertaining is Neville on the box, one is prepared to overlook his career in football management, at Valencia in LaLiga, and with the England national team at the Euros, whatever he was supposed to be doing there.

But this I can't forgive. Neville and his chum Ryan Giggs have teamed up with some Asian investors and plan to knock down an old bit of Manchester for a £200 million skyscraper development including 153 luxury flats, offices, prestige shops, topped off by two 'sky bars' and upscale restaurants where they no doubt drizzle stuff over other stuff and arrange it geometrically on the plate. No affordable housing, obviously.

All initially prompting little more than a sigh and a sad shake of the head, but the name of Neville's enterprise, the Jackson's Row Development Company, was like a dagger to the heart. Because Jackson's Row is the street in Manchester they want to knock down for their posh flats, on-site gym, 24-hour security, and cocktail bars with fabulous views over the whole of Manchester. And Jackson's Row is where my stuttering romantic life began.

There's an old synagogue there, where they used to have dances on a Saturday night. As it was a reform shul (Yiddish for synagogue), there was little chance of meeting up with Jew fundamentalists with their wacky insistence on two sets of plates and not switching on the light on a Saturday, and thus my Jewish (more 'ish' than Jew) parents thought it an ideal place for me to meet girls of my own unobserved religion, and not succumb to the lure of the shiksa (gentile woman) – 'shiks appeal', as *Seinfeld* dubbed it.

As it happened, as a pupil at a boys' grammar school, I was pretty useless with girls of any faith, but I do remember dancing at one of these socials with a girl called Michelle, mainly because of the Beatles' song of the same name which was around at the time. I may even have essayed a chaste kiss with her.

Look, I'm not suggesting a blue plaque or anything, but I resent losing a piece of history – and the building is a prime example of 1950s synagogue design – so that the nouveau riche wives and girlfriends of Premier League footballers can quaff cocktails looking down on the peasants below.

And it's not just the synagogue but a 1930s police station where I once answered questions in connection with a Road Traffic Incident, and a 19th Century inn believed to have inspired the pub in the TV series *Life On Mars* are also destined to go under Neville's bulldozers. Historic England are fighting the plans, and I'm with them. I guess Neville's purchase – together with brother Phil, Giggs, Paul Scholes, and Nicky Butt – of Salford City Football Club, is him 'giving something back', for which I admire him.

The first series, which followed the Class of 92's club to promotion, via managerial sackings, tea bar crises, toilet reconstruction, and other vicissitudes of life in the lower reaches of the football pyramid was hugely entertaining.

I doubted there was enough there for a second series, but it got off to a promising start on Thursday, covering Salford's successful run in the FA Cup, and something of a collapse in league form which currently sees them in danger of missing out on promotion.

There will be a small proportion of the audience for whom there will be no suspense, because they follow the lower leagues, but for those of us for whom doings in the Dobson The Butcher Northwest Premier Division B, or wherever it is Salford play, remain a mystery, it's a rattling good yarn.

The show's not about the football anyway. It's about whether the tea bar can overcome its one-star rating and newspaper headlines about E-Coli dangers. Where next for the pies, peas, and watery gravy?

And it's about the really lovely, personable thirty-odd year-old striker Gareth Seddon's future, as he pounds the streets in a probably vain bid to prolong his career, as younger players are brought in at Salford to replace him.

He's bought a cheese shop with his girlfriend Melissa to prepare for life after football. 'A cheese shop?' comments an incredulous and highly amused Gary Neville. 'Why's he got a cheese shop?' Well, possibly because he can't rustle up a bunch of Asian investors to finance a scheme to knock down part of Manchester.

The Ballad of Ashley Cole, sticking it to the man

Screen Break, The Guardian, *8 October 2012*

Ashley Cole, Man of the People. Overstatement maybe, but his muscular response to the FA's comments about him undoubtedly chimed in with the mood of the nation like nothing he has said or done before. I feel sure my reaction to the full back's *cri de cœur* was not untypical: 'Ah, the old bunch-of-twats argument, I've used it myself.'

Who among us has not used similar terms to describe those in authority; employers, law enforcers, Government, in-laws? Sure, as a rallying cry, 'bunch of twats' might not quite be up there with 'Power to the people' or 'Give me liberty or give me death,' but in the current economic climate particularly, Cole's now notorious hashtag spoke eloquently for the common man struggling under the yoke.

And the FA seems an entirely suitable target for Cole's broadside. Its convolutions over the John Terry case – *l'affaire John Terry*, as we're calling it on the streets – mishandling of various England managerial appointments, and even its role in the Hillsborough tragedy, leads one to the view that Ashley Cole's hashtag should maybe be incorporated into its coat of arms.

So impressed was I by Cole's pithy assessment, I felt compelled to hashtag #faircommentonamatterofpublicinterest back and I am prepared to give evidence in the inevitable 14-month, meticulous, expensively-lawyered, investigation into whether the FA is a bunch of what Cole says they are.

I love Twitter incidentally, unlike Alan Shearer, who said on the BBC's *Football Focus*, 'I don't get this Twitter lark, I have to tell you,' and recommended footballers be banned from using it, adding somewhat tangentially, 'They do it with motor bikes.'

On the contrary, I think footballers should be encouraged to use Twitter, and fined if their comments are bland and predictable. Twitter is one of the few chances we the people have of hearing directly from footballers, unless you count the PR mush masquerading as interview that *Football Focus* served us on Saturday; Steven Gerrard plugging his autobiography, and Victor Moses hawking a new computer game, for goodness sake.

The Gerrard piece was forgivable given the player's profile, but if you are obliged to screen a shot of some glorified pinball game in order to get access to a Chelsea reserve, is it not time for a public service broadcaster to respond in the style of Ashley Cole, and show some old goals or archive of John Motson in his sheepskin coat instead?

The row over Cole's tweet – twatgate, as I like to think it will soon be called – rumbled on all weekend. Garth Crooks suggested on the BBC's *Final Score* that suitable punishment would be to ban Cole from playing in England's World Cup qualifier on Friday, which seems eminently sensible given that we could probably play Hugh Fearnley-Whittingstall at left back against San Marino and get a result.

Roberto Di Matteo's announcement that Cole was to be disciplined by Chelsea was felt important enough to be breaking news during ESPN's coverage of West Ham-Arsenal, thankfully not interrupting Sam Allardyce's interview where he was asked if Andy Carroll was ready to return and said, 'He's biting at the bit, as the old cliché goes,' one I'm sure that's rarely far from any of our lips.

I happened to catch the match after watching an episode of the excellent documentary series *Sporting Greats*, featuring baseball legend Babe Ruth, and that was when the parallels between the American folk hero and our own pantomime villain struck.

When Babe played for the Boston Red Sox, he was 'a kinda pain in the neck,' writer Peter Golenbock told the show (see why Cole came to mind?). 'There was always some trouble, he was always hitting Harry Frazee (Red Sox owner) for a bit more money.' Frazee sold Babe to New York Yankees, said Golenbock, 'to get him out of his hair.'

Ruth was described as an everyman figure who 'ate large, drank large, and womanised large,' which is where Cole departs from his baseball counterpart, most of his floozies having been built on more trim lines. Ruth was also described as having 'a face that people could relate to,' so there is some work for Ashley to do there as well.

Maybe for true folk heroism, we should look to the performance of Leeds Rhinos' captain Kevin Sinfield in the Super League grand final. After being laid out in a clash of heads that would have had a small army of medics invading the pitch in other sports, Sinfield shook his head, swallowed and spat, and moments later stepped up to faultlessly convert a penalty.

And after 80 minutes of that kind of stuff, he took the mic and delivered to the crowd an articulate, modest, and gracious speech, remembering to thank everyone who needed to be thanked. His captaincy and all-round performance were exceptional, and the match was about half as good as Sky's commentators kept telling us it was, which meant it was very good indeed.

England expects – another great tennis hope emerges

Screen Break, The Guardian, *7 July 2008*

It is important to manage expectations, and the last thing we would want to do is pile any extra pressure on a girl who is only 14 years old, but Laura Robson, wow. I mean, LAURA ROBSON!! Phew. ENGLAND'S LAURA ROBSON, Champion of the World or what??? Come on, Laura.

That was more or less the tenor of Chris Bailey and Sam Smith's commentary on BBC TV as England's Laura beat Noppawan Lertcheewakarn in the girls' championship at Wimbledon on Saturday. 'Unfortunately, the hype around Laura is going to be unstoppable,' said Bailey, as the commentary team ratcheted it up a notch or two.

'I can see her being the new pin-up,' burbled Sam. 'She could be a cover girl for magazines like *Jackie*.' That would indeed be some achievement as *Jackie* went out of business around the time Sam herself was Britain's number one and subject to similar weight of unfeasible expectations. 'There's the crowd on Henman Hill,' continued the former British number one, and world number 57. 'In a few years' time we might be calling it Robson Ridge.'

'We don't want to put too much pressure on her,' one of the commentators said (dear me, no, we are all agreed on that), 'but she looks like a young Ana Ivanović – same sort of hairstyle, same hair colouring.' (I am not sure who was responsible for this gem, as I was busy managing my expectations at the time).

Other names invoked, as Come-on-Laura – as she will henceforth be known – swept to victory, included Martina Hingis and Amélie Mauresmo, previous winners of the girls' title, and Maria Sharapova, who apparently was lower in the junior rankings when she was the same age as Come-on-Laura.

A name not invoked quite as much was that of Annabel Croft, the last British winner of the title, in 1984, who, by the age of 21, had retired from the game. Croft gave a frank interview on *BBC Breakfast* in which she described tennis as 'a selfish sport', and herself as unable to make the sacrifices needed to continue with her career. 'It's very full-on,' said the former British number one, *Treasure Hunt* presenter, and winner of ITV's *Celebrity Wrestling*.

Actually, there are so many former British number ones floating round the various Wimbledon commentary boxes, I sometimes wonder whether becoming British number one is little more than a step to a media career.

If it comes down to a choice between spending three years at whatever they are calling Cardiff Polytechnic these days, watching Jeremy Kyle, eating bad food, and begging for work experience at the *Gloucestershire Echo*, and putting some time in on your ground strokes, the tennis might not seem like such a sacrifice.

But as Annabel wisely pointed out, what seems like a good idea at 14 might seem less attractive in later teenage years. Girls change, said the former presenter of ITV's *Interceptor*. Prodigious talent or not, Come-on-Laura's further progress remains an open question.

I agree. I may not know much about tennis but consider myself something of an expert on teenage girls having had two under my tutelage in recent years. I can confirm it is awfully difficult to keep them focused on making the most of talents displayed in early teenage years. It is also very difficult to get them to turn the lights off when they leave a room.

On which topic, there is a ritual attached to the emergence of a precocious talent like Come-on-Laura's which involves the parents giving interviews stressing that the prodigy is being brought up as 'just a normal kid'. Laura's mum Kathy, for instance – who will have to get used to being the star of a thousand cutaways when Laura plays Wimbledon next year – said the family's celebration meal would be in Pizza Hut.

Far be it from me to doubt her, but I am sure a family living in prosperous South West London, with a Shell executive as head of the household, could do better than Pizza Hut. (Not that I am casting aspersions on Pizza Hut, although their salad bar sometimes seems too heavily reliant on overly chilled green peppers and thousand island dressing.)

It is just that tennis in Britain, despite encouraging noises from the LTA, still mostly played by those who get their pizzas from authentic wood-fired ovens. There is no immediate sign of a British equivalent of the Williams sisters emerging.

At least it is not quite as middle class as Woody Allen perceives it. After the men's doubles on Saturday, I made the grave mistake of turning to Woody's film *Match Point* on one of the Sky movie channels. This may be not just Woody Allen's worst film but the worst film ever made.

I was reading in this paper on Saturday about a British film called *Crust* featuring a 7ft boxing shrimp, and another, a comedy called *Nine Dead Gay Guys,* both allegedly designed to be flops for tax reasons. Amateurs, I say. *Citizen Kane* compared to *Match Point,* which is as though the great Woody had seen a bunch of Hugh Grant-Working Title movies and decided he liked them, but without all the gritty realism.

Sometimes, though, foreign eyes help show us the truth about ourselves. Pat Cash, on BBC 5 Live yesterday, congratulated Come-on-Laura but pointed out that many female tennis players turn professional at 16 these days. 'You think she has beaten the best young players in the world, but it's far from that,' he said. He also claimed Laura was technically Australian. Spoilsport.

Whatever happened to Tear 'n' Share crisps?

Edited blog post, 2017-ish

The latest weapon in the war on obesity is Walkers Tear 'n' Share crisps. All right, it's the other side's weapon, but know your enemy and all that and, be honest, what a concept.

I saw them advertised during yesterday's Manchester United-Arsenal match: 'A bag of crisps that turns into a bowl.' Yes, that's right, a bag of crisps that turns into a bowl.

How it works is that you tear off the top of a flat-looking bag, which opens up the whole shebang into a bowl-like shape, enabling you to hand them round, and your companions to take a handful without the tiresome business of reaching into the bag, or indeed plunging their mitts right into the crisps, with all the attendant health risks – although personally I try not to associate with the kind of people who can't be trusted to wash their hands after the toilet.

In the advert, the crisps are being shared by much-loved TV personalities and former international footballers Jamie Redknapp, Alan Hansen, and Gary Lineker, dipping in without taking their eyes off the screen. See, when someone passes round an ordinary bag you have to look away for an instant to check on the exact position of the bag, width of opening and so on, and you could miss a goal. And if you do, there's, er, very little chance Sky Sports will show it again.

I watched the football too, unimpressed by Arsenal's limp surrender, but not as unimpressed as pundit Graeme Souness, from whose ears metaphorical smoke plumed as he embarked on an extraordinary rant, Arsenal's performance 'bordering on a joke.' What you need, in order to compete in football matches is a word I can't use here. Arsenal,' he said, 'lacked it in abundance'. Whether it's possible to lack something in abundance is a moot philosophical point, but I assume what Arsenal were short of according to Souness was 'balls', which is a word I can use here.

In fact, I can use any word I want. That is the joy of appearing purely on my own website. Sure, I miss out on a freelance payment, and the prestige of appearing in a well-respected national newspaper, or even *The Guardian* (I'm joking, I'm joking), but I am free to use any words I wish. Cockmonger, arse-biscuit, minge-rabbit, even foreign terms like *Scheidenpilz*, are all there for me, should necessity arise.

Wrestling in Honey

Free at last. Readers who have followed what I laughingly call my career through its various sackings will know that among the invaluable collection of reference books I keep on my desk is *Viz* comic's *Roger's Profanisaurus*, one of whose saucy euphemisms I have very occasionally managed to smuggle into a column. Well now the whole volume is fair game, quite literally an open book; gobbler's cough, grumblehound, festival flange, I can pick where I like.

No longer need I spend Sunday afternoons debating with *Guardian* sub-editors the relevance of some salty colloquialism I had decided to sully its pages with in pursuit of my art, although in fairness to the fine folk at that paper, it was more likely to be a dispute over the position of the apostrophe in 'gobbler's cough.'

Meanwhile, if you're looking for the most otiose three-and-a-half minutes of television, and you can't face *BBC Breakfast* or *The One Show*, may I direct you to the post-match interviews of the indefatigable Geoff Shreeves.

It's Geoff's job to lurk in the players' tunnel and beard whichever muddied oaf has just been awarded the Barclays Man of the Match Trophy, questioning the uninterviewable with the unanswerable. For instance, his opener yesterday to the young boy we are contractually obliged to call two-goal hero Marcus Rashford was: 'How much is this the stuff of dreams?' 'On a scale of one to ten, I should say about 6.5,' replied young Marcus, 'but was it not Shakespeare who said "We are such stuff as dreams are made on?"'

I made that quote up, but here's one I didn't.

Commentator Martin Tyler, over a shot of injured rivals Calum Chambers and Luke Shaw sitting together in the stand: 'It's lovely to see two young men enjoying each other's company.'

As I've been consulting *Viz*, I simply say fnarr, fnarr.

Afterword

Edited extract of unpublished memoir, 2017

I wanted to get some of this stuff down before I die, in case anyone is interested in an obituary. I mean, 'DJ Dies' would probably cover it, with a brief resumé of career 'highlights' because, frankly, people are dying all the time and who cares?

It's just that I have a particular interest in obituaries having been an obituarist myself, of sorts.

After a spectacularly unsuccessful University career, my first job was with Bristol United Press, who ran the *Bristol Evening Post*, and the *Western Daily Press*, a morning paper for the West Country, as well as a couple of regional weeklies in the outer suburbs, on which they gave junior reporters a six-month probationary period, to see if we had the right stuff.

I was assigned to the *Kingswood Observer*, covering suburbs North East of Bristol, which had been proper places in their own right before the Second World War, but were rapidly being subsumed into the city itself.

On my first Monday morning I was introduced to Roy Alderwick, Kingswood's local undertaker. Recenty, I googled him and found I had remembered the name correctly, such a great one for a local worthy of the type who dominated our contacts books, so I had to share it. Roy Alderwick.

(Unlike Sam and Josh, and those Thomas Hardy names that have been given a second lease of life, for some reason Roy remains resolutely unfashionable. My late friend Caroline

Aherne cleverly chose the name for the hen-pecked husband character in his sensible cardigans in the TV sketch programme *The Fast Show* – 'What did I say, Roy?')

I was introduced to Roy Alderwick by Tom, a chain-smoking old hack – he was probably about 40 but seemed old to me – who also took me round to the local vicars and Methodist ministers on my patch, showed where to get an economically priced cup of tea and a bacon sandwich close to Staple Hill magistrates court, and passed on important life skills such as how to brush cigarette ash off an Olivetti portable typewriter without interrupting your flow.

Roy Alderwick was first call on a Monday morning, the very first person I ever interviewed professionally, leading subsequently to a career in conversation with people as varied as Jerry Lee Lewis's sister, a championship standard whistler, and Anthony Wedgwood Benn.

I remember Roy as a chubby fellow with a combover, which in the early 'Seventies was not the source of mocking humour it is now. In fact, it was a very popular style for men in their forties or fifties suffering male pattern baldness.

I may, of course, have misremembered, and be mixing Roy up with characters from sitcoms I've seen, or Leonard Rossiter's undertaker in the film *Billy Liar*. That's the problem with memoir. Unless you keep a diary it's hard to separate what really happened from stuff you've imagined or read about, or seen in the movies, and I should confess I wasn't paying attention most of the time.

You aren't when you're younger, unless you're a poet or something and I wasn't, so those of you who remember Kingswood's premier undertaker's dome being replete with golden locks have as much chance as me of being right.

My business at Roy's place on a Monday morning was to get names and addresses of any fresh corpses the district was dealing with at the start of a new week, write the details down in my notebook, and turn up at the house of the dearly departed to quiz relatives on his or her (usually his) life and times. It hardly seems credible now, but intrusion on private grief was not just an unfortunate by-product of journalistic endeavour, but in this case its very *raison d'être*.

This is how it worked. Intrepid reporter rings doorbell. Leaves suitably respectful gap before ringing again, and eventually door is answered.

'Hello, Mrs Bennett. I'm terribly sorry to trouble you at this difficult time. I'm from *The Observer* and we were awfully sorry to learn about your husband's death. I wonder if you could spare me a few moments to talk about George so we can put a little write-up about him in the paper this weekend?'

'Ooh, I don't know about that.'

'It's just to make sure we get all the facts right. We wouldn't want to put anything in the paper that's wrong.'

'Hold on a minute.' (Shouting to daughter who's with an aunt or uncle in the sitting room.) 'Lesley, there's a chap 'ere, says he's from the *Observer*. He wants to do an article about Dad.'

Lesley, blonde, plump, fluffy slippers, comes to the front door and looks junior reporter up and down. 'Ah, a Jew. We don't see many of them round these parts.'

Not really, but thinking about those days I just remembered how very white, Christian, non-Metropolitan, that part of the world was back then. Just a few miles outside the eighth biggest city in England, and it was like going back to a world of cycling midwives, Ealing comedies and 'bobbies on bicycles two by two,' (a prehistoric reference even when Roger Miller used it in his 1966 chartbuster 'England Swings').

Anyway, a certain plausibility and a neatly knotted tie

must have gone a long way in those days, because I was invariably invited in by the newly-widowed. They sometimes gave me a cup of tea and a digestive biscuit (McVitie's Hob Nobs were still fifteen years in the future, which gives you some idea of how different the world was back then) while we chatted about the latest occupant of one of Roy Alderwick's mahogany-style boxes.

Though actually we didn't much. I was new to the business, and not entirely comfortable going into people's houses and asking personal questions. For a start, their houses were so different from our suburban Jewish home back in North Manchester.

Our house was noisy, and smelt of food – and so did those of my (mainly Jewish) friends. My mum always had some brisket or hamishe (home pickled) cucumbers on the go, or she'd fried some fish, so there were food odours; garlic, caraway seeds (?), fried onions. These houses in North East Bristol smelt of nothing. Furniture polish a bit, I suppose, and boiled ham sandwiches with lettuce (limp leaves, if memory serves, iceberg never came in until after Channel 4) in white sliced bread.

So the conversation tended to be as neutral and non-committal as the ambience. Despite the fact that many of the recently departed had seen service with the Gloucestershire Regiment, the so-called Glorious Glosters, an infantry outfit that played a key role in both of the 20th Century's two World Wars, we rarely touched on the subject's wartime experiences.

In many cases, I don't think the widows could have helped me in that area even if they'd wanted to. This was an era when lips were almost universally stiff and upper, especially in that very English part of England.

The returning soldier, I imagined, would place his boots by the fire, and after a cup of tea and a toasted teacake, and maybe in view of the circumstances a return to marital relations, would take up or resume peacetime life. All that *Ryan's Daughter* stuff was fine for the Irish, and passed an absorbing couple of hours at the ABC in Bristol Centre, but had no place in the borough of Kingswood.

What the widows could talk about was the old man's work. Kingswood was more or less a one-company town, with the boot and shoe manufacturer GB Britton expanding rapidly through the 1960s and 1970s thanks to the success of its TUF boot, a 'light and flexible men's working boot' according to a 1960s catalogue. My obit in the *Kingswood Observer* – 'Shoe Factory Worker Dies', or 'Finisher at GB Britton Dies' – would at least give the boot and shoe community an opportunity to learn which of their former colleagues had fallen off the perch.

There was a good chance they might have played together at the GB Britton Bowls Club – still going in 2020, unlike the shoe factory – set up by workers returning from the First World War, encouraged by George Bryant Britton, one of those classic Victorian entrepreneurs with a social conscience, but who never lost sight of the value of a half crown.

He was a councillor, an alderman, and later a Liberal MP and, unlike many other Bristol business titans, unsullied by connections with the slave trade as far as I know, not that the *Kingswood Observer* – or anybody else in Bristol back then – would have bothered to mention it if he had been.

On the employment history of the recently deceased, we stuck to facts. In truth, it was more a *cv* than an obituary. Even when my awkwardness disappeared, and I relaxed more among the mourners, I tended not to broach interesting questions that might have given a clue to the character of my subject, like, 'What was he like at the works' Christmas party? Was he tongue-tied and ill at ease when he introduced you to his boss? Did he ever spot a girl from the office he was vaguely aware of dancing with her boyfriend over the other side of the room, and did he think about her every single day for the rest of his life without ever seeing her again?'

We did ask about hobbies and interests, but there was rarely much of a story there. The days of older folk retiring and doing a sociology degree at the Open University or hiking through the Hindu Kush were twenty or thirty years in the future, which meant less than captivating headlines like 'Keen Gardener Dies'.

I did wedding reports as well, where the family filled in a form from which I picked out a 'news angle', and wrote up. Machinist Weds, Honeymoon In Caribbean, Met At Local Youth Club; those were some of mine.

Both the chaps who sub-edited the paper were called Norman. The head Norman was round about 60, I suppose, maybe a little younger, a chain-smoking veteran of Bristol journalism who must have done something awful in his career on the *Post* or the *Daily Press* to be imprisoned in a cramped local weekly office, knocking the efforts of barely literate teenagers into a kind of journalese, two floors down from where the 24-hour newsroom action was.

I never remember this Norman sharing with us anything that could have been useful in our future careers, or engaging with us at all. On those occasions when banter flew round the office, his incessant two-finger typing would slow to a low hum, and a faint suggestion of an indulgent smile would be just perceptible to us Norm-watchers. I think he was a good chap, but I have little to base this on apart from the fact that he never lost his temper at some of the bilge I turned out like he did with others and I was signed to a three-year apprenticeship when my six-month probation ended.

The other Norm was thirtyish, keener to befriend his

young charges than his boss and thus probably more likely to be treacherous as we scrapped for our indentureships. He'd sympathise with us over our run-ins with Senior Norm, tut-tutting and agreeing when we complained about SN being out of touch with modern times and so on.

He invited me for tea to his ramshackle, damp cottage in Oldland Common, a proper old school village to the North of Bristol, one of the last places to have coal mines in the area, probably all poshed up and desirable now, but in those days just somewhere to live if you didn't have much money.

It was all a little chaotic – I'm not sure Mrs Norm was expecting me. While Norm prepared a disappointingly lukewarm mug of tea – as my dad used to say, 'What is it with the goyim and all the milk in the tea?' – I watched his two small scruffy children playing on a makeshift swing optimistically attached to a tree branch, but not in any way compliant with health and safety, had such a thing have existed in those days.

Both the little ones had stinking colds, so I had to manage their surprisingly abundant yellow-green streams, given the cute, tiny button-noses they were streaming from, while entertaining them with vigorous pushing, and simultaneously trying to keep bones unbroken.

If you were around in the early 1970s, you'd recognise Mr and Mrs Norm. He was a little paunchy, thinning hair, full beard – out of the suit and into polo-neck jumper and corduroy trousers once home – and she was what back then was known as an Earth Mother type, again carrying a few surplus pounds, you should pardon me for saying, mid-calf length floral print dress, billowing – is that the word? – sandals, no make-up, hairstyle as much like Joan Baez as it was possible for an English grammar school girl with curly hair to achieve.

It was so much easier in the 1970s to find out what tribe

people belonged to. There was a *Guardian*, an old *Observer* magazine and a paperback of *The Female Eunuch* on the big wooden table in Norm's living room, and a shelf full of vinyl LPs; Pentangle, Fairport Convention, Pink Floyd, Jefferson Airplane, early Dylan, Bert Jansch, Steeleye Span, Roy Harper, a lot of British stuff, folk and folk rock veering gently into psychedelia. You knew exactly where you were.

These days, nobody's walking round with a paperback in their pocket, and where the long-playing records used to sit there are houseplants and a book on Thai cooking.

It occurred to me recently that if Norm had not stacked the albums on a rackety shelf, not let his *enfants sauvages* crayon all over the covers and, most importantly, not played the damned things, he would have had a nice pension. But who knew? If my mum had held on to the slum in Hackney where she was born after the First World War, her grand-children could've been privately and expensively educated.

As it turned out, I never really worked out how to make money – as was pointed out to me 40 years later, when a colleague said I'd always managed to earn decent money, but not make any, an important distinction. I never really learnt to do anything of value as it happens; basic motor mechanics, home improvements, tantric sex, all remain firmly closed books. But what I did learn – from hippy Norm with the snotty kids – was how to write a story for a newspaper.

About two weeks into my job – I can't believe, incidentally, that at just 19 years old I packed a few clothes and a couple of Beatles LPs and travelled to a strange, virtually Jew free town to be a journalist – the first story I ever found, which wasn't about someone dying, getting married, or doing a sponsored swim for charity, was about a chap in a two-year stand-off with the council because the road he lived on was full of potholes. I think it was something to do with the road not being properly 'adopted' by the council, and thus the vast cost of repairs falling on the residents.

The unfortunate who vouchsafed this scandal to me had folders full of correspondence about the issue. He was a divorced chap who invited me into his not-too-tidy house, gave me another in a series of disappointing cups of tea, and treated me to a blow by blow account of his dealings with local officialdom until I was as fed up with him as the Council undoubtedly was.

In fairness, he did seem to have been treated shoddily, but was one of those guys whose lives seemed to be a series of hard luck stories. Wife gone, hair going, and quite frankly the suspension on his 1965 Hillman Husky shot to bits thanks to the negligence of Warmley Rural District Council.

Back in the office, in a state of some excitement, I gave this saga the type of treatment Robert Redford and Dustin Hoffman would later turn into Oscar-winning gold in the 1976 film *All The President's Men*. I submitted the magnum opus to junior Norm, who duly submitted it back to me, suggesting the 1,500 words I'd devoted to this tale of suburban revolt was a little excessive, and some of the more Wat Tyler elements I'd ascribed to its hero belonged on the spike (a literal spike in those days).

'What's the name of this benighted thoroughfare?' he asked. 'Grimsbury Road.' 'Well, how about 'Grimsbury Road has been living up to its name these past eighteen months, some quotes from the residents, not too much with Che Guevara, he sounds like a bit of a loser, reaction from the council, and it's all over in 700 words, a crime with no victims.'

'It's a decent tale,' he continued, 'but I doubt it'll have the editor of the...' Rival newspaper mentioned here; I want to say the *South Gloucestershire Gazette* but the Internet tells me that went out of print in 1935, which acts as a useful reminder that these fragments of memoir are not to be taken as gospel. Anyway, he doubted that my very first page lead would have our rival driving up onto the Mendip Hills, attaching a length of hose to his exhaust pipe and filling his car with deadly fumes.

I would love to bring you that story, either in its original form or the new improved Norm version, but the *Kingswood Observer* long ago went the way of the *South Gloucestershire Gazette*. I never kept cuttings, from that paper or the *Western Daily Press,* the regional daily paper to which I graduated.

These days you might be able to rely on a parent keeping a scrapbook, but parenting was different back then. Whereas my wife and I have kept every daubing, Girl Guide certificate, record of achievement, major or minor, of my beloved children, my parents were vaguely aware that I'd dropped out of university and gone to work in newspapers in the West Country, mainly because I telephoned them once a week to confirm I was still alive and 'eating OK' – key query, I lied mostly – they were hardly archivists.

They may have been secretly proud I was learning an arguably useful trade and, more importantly (Jewish family), taking on board all essential nutrients, but my professional life was not a daily concern, as my children's is to me, to the extent that when one of my daughters got a job at Sky News, I found myself locked into the channel all day, barely even considering the damage to mental health that sixteen hours constant exposure to broadcast news can cause.

As for the collection of words you now hold in your hands with such obvious pleasure – they represent just a few of the hundreds of thousands of mine now littering the information superhighway, not exactly full of sound and fury, but definitely told by an idiot and signifying nothing.

Acknowledgements

Before being woke was a thing – in fact, before being a thing was a thing – I thought of myself as woke, as we understood it a couple of decades ago.

I grew up in a *Guardian* household, continued to read the paper at university, and have retained affection for it, despite occasionally trying circumstances, not least being 'let go' from my position as a columnist in the sports section in order to pursue my first love, unemployment.

Although less than thrilled to be thrown out onto the street with the workhouse beckoning, I tried hard not to be bitter, and reading back through some of the pieces I wrote for the paper, it seems at this remove that the paper may have made the right decision.

While I like to think I have remained the kind of pinko liberal softy perfectly at home among the chattering classes, there are aspects of *Guardian* culture I might have struggled with as the years passed and the arteries hardened; transgender issues, chickpeas, women's football, that kind of thing.

So I am happy to have passed on the baton to a new generation of *Guardian* writers, who keep the flame of quirky and sometimes semi-humorous sportswriting burning brightly, even occasionally making it into *Private Eye*'s Pseuds Corner, a badge of honour I never quite managed to secure.

So I salute my alma mater, thank all the sub-editors – a breed now very much in the wheeltapper, shunter, and lamplighter category – who helped keep the pieces reprinted in this book semi-literate and mostly free of glaring cock-ups.

I'd also like to thank the current sports department and the rights people at *The Guardian* for being very sweet and allowing me to reprint the Screen Break columns, possibly because they felt they weren't worth very much to anyone anyway, but still...

Some of the pieces not from *The Guardian* are from the *Racing Post,* who provided an outlet for me post-Screen Break despite my connection with horse and greyhound racing being tangential at best – although in my experience if the dog you've backed is not in the lead at the first bend you might as well kiss your investment goodbye. I'm eternally grateful to Bruce Millington at the *Post* for the gig and for allowing reprint of the articles, in return for a free book.

Other pieces in the collection are either unpublished – mostly book ideas that came to nothing – or from my current perch, at *Forty20,* an excellent monthly rugby league magazine that continues to publish me, despite any mention of the superior code of rugby being coincidental. So thanks to Phil Caplan and Tony Hannan at *Forty20* who are not entirely unconnected with publication of this volume. Thank you also to Jody Ineson for compiling the index.

Finally, apologies if you find the same joke appearing in two or more of the pieces in this book. But in the spirit of chickpeas and all that, I have tried to be ecologically sound, and recycled material wherever possible, on the basis that one joke carefully used can last a lifetime.

Index

Index